ISBN 978-0-483-58754-0

PIBN 10699868

JONES's

BRITISH THEATRE.

VOL. V.

CONTAINING,

I.

THE SCHOOL FOR SCANDAL.

II.

THE CRITIC.

III.

THE RIVALS.

IV.

A TRIP TO SCARBOROUGH.

DUBLIN:

PRINTED BY JOHN CHAMBERS,

FOR WILLIAM JONES, No. 86, DAME-STREET.

1795.

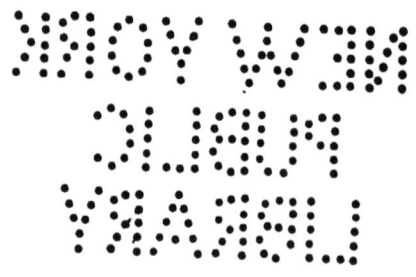

THE

SCHOOL FOR SCANDAL.

COMEDY.

BY R. B. SHERIDAN, ESQ.

ADAPTED FOR

THEATRICAL REPRESENTATION,

AS PERFORMED AT THE

THEATRE-ROYAL,

DRURY-LANE.

REGULATED FROM THE PROMPT-BOOK.

By Permiſſion of the Managers,

" The Lines diſtinguiſhed by inverted Commas, are omitted in the Repreſentation."

DUBLIN :

PRINTED BY WILLIAM PORTER,

FOR WILLIAM JONES, NO. 86, DAME-STREET.

M DCC XCII.

PROLOGUE.

WRITTEN BY MR. GARRICK.

SPOKEN BY MR. KING.

A School for Scandal! tell me, I befeech you,
Needs there a fchool—this modifh art to teach you ?
No need of leffons now—the knowing think
We might as well be taught to eat and drink.
Caus'd by a dearth of Scandal, fhould the vapours
Diftrefs our fair ones—let them read the papers ;
Their powerful mixtures fuch diforders hit,
Crave what they will, there's quantum fufficit.
    " Lord !" cries my Lady Wormwood, *(who loves*
    tattle,
And puts much falt and pepper in her prattle)
Juft ris'n at noon, all night at cards when threfhing
Strong tea and fcandal—blefs me, how refrefhing !
Give me the papers, Lifp—how bold and free ! (fips)
" Laft night Lord L. (fips) *was caught with Lady*
D."
For aching heads, what charming fal volatile !—(fips)
" If Mrs. B. will ftill continue flirting,
" We hope fhe'll draw *or we'll* undraw *the curtain."*
Fine fatire, pox—in public all abufe it ;
But, by ourfelves—(fips) *our praife we can't refufe it.*
Now, Lifp, read you—there at that dafh and ftar—
Yes, Ma'am—" A certain Lord had beft beware,
" Who lives not twenty miles from Grofvenor-fquare :

A 2

" *For should he Lady W— find willing—*
" Wormwood *is bitter."—Oh! that's me—the villain!*
Throw it behind the fire, and never more
Let that vile paper come within my door.

    Thus at our friends we laugh, who feel the dart;
To reach our feelings, we ourselves must smart.
Is our young bard so young—to think that he
Can stop the full spring tide of calumny?
Knows he the world so little, and its trade?—
Alas! the devil's sooner rais'd *than* laid.
So strong, so swift the monster, there's no gagging;
Cut Scandal's head off—still the tongue is wagging.
Proud of your smiles, once lavishly bestow'd,
Again our young Don Quixote takes the road;
To shew his gratitude—he draws his pen,
And seeks the hydra, Scandal, in its den;
From his fell gripe the frighted fair to save,
Tho' he should fall—th' attempt must please the brave.
For your applause, all perils he would thro'—
He'll fight—that's write—a cavalier so true,
Till ev'ry drop of blood—that's ink—is spilt for you.

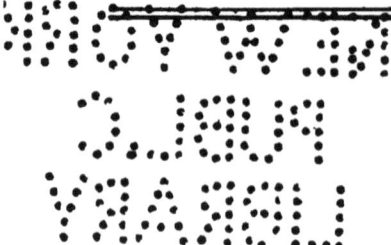

Men.

Sir Peter Teazle, - - -	Mr. King.
Sir Oliver Surface, - - -	Mr. Yates.
Joseph, and - - - -	Mr. Palmer.
Charles Surface, - - -	Mr. Smith.
Rowley, - - - - -	Mr. Aicken.
Crabtree, - - - - -	Mr. Parsons.
Sir Benjamin Backbite, - -	Mr. Dodd.
Moses, - - - - -	Mr. Baddely.
Snake, - - - - -	Mr. Packer.
Trip, - - - - - -	Mr. Lemash.
Careless and others, Companions to Charles,	{ Mr. Farran, Mr. Norris, &c.

Women.

Lady Teazle, - - - -	Mrs. Abington.
Maria, (Sir Peter's *Ward*) - -	Miss P. Hopkins.
Lady Sneerwell, - - -	Miss Sherry.
Mrs. Candour, - - - -	Miss Pope.

THE

SCHOOL FOR SCANDAL.

ACT I. SCENE I.

Lady SNEERWELL'*s houfe.*

Lady SNEERWELL *and* SNAKE *difcovered at a tea table.*

Lady Sneerwell.

THE paragraphs, you fay, Mr. Snake, were all inferted.

Snake. They were, Madam; and as I copied them myfelf in a feigned hand, there can be no fuf-picion from whence they came.

L. Sneer. Did you circulate the report of Lady Brittle's intrigue with Captain Boaftall?

Snake. That's in as fine a train as your Lady-fhip could wifh. In the common courfe of things,

I think it muſt reach Mrs. Clacket's ears within twenty-four hours, and then the buſineſs, you know, is as good as done.

L. Sneer. Why yes, Mrs. Clacket has talents, and a great deal of induſtry.

Snake. True, Madam, and has been tolerably ſuccefsful in her days ; to my knowledge ſhe has been the cauſe of ſix matches being broken off, and three ſons diſinherited ; of four forced elopements, as many cloſe confinements, nine ſeparate mainte-nances, and two divorces ;—nay, I have more than once traced her cauſing a *tête-a-tête* in the Town and Country Magazine, when the parties never ſaw one another before in the whole courſe of their lives.

L. Sneer. Why yes, ſhe has genius, but her manner is too groſs.

Snake. True, Madam ; ſhe has a fine tongue, and a bold invention ; but then, her colouring is too dark, and the outlines rather too extravagant ; ſhe wants that delicacy of hint, and mellowneſs of ſneer, which diſtinguiſhes your ladyſhip's ſcandal.

L. Sneer. You are partial, Snake.

Snake. Not in the leaſt ; every body will allow that Lady Sneerwell can do more with a word or look, than many others with the moſt laboured de-tail, even though they accidentally happen to have a little truth on their ſide to ſupport it.

L. Sneer. Yes, my dear Snake, and I'll not deny the pleaſure I feel at the ſucceſs of my ſchemes ;. *(both riſes)* wounded myſelf, in the early part of my life, by the envenomed tongue of ſlander, I confeſs nothing can give me greater ſatisfaction, than reducing others to the level of my own injured reputation.

Snake. True, Madam; but there is one affair, in which you have lately employed me, wherein, I confefs, I am at a lofs to guefs at your motives.

L. Sneer. I prefume you mean with regard to my friend Sir Peter Teazle, and his family.

Snake. I do—here are two young men, to whom Sir Peter has acted as guardian fince their father's death—the eldeft poffeffing the moft amiable character, and univerfally well fpoken of; the youngeft the moft diffipated, wild, extravagant young fellow in the world—the former an avowed admirer of your ladyfhip, and apparently your favourite; the latter attached to Maria, Sir Peter's ward, and confeffedly admired by her : Now, on the face of thefe circumftances, it is utterly unaccountable to me, why you, the widow of a city knight, with a large fortune, fhould not immediately clofe with the paffion of a man of fuch character and expectation as Mr. Surface; and more fo, why you are fo uncommonly earneft to deftroy the mutual attachment fubfifting between his brother Charles and Maria.

L. Sneer. Then at once, to unravel this myftery, I muft inform you, that love has no fhare whatever in the intercourfe between Mr. Surface and me.

Snake. No!—

L. Sneer. No! his real views are to Maria, or her fortune, while in his brother he finds a favoured rival; he is therefore obliged to mafk his real intentions, and profit by my affiftance.

Snake. Yet ftill I am more puzzled why you fhould intereft yourfelf for his fuccefs.

L. Sneer. Heavens! how dull you are! Can't you furmife a weaknefs I have hitherto, through fhame, concealed even from you? Muft I confefs it that Charles, that profligate, that libertine, that bankrupt in fortune and reputation, that he it is for whom I am thus anxious and malicious; and to gain whom I would facrifice every thing.

Snake. Now, indeed, your conduct appears confiftent;—but pray, how came you and Mr. Surface fo confidential?

L. Sneer. For our mutual intereft; he pretends to, and recommends fentiment and liberality; but I know him to be artful, clofe and malicious. In fhort, a fentimental knave; while with Sir Peter, and indeed with moft of his acquaintance, he paffes for a youthful miracle of virtue, good fenfe, and benevolence.

Snake. Yes, I know Sir Peter vows he has not his fellow in England, and has praifed him as a man of character and fentiment.

L. Sneer. Yes; and with the appearance of being fentimental, he has brought Sir Peter to favour his addreffes to Maria, while poor Charles has no friend in the houfe, though I fear he has a powerful one in Maria's heart, againft whom we muft direct our fchemes.

Enter SERVANT.

Ser. Mr. Surface, Madam.

L. Sneer. Shew him up—*(Exit Servant)*—he generally calls about this hour—I don't wonder at people's giving him to me for a lover.

Enter Joseph Surface.

Jof. Lady Sneerwell, good morning to you.— Mr. Snake, your moſt obedient.

L. Sneer. Snake has juſt been rallying me upon our attachment, but I have told him our real views; I need not tell you how uſeful he has been to us, and believe me, our confidence has not been ill-placed.

Jof. Oh, Madam, 'tis impoſſible for me to fuſpect a man of Mr. Snake's merit and accompliſhments.

L. Sneer. Oh, no compliments; but tell me when you faw Maria, or what's more material to us, your brother.

Jof. I have not feen either finee I left you; but I can tell you they never met. Some of your ſtories have had a good effect in that quarter.

L. Sneer. The merit of this, my dear Snake, belongs to you; but do your brother's diſtreſſes increaſe?

Jof. Every hour—I am told he had another execution in his houfe yeſterday—in ſhort, his diſſipation and extravagance exceeds any thing I ever heard.

L. Sneer. Poor Charles!

Jof. Aye, poor Charles indeed! notwithſtanding his extravagance one cannot help pitying him;

I wifh it was in my power to be of any effential fervice to him ; for the man who does not feel for the
diftreffes of a brother, even though merited by his
own mifconduct, deferves to be—

L. Sneer. Now you are going to be moral and
forget you are among friends.

Jof. Gad, fo I was, ha ! ha !—I'll keep that
fentiment 'till I fee Sir Peter, ha ! ha ! however it
would certainly be a generous act in you to refcue
Maria from fuch a libertine, who, if he is to be
reclaimed at all, can only be fo by a perfon of your
fuperior accomplifhments and underftanding.

Snake. I believe Lady Sneerwell, here's company coming ; I'll go and copy the letter I mentioned to your ladyfhip. Mr. Surface your moft
obedient.   [*Exit Snake.*

Jof. Mr. Snake, your moft obedient. I wonder, Lady Sneerwell, you would put any confidence in that fellow.

L. Sneer. Why fo ?

Jof. I have difcovered he has of late had feveral
conferences with old Rowley, who was formerly my
father's fteward ; he has never, you know, been a
friend of mine.

L. Sneer. And do you think he would betray us ?

Jof. Not unlikely ; and take my word for it,
Lady Sneerwell, that fellow has not virtue enough
to be faithful to his own villanies.

Enter MARIA.

L. Sneer. Ah, Maria, my dear, how do you
do ?—What's the matter ?

Maria. Nothing, Madam, only this odious lover of mine, Sir Benjamin Backbite, and his uncle Crabtree, juft called in at my guardian's, but I took the firft opportunity to flip out, and run away to your ladyfhip.

L. Sneer. Is that all?

Jof. Had my brother Charles been of the party you would not have been fo much alarmed.

L. Sneer. Nay, now you are too fevere; for I dare fay the truth of the matter is, Maria heard you was here, and therefore came.—But pray, Maria, what particular objection have you to Sir Benjamin that you avoid him fo?

Maria. Oh, Madam, he has done nothing; but his whole converfation is a perpetual libel upon all his acquaintance.

Jof. Yes, and the worft of it is, there is no advantage in not knowing him, for he would abufe a ftranger as foon as his beft friend, and his uncle is as bad.

Maria. For my own part, I own wit lofes its refpect with me, when I fee it in company with malice;—what think you, Mr. Surface?

Jof. To be fure, Madam—to fmile at a jeft that plants a thorn in the breaft of another, is to become a principal in the mifchief.

L. Sneer. Pfha—there is no poffibility of being witty without a little ill-nature; the malice in a good thing is the barb that makes it ftick.—What is your *real* opinion, Mr. Surface?

Jof. Why, my opinion is, that where the spirit of raillery is suppressed, the conversation must be naturally insipid.

Maria. Well, I will not argue how far slander may be allowed, but in a man, I am sure it is despisable.—We have pride, envy, rivalship, and a thousand motives to depreciate each other; but the male slanderer, must have the cowardice of a woman, before he can traduce one.

Enter SERVANT.

Serv. Mrs. Candour, Madam, if you are at leisure, will leave her carriage.

L. Sneer. Desire her to walk up *(Exit Servant.)* Now, Maria, here's a character to your taste; though Mrs. Candour is a little talkative, yet every body allows she is the best natured sort of woman in the world.

Maria. Yes—with the very grofs affectation of good nature, she does more mischief, than the direct malice of old Crabtree.

Jof. Faith it's very true; and whenever I hear the current of abuse running hard against the characters of my best friends, I never think them in such danger, as when Candour undertakes their defence.

L. Sneer. Hush! hush! here she is.

Enter Mrs. CANDOUR.

Mrs. Can. Oh! my dear Lady Sneerwell; well, how do you do? Mr. Surface, your most obedient—Is there any news abroad? No!—nothing good I fuppofe—No! nothing but fcandal!—nothing but fcandal!

Jof. Juft fo indeed, Madam.

Mrs. Can. Nothing but fcandal!—Ah, Maria, how do you do child; what, is every thing at an end between you and Charles? What, he is too extravagant—Aye! the town talks of nothing elfe.

Maria. I am forry, Madam, the town is fo ill employed.

Mrs. Can. Aye, fo am I child—but what can one do? we can't ftop peoples tongues :—They hint too, that your guardian and his Lady don't live fo agreeable together as they did.

Maria. I am fure fuch reports are without foundation.

Mrs. Can. Aye, fo thefe things generally are—'tis like Mrs. Fafhion's affair with Colonel Coterie ; though, indeed, that affair was never rightly cleared up; and it was but yefterday Mifs Prim affured me, that Mr. and Mrs. Honeymoon are now become mere man and wife, like the reft of their acquaintance. She likewife hinted, that a certain widow in the next ftreet, had got rid of her dropfy, and recovered her fhape in a moft furprizing manner.

Jof. The licence of invention, fome people give themfelves, is aftonifhing.

Mrs. Can. 'Tis fo—but how will you ftop peoples tongues? 'Twas but yefterday Mrs. Clacket informed me, that our old friend, Mifs Prudely, was going to elope, and that her guardian caught her juft ftepping into the York Diligence, with her

dancing mafter. I was informed too, that Lord
Flimfy caught his wife at a houfe of no extraordi-
nary fame, and that Tom Saunter and Sir Harry
Idle, were to meafure fwords on a fimilar occafion—
But I dare fay there is no truth in the ftory, and I
would not circulate fuch a report for the world.

Jof. You report!—No, no, no.

Mrs. Can. No, no—tale-bearers are juft as bad
as the tale-makers.

Enter SERVANT.

Serv. Sir Benjamin Backbite and Mr. Crabtree.
                                    [*Exit Servant.*

Enter Sir BENJAMIN *and* CRABTREE.

Crab. Lady Sneerwell, your moft obedient humble fervant. Mrs. Candour, I believe you don't
know my nephew, Sir Benjamin Backbite ; he has
a very pretty tafte for poetry, and fhall make a rebus
er a charade with any one.

Sir Benj. Oh fie ! uncle.

Crab. In faith he will—Did you ever hear the
lines he made at Lady Ponto's route, on Mrs. Friz-
zle's feathers catching fire ; and the rebufes—his
firft is the name of a fifh ; the next a great naval
commander, and—

Sir Benj. Uncle, now prythee.

L. Sneer. I wonder, Sir Benjamin, you never
publifh any thing.

Sir Benj. Why, to fay the truth, 'tis very vulgar to print—and as my little productions are chiefly
fatires, and lampoons on particular perfons, I find

they circulate better by giving copies in confidence to the friends of the parties ;—however I have some love elegics, which, when favoured by the lady's smiles, *(to Maria)* I mean to give to the public.

Crab. 'Foregad, Madam, they'll immortalize you, *(to Maria)* you will be handed down to posterity; like Petrarch's Laura, or Waller's Sachariffa.

Sir Benj. Yes, Madam, I think you'll like them, *(to Maria)* when you shall fee them on a beautiful quarto type, where a neat rivulet of text shall murmur thro' a meadow of margin ;—'foregad they'll be the most elegant things of their kind.

Crab. But, odfo, Ladies, did you hear the news ?

Mrs. Can. What—do you mean the report of— .

Crab. No, Madam, that's not it—Mifs Nicely going to be married to her own footman.

Mrs. Can. Impoffible !

Sir Benj. 'Tis very true, indeed Madam ; every thing is fixed, and the wedding liveries befpoke.

Crab. Yes, and they do fay there were very preffing reafons for it.

Mrs. Can. I heard fomething of this before.

L. Sneer. Oh ! it cannot be ; and I wonder they'd report fuch a thing of fo prudent a lady.

Sir Benj. Oh ! but Madam, that is the very reafon that it was believed at once ; for fhe has always been fo very cautious and referved, that every body was fure there was fome reafon for it at bottom.

Mrs. Can. It is true, there is a fort of puny, fickly reputation, that would outlive the robufter character of an hundred prudes.

Sir Benj. True, Madam; there are Valetudinarians in réputation as well as conftitution, who being confcious of their weak part, avoid the leaft breath of air, and fupply their want of ftamina by care and circumfpection.

Mrs. Can. I believe this may be fome miftake; you know, Sir Benjamin, very trifling circumftances have often given rife to the moft ingenious tales.

Crab. Very true;—but odfo, ladies, did you hear of Mifs Letitia Piper's lofing her lover and her character at Scarborough—Sir Benjamin, you remember it.

Sir Benj. Oh, to be fure, the moft whimfical circumftance!

L. Sneer. Pray let us hear it.

Crab. Why, one evening at Lady Spadille's affembly, the converfation happened to turn upon the difficulty of breeding Nova Scotia fheep in this country; no, fays a lady prefent, I have feen an inftance of it, for a coufin of mine, Mifs Letitia Piper, had one that produced twins. What, what, fays old Lady Dundizzy, (whom we all know is as deaf as a poft) has Mifs Letitia Piper had twins.—This you may eafily imagine, fet the company in a loud laugh; and the next morning it was every where reported, and believed, that Mifs Letitia Piper had actually been brought to bed of a fine boy and girl.

Omnes. Ha, ha, ha, ha.

Crab. 'Tis true, upon my honour.—Oh, Mr. Surface, how do you do; I hear your uncle, Sir Oliver, is expected in town ; fad news upon his arrival, to hear how your brother has gone on.

Jof. I hope no bufy people have already prejudiced his uncle againft him—he may reform.

Sir Benj. True, he may ; for my part, I never thought him fo utterly void of principles as people fay—and though he has loft all his friends, I am told no body is better fpoken of amongft the Jews.

Crab. 'Foregad if the Old-Jewry was a ward, Charles would be an alderman, for he pays as many annuities as the Irifh Tontine ; and when he is fick, they have prayers for his recovery in all the Synagogues.

Sir Benj. Yet no man lives in greater fplendour.— They tell me, when he entertains his friends, he can fit down to dinner with a dozen of his own fecurities, have a fcore of tradefmen waiting in the anti-chamber, and an officer behind every gueft's chair.

Jof. This may be entertaining to you, gentlemen—but you pay very little regard to the feelings of a brother.

Maria. Their malice is intolerable. *(Afide)* Lady Sneerwell, I muft wifh you a good morning; I'm not very well.   [*Exit* Maria.

Mrs. Can. She changes colour.

L. Sneer. Do, Mrs. Candour, follow her.

Mrs. Can. To be fure I will—poor dear girl, who knows what her fituation may be ?

[*Mrs.* Candour *follows.*

L. Sneer. 'Twas nothing, but that ſhe could not bear to hear Charles reflected on, notwithſtanding, their difference.

Sir Benj. The young lady's penchant is obvious.

Crab. Come, don't let this diſhearten yon—fol-low her, and repeat ſome of your odes, to her, and I'll aſſiſt you.

Sir Benj. Mr. Surface, I did not come to hurt you, but depend on't your brother is utterly un-done.

Crab. Oh! undone as ever man was—can't raiſe a guinea.

Sir Benj. Every thing is ſold, I am told, that was moveable.

Crab. Not a moveable left, except ſome old bot-tles, and ſome pictures, and they ſeemed to be framed in the wainſcot, egad.

Sir Benj. I am ſorry to hear alſo ſome bad ſtories of him.

Crab. Oh! he has done many mean things, that's certain.

Sir Benj. But, however, he's your brother.

Crab. Aye! as he's your brother—we'll tell you more another opportunity.

Sir Benj. Yes! as he's your brother—we'll tell you more another opportunity.

[*Exeunt* Crab *and* Sir Benjamin.

L. Sneer. 'Tis very hard for them, indeed, to leave a ſubject they have not quite run down.

Joſ. And I fancy their abuſe was no more ac-ceptable to your ladyſhip than to Maria.

L. Sneer. I doubt her affe&ions are further en-
,gaged than we imagine ;—but the family are to be
here this afternoon, fo you may as well dine where
you are ; we fhall have an opportunity of obferving
her further ;—in the mean time I'll go and plot
mifchief, and you fhall ftudy.   [*Exeunt.*

SCENE II.

Sir **Peter Teazle's** *Houfe.*

Enter Sir **Peter Teazle**.

Sir Pet. When an old batchelor marries a young
wife, what is he to expe& ?—'Tis not above fix
months fince my Lady Teazle made me the happieft
of men—and I have been the moft miferable dog
ever fince.—We tifted a little going to church,
and fairly quarrelled before the bells were done
ringing. I was more than once nearly choaked with
gall during the honey-moon, and had loft every fa-
tisfa&ion in life, before my friends had done wifh-
ing me joy—and yet, I chofe with caution a girl
bred wholly in the country, who had never known
luxury, beyond one filk gown, or diffipation beyond the annual gala of a race ball.—Yet now fhe
plays her part in all the extravagant fopperies of the
town, with as good a grace as if fhe had never feen
a'bufh, or a grafs plot out of Grofvenor-fquare.—I
am fneered at by all my acquaintance—paragraphed
in the newfpapers—fhe difputes my fortune, and con-

tradicts all my humours.—And yet, the worft of it
is, I doubt I love her, or I fhould never bear all
this—but I am determined never to be weak enough
to let her know it—No! no! no!

Enter Rowley.

Row. Sir Peter your fervant, how do you find
yourfelf to day?

Sir Pet. Very bad, mafter Rowley; very bad
indeed.

Row. I'm forry to hear that—what has happened to make you uneafy fince yefterday?

Sir Pet. A pretty queftion truly to a married
man.

Row. Sure my lady is not the caufe!

Sir Pet. Why! has any one told you fhe was
dead?

Row. Come, come, Sir Peter, notwithftanding
you fometimes difpute and difagree, 1 am fure you
love her.

Sir Pet. Aye, mafter Rowley; but the worft of
it is, that in all our difputes and quarrels, fhe is
ever in the wrong, and continues to thwart and
vex me;—I am myfelf the fweeteft tempered man
in the world, and fo I tell her an hundred times a
day.

Row. Indeed, Sir Peter!

Sir Pet. Yes—and then there's Lady Sneerwell,
and the fet fhe meets at her houfe, encourage her
to difobedience; and Maria, my ward, fhe too prefumes to have a will of her own, and refufes the
man I propofe for her; defigning, I fuppofe, to

beſtow herſelf and fortune upon that profligate his brother.

Row. You know, Sir Peter, I have often taken the liberty to differ in opinion with you in regard to theſe two young men; for Charles, my life on't, will retrieve all one day or other.—Their worthy father, my once honoured maſter, at his years, was full as wild and extravagant as Charles now is; but at his death he did not leave a more benevolent heart to lament his loſs.

Sir Pet. You are wrong, maſter Rowley, you are very wrong. By their father's will, you know, I became guardian of theſe young men, which gave me an opportunity of knowing their different diſpoſitions; but their uncle's Eaſtern liberality ſoon took them out of my power, by giving them an early independence.—But for Charles, whatever good qualities he might have inherited, they are long ſince ſquandered away with the reſt of his fortune.—Joſeph, indeed, is a pattern for the young men of the age—a youth of the nobleſt ſentiments, and acts up to the ſentiments he profeſſes.

Row. Well, well, Sir Peter, I ſhan't oppoſe your opinion at preſent, though I am ſorry you are prejudiced againſt Charles, as this may probably be the moſt critical period of his life, for his uncle, Sir Oliver, is arrived, and now in town.

Sir Pet. What! my old friend, Sir Oliver, is he arrived? I thought you had not expected him this month.

Row. No more we did, Sir, but his paſſage has been remarkably quick.

Sir Pet. I fhall be heartily glad to fee him—'tis fixteen years fince old Nol and I met—but does he ftill enjoin us to keep his arrival a fecret from his nephews ?

Row. He does, Sir; and is determined, under a feigned charaƈter, to make trial of their different difpofitions.

Sir Pet. Ah ! there is no need of it, for Jofeph I am fure, is the man—but hark'y, Rowley, does Sir Oliver know that I am married ?

Row. He does, Sir, and intends fhortly to wifh you joy.

Sir Pet. What, as we wifh health to a friend in a confumption.—But I muft have him at my houfe —do you conduƈt him, Rowley : I'll go and give orders for his reception *(going).* We ufed to rail at matrimony together—he has ftood firm to his text.— But, Rowley, don't give him the leaft hint that my wife and I difagree, for I would have him think *(Heaven forgive me)* that we are a very happy couple.

Row. Then you muft be careful not to quarrel whilft he is here.

Sir Pet. And fo we muft—but that will be im-poffible !—Zounds, Rowley, when an old batchelor marries a young wife, he deferves—aye, he deferves —no—the crime carries the punifhment along with it.

ACT II. SCENE I.

Sir Peter Teazle's *Houſe.*

Enter Sir Peter *and* Lady Teazle.

Sir Peter.

Lady Teazle, Lady Teazle, I won't bear it.

L. Teaz. Very well, Sir Peter, you may bear it or not, juſt as you pleaſe ; but I know I ought to have my own way in every thing, and what's more, I will.

Sir Pet. What, Madam ! is there no reſpect due to the authority of a huſband ?

L. Teaz. Why, don't I know that no woman of faſhion does as ſhe is bid after her marriage.— Though I was bred in the country, I'm no ſtranger to that : if you wanted me to be obedient, you ſhould have a'opted me, and not married me—I'm ſure you are old enough.

Sir Pet. Aye, there it is—Oons, Madam, what right have you to run me into all this extravagançe ?

L. Teaz. I'm ſure I am not more extravagant than a woman of quality ought to be.

Sir Pet. 'Slife, Madam, I'll have no more ſums ſquandered away upon ſuch unmeaning luxuries ; you have as many flowers in your dreſſing-room, as

B

would turn the Pantheon into a green-houfe; or make a Féte Champetré at Chriftmas.

L. Teaz. Lord, Sir Peter, am I to blame that flowers don't blow in cold weather; you muft blame the climate, and not me—I'm fure, for my part, I wifh it was Spring all the year round, and that rofes grew under our feet.

Sir Pet. Zounds, Madam, I fhould not wonder at your extravagance if you had been bred to it—Had you any of thefe things before you married me?

L. Teaz. Lord, Sir Peter, how can you be angry at thofe little elegant expences?

Sir Pet. Had you any of thofe little elegant expences when you married me?

L. Teaz. For my part, I think you ought to be pleafed your wife fhould be thought a woman of tafte.

Sir Pet. Zounds, Madam, you had no tafte when you married me.

L. Teaz. Very true, indeed; and after having married you, I never fhould pretend to tafte again.

Sir Pet. Very well, very well, Madam—You have entirely forgot what your fituation was when firft I faw you.

L. Teaz. No, no, I have not; a very difagreeable fituation it was, or I'm fure I never fhould have married you.

Sir Pet. You forget the humble flate I took you from—the daughter of a poor country 'Squire—When I came to your father's, I found you fitting at your tambour, in a linen gown, a bunch of keys to your fide, and your hair combed fmoothly over a roll.

L. Teaz. Yes, I remember very well ;—my daily occupation was to overlook the dairy, fuperintend the poultry, make extracts from the family receipt book, and comb my aunt Deborah's lap dog.

Sir Pet. Oh ! I am glad to find you have fo good a recollection.

L. Teaz. My evening employments were to draw patterns for ruffles, which I had no materials to make up ; play at Pope Joan with the Curate ; read a fermon to my aunt Deborah, or perhaps be ftuck up at an old fpinnet to tune my father to fleep after a fox chace.

Sir Pet. Then you was glad to take a ride out behind the butler, upon the old dock'd coach horfe.

L. Teaz. No, no, I deny the butler and the coach horfe.

Sir Pet. I fay you did. This was your fitua-tion—Now, Madam, you muft have your coach, vis-a-vis, and three powdered footmen to walk be-fore your chair ; and in fnmmer, two white cats to draw you to Kenfington Gardens : and inftead of your living in that hole in the country, I have brought you home here, made a woman of fortune of you, a woman of quality—in fhort, Madam, I have made you my wife.

L. Teaz. Well, and there is but one thing more you can now do to add to the obligation, and that is——

Sir Pet. To make you a widow, I fuppofe.

L. Teaz. Hem!——

Sir Pet. Very well, Madam, very well; I am much obliged to you for the hint.

L. Teaz. Why then will you force me to fay fhocking things to you. But now we have finifhed our morning converfation, I prefume I may go to my engagements at Lady Sneerwell's.

Sir Pet. Lady Sneerwell!—a precious acquaintance you have made with her too, and the fet that frequent her houfe—Such a fet, mercy on us!—Many a wretch who has been drawn upon a hurdle, has done lefs mifchief than thofe barterers of forged lies, coiners of fcandal, and clippers of reputation.

L. Teaz. How can you be fo fevere; I'm fure they are all people of fafhion, and very tenacious of reputation.

Sir Pet. Yes, fo tenacious of it, they'll not allow it to any but themfelves.

L. Teaz. I vow, Sir Peter, when I fay an ill-natured thing I mean no harm by it, for I take it for granted they'd do the fame by me.

Sir Pet. They've made you as bad as any of them.

L. Teaz. Yes——I think I bear my part with a tolerable grace.——

Sir Pet. Grace, indeed!——

L. Teaz. Well, but Sir Peter, you know you promifed to come.

Sir Pet. Well, I fhall juft call in to look after *my own character.*

L. Teaz. Then upon my word, you muſt make haſte after me, or you'll be too late.

[*Exit* L. Teazle.

Sir Pet. I have got much by my intended expoſtulation—What a charming air ſhe has !—what a neck, and how pleaſingly ſhe ſhews her contempt of my authority !—Well, though I can't make her love me, 'tis ſome pleaſure to teize her a little, and I think ſhe never appears to ſuch advantage, as when ſhe is doing every thing to vex and plague me. [*Exit.*

SCENE II.

Lady SNEERWELL's *Houſe.*

Enter Lady SNEERWELL, CRABTREE, Sir BENJAMIN, JOSEPH, Mrs. CANDOUR, *and* MARIA.

L. Sneer. Nay, poſitively we'll have it.

Joſ. Aye, aye, the epigram by all means.

Sir Benj. Oh ! plague on it, it's mere nonſenſe.

Crab. Faith, Ladies, 'twas excellent for an extempore.

Sir Benj. But, Ladies, you ſhould be acquainted with the circumſtances——You muſt know that one day laſt week, as Lady Bab Curricle was taking the duſt in Hyde-Park, in a ſort of duodecimo phæton, ſhe deſired me to write ſome verſes on her ponies; upon which I took out my pocket book, and in a moment produced the following :——

> " Sure never were feen two fuch beautiful po-
>   nies,
> " Other horfes are clowns,—but thefe macaro-
>   nies ;
> " To give them this title I'm fure can't be
>   wrong,
> " Their legs are fo flim and their tails are fo
>   long."

Crab. There, Ladies——done in the crack of a whip—and on horfeback too!

Jof. Oh! a very Phœbus mounted——

Mrs. Can, 1 muft have a copy.

Enter Lady TEAZLE.

L. Sneer, Lady Teazle, how do you do—I hope we fhall fee Sir Peter.

L. Teaz. I believe he will wait on 'your lady-fhip prefently.

L. Sneer. Maria my love, you look grave ; come, you fhall fit down to piquet with Mr. Surface.

Maria. I take very little pleafure in cards—but I'll do as your ladyfhip pleafes.

L. Teaz. I wonder he would fit down to cards with Maria.—I thought he would have taken an opportunity of fpeaking to me before Sir Peter came.   [*Afide.*

Mrs. Can. Well, now I'll forfwear his fociety.
                                    [*Afide.*

L. Teaz. What's the matter, Mrs. Candour ?

Mrs. Can. Why, they are fo cenforious they won't allow our friend, Mifs Vermillion, to be hand-fome.

L. Sneer. Oh, furely fhe's a pretty woman.

Crab. I'm glad you think fo.

Mrs. Can. She has a charming frefh colour.

L. Teaz. Yes, when it is frefh put on.

Mrs. Can. Well, I'll fwear its natural, for I've feen it come and go.

L. Teaz. Yes, it comes at night, and goes again in the morning.

Sir Benj. True, Madam, it not only goes and comes, but what's more, egad her maid can fetch and carry it.

Mrs. Can. Well,——and what do you think of her fifter?

Crab. What, Mrs. Evergreen—'foregad, fhe's fix and fifty if fhe's a day.

Mrs. Can. Nay, I'll fwear two or three and fifty is the outfide——I don't think fhe looks more.

Sir Benj. Oh, there's no judging by her looks, unlefs we could fee her face.

L. Sneer. Well, if Mrs. Evergreen does take fome pains to repair the ravages of time, fhe certainly effects it with great ingenuity, and furely that's better than the carelefs manner in which the widow Oaker chalks her wrinkles.

Sir Benj. Nay, now my lady Sneerwell, you are too fevere upon the widow—Come, it is not that *fhe paints fo ill*, but when fhe has finifhed her face, *fhe joins it fo* badly to her neck, that fhe looks

like a mended ſtatue, in which the connoiſſeur may
ſee at once, that the head is modern, though the
trunk's antique.

Crab. What do you think of Miſs Simper?

Sir Benj. Why, ſhe has pretty teeth.

L. Teaz. Yes, and upon that account never ſhuts
her mouth, but keeps it always a-jar, as it were,
thus *(ſhews her teeth)*.

Omnes. Ha, ha, ha.

L. Teaz. And yet I vow that's better than the
pains Mrs. Prim takes to conceal her loſſes in front;
ſhe draws her mouth till it reſembles the aperture
of a poor-box, and all her words appear to ſlide
out edge-ways as it were, thus——

" *How do you do, madam?—Yes, madam."*

L. Sneer. Ha, ha, ha; very well, Lady Teazle—I vow you appear to be a little ſevere.

L. Teaz. In defence of a friend, you know, it
is but juſt.—But here comes Sir Peter to ſpoil our
pleaſantry.

Enter Sir PETER.

Sir Pet. Ladies your ſervant—mercy upon me!—
The whole ſet—a character dead at every ſentence.

[*Aſide.*

Mrs. Can. They won't allow good qualities to
any one—not even good-nature to our friend Mrs.
Purſey.

Crab. What! the old fat dowager that was at
Mrs. Quadrille's laſt night.

Mrs. Can. Her bulk .is her misfortune ; and when fhe takes fuch pains to get rid of it, you ought not to refleâ on her.

L. Sneer. That's very true, indeed.

L. Teaz. Yes,—I'm told fhe abfolutely lives upon acids and fmall whey, and laces herfelf with pullies. Often in the hotteft day in fummer, you fhall fee her on a little fquat poney, with her hair platted and turned up like a drummer, and away fhe goes puffing round the ring in a full trot.

Sir Pet. Mercy on me ! this is her own relation ; a perfon they dine with twice a week. [*Afide.*

Mrs. Can. I vow you fhan't be fo fevere upon the dowager; for let me tell you, great allowances are to be made for a woman who ftrives to pafs for a flirt at fix and thirty.

L. Sneer. Though furely fhe's handfome ftill ; and for the weaknefs in her eyes, confidering how much fhe reads by candle-light, 'tis not to be wondered at.

Mrs Can. Very true ; and for her manner, I think it very graceful, confidering fhe never had any education ; for her mother, you know, was a Welch milliner, and her father a fugar-baker at Briftol.

Sir Benj. Aye, you are both of you too good-natured

Mrs. Can. Well, I will never join in the ridicule of a friend ; fo I tell my coufin Ogle, and you all know what pretenfions fhe has to beauty.

Crab. She has the oddeft countenance—a collection of features from all corners of the globe.

Sir Benj. She has, indeed, an Irifh front.

Crab. Caledonian locks.

Sir Benj. Dutch nofe.

Crab. Auftrian lips.

Sir Benj. The complexion of a Spaniard.

Crab. And teeth a la Chinoife.

Sir Benj. In fhort, her face refembles a table d'hote at Spa, where no two guefts are of a nation.

Crab. Or a Congrefs at the clofe of a general war, where every member feems to have a different intereft, and the nofe and chin are the only parties likely to join iffue.

Sir Benj. Ha, ha, ha.

L. Sneer. Ha, ha.—Well, I vow you are a couple of provoking toads.

Mrs. Can. Well, I vow you fhan't carry the laugh fo—let me tell you that, Mrs. Ogle—

Sir Pet. Madam, madam, 'tis impoffible to ftop thofe good gentlemen's tongues; but when I tell you, Mrs. Candour, that the lady they are fpeaking of is a particular friend of mine, I hope you will be fo good as not to undertake her defence.

L. Sneer. Well faid, Sir Peter; but you are a cruel creature, too phlegmatic yourfelf for a wit, and too peevifh to allow it to others.

Sir Pet. True wit, madam, is more nearly allied to good nature than you are aware of.

L. Teaz. True, Sir Peter; I believe they are fo near a-kin that they can never be united.

Sir Benj. Or rather, madam, fuppofe them to be man and wife, one fo feldom fees them together.

L. Teaz. But Sir Peter is fuch an enemy to fcandal, I believe he would have it put down by Parliament.

Sir Pet. 'Foregad, madam, if they confidered the fporting with reputations of as much confequence as poaching on manors, and paffed an act for the prefervation of fame, they would find many would thank them for the bill.

L. Sneer. Oh lud!—Sir Peter would deprive us of our *privileges.*

Sir Pet. Yes, madam ; and none fhould then have the liberty to kill characters, and run down reputations, but *privileged* old maids, and *difappointed* widows.

L. Sneer. Go, you monfter !

Mrs. Can. But fure you would not be fo fevere on thofe who only report what they hear ?

Sir Pet. Yes, madam, I would have law for them too ; wherever the drawer of the lie was not to be found, the injured party fhould have a right to come on any of the indorfers.

Crab. Well, I verily believe there never was a fcandalous ftory without fome foundation.

Sir Pet. Nine out of ten are formed on fome malicious invention, or idle reprefentation.

L. Sneer. Come, ladies, fhall we fit down to cards in the next room ?

Enter a Servant, *who whispers* Sir Peter.

Sir Pet. I'll come directly—I'll steal away un-perceived.   [*Aside.*

L. Sneer. Sir Peter, you're not leaving us.

Sir Pet. I beg pardon, ladies, 'tis particular bu-sinefs, and I muft—but I leave my character behind me.   [*Exit* Sir Peter.

Sir Benj. Well, certainly Lady Teazle, that lord of yours is a ftrange being ;-I could tell you fome ftories of him would make you laugh heartily, if he was not your hufband.

L. Teaz. Oh, never mind that—this_way.

[*They walk up and exeunt.*

Jof. You take no pleafure in this fociety. (*To Maria*).

Maria. How can I ? If to raife a malicious fmile at the misfortunes and infirmities of thofe who are unhappy, be a proof of wit and humour, Heaven grant me a double portion of dulnefs.

Jof. And yet, they have no malice in their hearts.

Maria. Then it is the more inexcufable, fince nothing but an ungovernable depravity of heart, could tempt them to fuch a practice.

Jof. And is it poffible, Maria, that you can thus feel for others, and yet be cruel to me alone ?—Is hope to be denied the tendereft paffion ?

Maria. Why will you perfift to perfecute me on a fubject on which you have long fince known my fentiments.

Jof. Oh, Maria, you would not be thus deaf to me, but that Charles, that libertine, is ftill a fa-voured rival. ‑

Maria. Ungeneroufly urged; but whatever my fentiments are, with regard to that unfortunate young man, be affured, I fhall not confider myfelf more bound to give him up, becaufe his misfor-tunes have loft him the regards—even of a brother—
[*Going out.*

Jof. Nay, Maria, you fhall not leave me with a frown ; by all that's honeft I fwear—*(Kneels, and fees* Lady Teazle *entering behind)* Ah ! Lady Tea-zle, ah ! you fhall not ftir—*(To Maria)* I have the greateft regard in the world for Lady Teazle, ‑but if Sir Peter was once to fufpect—

Maria. Lady Teazle !— .

L. Teaz. What is all this, child ?—You are wanting in the next room. *(Exit Maria)*—What is the meaning of all this?—What! did you mif-take her for me ?

Jof. Why, you muft know—Maria—by fome means fufpecting—the—great regard I entertain for your ladyfhip—was—was—threatening—if I did not defift, to acquaint Sir Peter—and I—I—was juft reafoning with her—

L. Teaz. You feem to have adopted a very ten-der method of reafoning—pray, do you ufually argue on your knees ?

Jof. Why, you know, fhe's but a child, and I thought a little bombaft might be ufeful to keep her filent.—But, my dear Lady Teazle, when will you come and give me your opinion of my library ?

L. Teaz. Why, I really begin to think it not fo proper, and you know I admit you as a lover no farther than fafhion dictates.

Jof. Oh, no more ;—a mere platonic Cicifbeo, that every lady is entitled to.

L. Teaz. No further—and though Sir Peter's treatment may make me uneafy, it fhall never provoke me—

Jof. To the only revenge in your power.

L. Teaz. Go, you infinuating wretch—but we fhall be miffed, let us join the company.

Jof. I'll follow your ladyfhip.

L. Teaz. Don't ftay long, for I promife you Maria fhan't come to hear any more of your reafoning.   [*Exit* Lady Teazle.

Jof. A pretty fituation I am in—by gaining the wife I fhall lofe the heirefs—I at firft intended to make her ladyfhip only the inftrument in my defigns on Maria, but—I don't know how it is—I am become her ferious admirer. I begin now to wifh I had not made a point of gaining fo very good a character, for it has brought me into fo many confounded rogueries, that I fear I fhall be expofed at laft.

[*Exit* Jofeph.

SCENE III.

Sir Peter Teazle's *Houſe.*

Enter Sir Oliver *and* Rowley.

Sir Oliv. Ha, ha, and ſo my old friend is married at laſt, eh Rowley—and to a young wife out of the country, ha, ha, ha.   That he ſhould buff to old batchelors ſo long, and ſink into a huſband at laſt.

Row. But let me beg of you, Sir, not to rally him upon the ſubject, for he cannot bear it, though he has been married theſe ſeven months.

Sir Oliv. Then he has been juſt half a year on the ſtool of repentance.   Poor Sir Peter !—But you ſay he has entirely given up Charles—never ſees him, eh.

Row. His prejudice againſt him is aſtoniſhing, and I believe it is greatly aggravated by a ſuſpicion of a connexion between Charles and Lady Teazle, and ſuch a report I know has been circulated and kept up, by means of Lady Sneerwell, and a ſcandalous party who aſſociate at her houſe ; whereas I am convinced, if there is any partiality in the caſe, that Joſeph is the favourite.

Sir Oliv. Aye, aye—I know there are a ſet of miſchievous prating goſſips, both male and female, who murder characters to kill time, and rob a young fellow of his good name, before he has ſenſe enough to know the value of it :—But I am not to be prejudiced againft my nephew by any fuch, I promife you—No, no, if Charles has done nothing falfe or mean, I fhall compound for his extravagance.

Row. I rejoice, Sir, to hear you fay fo ; and am happy the fon of my old mafter has one friend left however.

Sir Oliv. What ! fhall I forget, Mafter Rowley, when I was at his years myfelf?—egad, neither my brother or I were very prudent youths, and yet, I believe, you have not feen many better men than your old mafter was.

Row. 'Tis that reflection I build my hopes on— and, my life on't ! Charles will prove deferving of your kindnefs.—But here comes Sir Peter.

Enter Sir PETER.

Sir Pet. Where is he ? Where is Sir Oliver ?— Ah, my dear friend, I rejoice to fee you !—You are welcome—indeed you are welcome—you are welcome to England a thoufand—and a thoufand. times !—

Sir Oliv. Thank you, thank you, Sir Peter— and I am glad to find you fo well, believe me.

Sir Pet. Ah, Sir Oliver !—It's fixteen years fince laft we faw each other—many a bout we have had together in our time !

Sir Oliv. Aye I have had my fhare.—But what, I find you are married—hey old boy !—Well, well, it can't be helped, fo I wifh you joy with all my. heart.

Sir Pet. Thank you, thank you—Yes, Sir Oliver, I have entered into that happy ſtate—but we won't talk of that now.

Sir Oliv. That's true, Sir Peter, old friends ſhould not begin upon grievances at their firſt meeting, no, no, no.

Row. (*Aſide to Sir Oliver*) Have a care, Sir;—don't touch upon that ſubjeć.

Sir Oliv. Well—So one of my nephews, I find, is a wild young rogue.

Sir Pet. Oh, my dear friend, I grieve at your diſappointment there—Charles is, indeed, a ſad libertine—but no matter, Jóſeph will make you ample amends—every body ſpeaks well of him.

Sir Oliv. I am very ſórry to hear it ; he has too good a charaćter to be an honeſt fellow—every body ſpeaks well of him !—'pſhaw—then he has bowed as low to knaves and fools, as to the honeſt dignity of genius and virtue.

Sir Pet. What the plague! are you angry with Joſeph for not making enemies ?

Sir Oliv. Why not, if he has merit enough to deſerve them.

Sir Pet. Well, well, ſee him, and you'll be convinced how worthy he is—he is a pattern for all the young men of the age.—He's a man of the nobleſt ſentiments.

Sir Oliv. Oh ! plague of his ſentiments.—If he ſalutes me with a ſcrap of morality in his mouth I ſhall be ſick direćtly—But don't however miſtake me, Sir Peter, I don't mean to defend Charles's errors ; but before I form my judgment of either of them, I intend to make a trial of their hearts, and my friend Rowley and I have planned something for that purpofe.

Sir Pet. My life on Jofeph's honour.

Sir Oliv. Well, well, give us a bottle of good wine, and we'll drink your lady's health, and tell you all our fchemes.

Sir Pet. Alons—done.

Sir Oliv. And don't Sir Peter, be too fevere againft your old friend's fon—Odds my life, I am not forry he has run a little out of the courfe—for my part, I hate to fee prudence clinging to the green fuckers of youth ; 'tis like ivy round the faplin, and fpoils the growth of the tree.   [*Exeunt omnes.*

ACT III. SCENE I.

Sir PETER's *Houfe.*

Enter Sir PETER, Sir OLIVER, *and* ROWLEY.

Sir Peter.

WELL, well, we'll fee this man firft, and then have our wine afterwards.—But Rowley, I don't fee the jeft of your fcheme.

Row. Why, Sir, this Mr. Stanley is a near relation of their mother's, and formerly an eminent merchant in Dublin—He failed in trade, and is greatly reduced; he has applied by letter to Mr. Surface and Charles for affiftance—from the former of whom he has received nothing but fair promifes ; while Charles, in the midft of his own diftreffes, is at prefent endeavouring to raife a fum of money, part of which I know he intends for the ufe of Mr. Stanley.

Sir Oliv. Aye—he's my brother's fon.

Row. Now, Sir, we propofe, that Sir Oliver fhall vifit them both, in the character of Mr. Stanley ; as I have informed them he has obtained leave of his creditors to wait on his friends in perfon—and in the younger, believe me, you'll find one, who, in the midft of diffipation and extravagance, has ftill, as our immortal bard expreffes it—*A tear for pity, and a hand open as day' for melting charity.*

Sir Pet. What fignifies his open hand and purfe, if he has nothing to give. But where is this perfon you were fpeaking of ?

Row. Below, Sir, waiting your commands— You muft know, Sir Oliver, this is a friendly Jew ; one who, to do him juftice, has done every thing in his power to affift Charles—Who waits—*(Enter a Servant)* defire Mr. Mofes to walk up.

[*Exit* Servant.

Sir Pet. But how are you fure he'll fpeak truth ?

Row. 'Why, Sir, I have perfuaded him, there's no profpect of his being paid feveral fums of money he has advanced for Charles, but through the bounty of Sir Oliver, who he knows is in town ; therefore you may depend on his being faithful to his intereft—Oh ! here comes the honeft Ifraelite.—

Enter MOSES.

Sir Oliver, this is Mr. Mofes.——Mr. Mofes, this
is Sir Oliver.

Sir Oliv. I underſtand you have lately had great
dealings with my nephew, Charles.

Mofes. Yes, Sir Oliver—I have done all I could
for him—but he was ruined before he came to me
for affiſtance.

Sir Oliv. That was unlucky truly, for you had
no opportunity of ſhewing your talent.

Mofes. None at all; I had not the pleaſure of
knowing his diſtreſſes, 'till he was ſome thouſands
worſe than nothing.

Sir Oliv. Unfortunate indeed! But I ſuppoſe
you have done all in your power for him.

Mofes. Yes, he knows that—This very evening I
was to have brought him a gentleman from the
city, who does not know him, and will advance
him ſome monies.

Sir Pet. What! a perſon that Charles has never
borrowed money of before, lend him any in his
preſent circumſtances!

Mofes. Yes.—

Sir Oliv. What is this gentleman's name?

Mofes. Mr. Premium, of Crutched Friars, formerly a broker.

Sir Pet. Does he know Mr. Premium?

Mofes. Not at all.

Sir Pet. A thought ſtrikes me—Suppoſe, Sir
Oliver, you was to viſit him in that character,
'twill be much better than the romantic one of an

old relation; you will then have an opportunity of feeing Charles in all his glory.

Sir Oliv. Egad I like that idea better than the other, and then I may vifit Jofeph afterwards as old Stanley.

Row. Gentlemen, this is taking Charles rather unawares; but Mofes, you underftand Sir Oliver, and I dare fay will be faithful.

Mofes. You may depend upon me.—This is very near the time I was to have gone.

Sir Oliv. I'll accompany you as foon as you pleafe, Mofes—But hold, I had forgot one thing—How the plague fhall I be able to pafs for a Jew?

Mofes. There is no need—the principal is a Chriftian.

Sir Oliv. Is he? 1 am very forry for it.—But then again, am I not too fmartly dreffed to look like a money-lender?

Sir Pet. Not at all—it would not be out of cha-racter if you went in your own chariot—would it, Mofes?

Mofes. Not in the leaft.

Sir Oliv. Well, but how muft I talk? There's certainly fome cant of ufury, or mode of treating, that I ought to know.

Sir Pet. As I take it Sir Oliver, the great point is be exorbitant in your demands.—Eh! Mofes!

Mofes. Yes, dat is very great point.

Sir Oliv. I'll anfwer for't I'll not be wanting in that, eight or ten *per cent.* on the loan at leaft.

Mofes. Oh! if you afk him no more as dat, you'll be difcovered immediately.

Sir Oliv. Hey, what the plague—how much then ?

Mofes. That depends upon the circumftances— if he appears not very anxious for the fupply, you fhould require only forty or fifty *per cent.* but if you find him in great diftrefs, and he wants money very bad—you muft afk double.

Sir Pet. Upon my word, Sir Oliver—Mr. Premium I mean—it's a very pretty trade you're learning.

Sir Oliv. Truly, I think fo ; and not unprofitable.

Mofes. Then you know you have not the money yourfelf, but are forced to borrow it of a friend.'

Sir Oliv. Oh ! I borrow it for him of a friend— do I ?

Mofes. Yes, and your friend's an unconfcionable dog—but you can't help dat.

Sir Oliv. Oh ! my friend's an unconfcionable dog—is he ?

Mofes. And then he himfelf has not the monies by him, but is forced to fell ftock at a great lofs.

Sir Oliv. He is forced to fell ftock at a great lofs—Well, really, that's very kind of him.

Sir Pet. But hark'ye Mofes, if Sir Oliver was to rail a little at the annuity bill, don't you think it would have a good effect ?

Mofes. Very much.

Row. And lament that a young man muft now come to years of difcretion, before he has it in his power to ruin himfelf.

Mofes. Aye ! a great pity.

Sir Pet. Yes, and abufe the public for allowing merit to a bill, whofe only object was to preferve youth and inexperience from the rapacious gripe of ufury, and to give the young heir an opportunity of enjoying his fortune, without being ruined by coming into poffeffion.

Sir Oliv. So—fo—Mofes fhall give me further inftructions as we go together.

Sir Pet. You'll fcarce have time to learn your trade, for Charles lives but hard by.

Sir Oliv. Oh! never fear—my tutor appears fo able, that tho' Charles lived in the next ftreet, it muft be my own fault if I am not a complete rogue before I have turned the corner.

[*Exeunt* Sir Oliver *and* Mofes.

Sir Pet. So, Rowley, you would have been partial, and given Charles the notice of our plot.

Row. No indeed, Sir Peter.

Sir Pet. Well, I fee Maria coming, I want to have fome talk with her.   [*Exit* Rowley.

Enter MARIA.

So Maria—What, is Mr. Surface come home with you?

Maria. No, Sir—he was engaged.

Sir Pet. Maria, I wifh you were more fenfible to his excellent qualities—does not every time you are in his company convince you of the merit of that amiable young man?

Maria. You know, Sir Peter, I have often told you, that of all the men that have paid me a par ticular attention, there is not one I would not sooner prefer than Mr. Surface.

Sir Pet. Aye, aye, this blindnefs to his merit proceeds from your attachment to that profligate brother of his. '

Maria. This is unkind—you know at your requeft, I have forbore to fee or correfpond with him, as I have long been convinced he is unworthy my regard; but while my reafon condemns his vices, my heart fuggefts fome pity for his misfortunes.

Sir Pet. Ah! you had beft refolve to think of him no more, but give your heart and hand to a worthier objeſt.

Maria. Never to his brother.

Sir Pet. Have a care Maria, I have not yet made you know what the authority of a guardian is—don't force me to exert it.

Maria. I know, that for a fhort time I am to obey you as my father—but muft ceafe to think you fo, when you would compel me to be miserable.   [*Exit in tears.*

Sir Pet. Sure never was man plagued as I am— I had not been married above three weeks, before her father, a heal, hearty man, died—on purpofe, I believe, to plague me with the care of his daughter: but here comes my help mate, fhe feems in mighty good humour; I wifh I could teize her into loving me a little.

Enter Lady Teazle.

L. Teaz. What's the matter, Sir Peter? What have you done to Maria? It is not fair to quarrel

━ -nd I not by.   ᴵ   4

Sir Pet. Ah! Lady Teazle, it is in your power to put me into a good humour at any time.

L. Teaz. Is it? I am glad of it—for I want you to be in a monſtrous good humour now—Come, do be good humoured, and let me have two hundred pounds.

Sir Pet. What the plague! can't I be in a good humour without paying for it—but look always thus, and you ſhall want for nothing. *(Pulls out a pocket-book.)* There, there's two hundred pounds for you, *(going to kiſs)* now ſeal me a bond for the re-payment.

L. Teaz. No, my note of hand will do as well.

[Giving her hand.

Sir Pet. Well, well, I muſt be ſatisfied with that—you ſhan't much longer reproach me for not having made you a proper ſettlement—I intend ſhortly to ſurprize you.

L. Teaz. Do you? You can't think, Sir Peter, how good humour becomes you—Now you look juſt as you did before I married you.

Sir Pet. Do I indeed?

L. Teaz. Don't you remember when you uſed to walk with me under the elms, and tell me ſtories of what a gallant you were in your youth, and aſked me if I could like an old fellow, who could deny me nothing.

Sir Pet. Aye, and you were ſo attentive and obliging to me then.

L. Teaz. Aye, to be ſure I was, and uſed to take your part againſt all my acquaintance; and when my couſin Sophy uſed to laugh at me, for

C

thinking of marrying a man old enough to be my
father, and call you an ugly, ftiff, formal old
batchelor, I contradicted her, and faid I did not
think you fo ugly by any means, and that I dar'd
fay, you would make a good fort of a hufband.

Sir Pet. That was very kind of you—Well, and
you were not miftaken, you have found it fo, have
not you?—But fhall we always live thus happy?

L. Teaz. With all my heart—I'm—I don't care
how foon we leave off quarrelling, provided you
will own you are tired firft.

Sir Pet. With all my heart.

L. Teaz. Then we fhall be as happy as the day
is long, and never, never—never quarrel more.

Sir Pet. Never—never—never—and let our future conteft be, who fhall be moft obliging.

L. Teaz. Aye!

Sir Pet. But, my dear Lady Teazle—my love—
indeed you muft keep a ftrict watch over your temper—for, you know, my dear, that in all our difputes and quarrels, you always begin firft.

L. Teaz. No, no, Sir Peter, my dear, 'tis always you that begins.

Sir Pet. No, no—no fuch thing.

L. Teaz. Have a care, this is not the way to
live happy if you fly out thus.

Sir Pet. No, no—'tis you.

L. Teaz. No—'tis you.

Sir Pet. Zounds!—I fay 'tis you.

L. Teaz. Lord! I never faw fuch a man in my
life—juft what my coufin Sophy told me.

Sir Pet. Your coufin Sophy is a forward, faucy, impertinent minx.

L. Teaz. You are a very great bear, I am fure, to abufe my relations.

Sir Pet. But I am well enough ferved for marrying you—a pert forward, rural coquette, who had refufed half the honeft 'fquires in the country.

L. Teaz. I am fure I was a great fool for marrying you—a ftiff, crop, dangling old batchelor, who was un-married at fifty, becaufe no body would have him.

Sir Pet. You was very glad to have me—you never had fuch an offer before.

L. Teaz. Oh, yes I had—There was Sir Tivey Terrier, who every body faid would be a better match ; for his eftate was full as good as yours, and—he has broke his neck fince we were married.

Sir Pet. Very—very well, Madam—you're an ungrateful woman ; and may plagues light on me, if I ever try to be friends with you again— You fhall have a feparate maintenance.

L. Teaz. By all means a feparate maintenance.

Sir Pet. Very well, Madam—Oh, very well. Aye, Madam, and I believe the ftories of you and Charles—of you and Charles, Madam—were not without foundation.

L. Teaz.—Take care, Sir Peter ; take care what you fay, for I won't be fufpected without a caufe, I promife you.

Sir Pet. A divorce !—

L. Teaz. Aye, a divorce.

Car. But come, Charles, you have not given us your real favourite.

Cha. Faith I have withheld her only in compassion to you, for if I give her, you must toast a round of her peers, which is impossible, *(sighs)* on earth.

Car. We'll toast some heathen deity or celestial goddess to match her.

Cha. Why then bumpers—bumpers all round,—Here's Maria—Maria.—*(Sighs)*

1st Gent. Maria—'Pshaw—give her sir-name.

Cha. 'Pshaw—Hang her sir name, that's too formal to be registered in Love's calendar.

1st Gent. Maria then.—Here's Maria.

Sir Toby. Maria—Come here's Maria.

Cha. Come, Sir Toby, have a care; you must give a beauty superlative.

Sir Toby. Then I'll give you——Here's——

Car. Nay, never hesitate.—But Sir Toby has got a song, that will excuse him.

Omnes. The song.——The song.

S O N G.

Here's to the maiden of blushing fifteen,
    Now to the widow of fifty ;
Here's to the flaunting, extravagant quean,
    And then to the housewife that's thrifty :
      Let the toast pass, drink to the lass,
      I warrant she'll find an excuse for the glass.

Here's to the charmer whofe dimples we prize,
　Now to the damfel with none, Sir;
Here's to the maid with her pair of blue eyes,
　And now to the nymph with but one, Sir;
　　Let the toaſt pafs, &c.

Here's to the maid with her bofom of fnow,
　Now to her that's as brown as a berry;
Here's to the wife with her face full of woe,
　And now to the damfel that's merry.
　　Let the toaſt pafs, &c.

For let them be clumfy, or let them be flim,
　Young or ancient I care not a feather;
So fill us a bumper quite up to the brim,
　And e'en let us toaſt them together.
　　Let the toaſt pafs, &c.

　　Trip *enters and whiſpers* Charles.

Cha. Gentlemen, I muſt beg your pardon;
(rifing) I muſt leave you upon bufinefs—Carelefs,
take the chair.

Car. What, this is fome wench—but we won't
lofe you for her.

Cha. No, upon my honour—it is only a jew and
a broker that came by appointment.

Car. A jew and a broker! we'll have 'em in.

Cha. Then defire Mr. Mofes to walk in.

Trip. And little Premium too, Sir.

Car. Aye, Mofes and Premium, (*Exit* Trip)
Charles *we'll give* the rafcals fome generous Bur-
gundy.

C 5

ticular attention, there is not one I would not
fooner prefer than Mr. Surface.

Sir Pet. Aye, aye, this blindnefs to his merit
proceeds from your attachment to that profligate
brother of his.

Maria. This is unkind—you know at your requeft, I have forbore to fee or correfpond with him,
as I have long been convinced he is unworthy my
regard; but while my reafon condemns his vices,
my heart fuggefts fome pity for his misfortunes.

Sir Pet. Ah! you had beft refolve to think of
him no more, but give your heart and hand to
a worthier object.

Maria. Never to his brother.

Sir Pet. Have a care Maria, I have not yet
made you know what the authority of a guardian
is—don't force me to exert it.

Maria. I know, that for a fhort time I am to
obey you as my father—but muft ceafe to think
you fo, when you would compel me to be miferable.   [*Exit in tears.*

Sir Pet. Sure never was man plagued as I am—
I had not been married above three weeks, before
her father, a heal, hearty man, died—on purpofe,
I believe, to plague me with the care of his daughter: but here comes my help mate, fhe feems in
mighty good humour; I wifh I could teize her into
loving me a little.

Enter LADY TEAZLE.

L. Teaz. What's the matter, Sir Peter? What
have you done to Maria? It is not fair to quarrel
and I not by.   4

Sir Pet. Ah! Lady Teazle, it is in your power to put me into a good humour at any time.

L. Teaz. Is it? I am glad of it—for I want you to be in a monſtrous good humour now—Come, do be good humoured, and let me have two hundred pounds.

Sir Pet. What the plague! can't I be in a good humour without paying for it—but look always thus, and you ſhall want for nothing. *(Pulls out a pocket-book.)* There, there's two hundred pounds for you, *(going to kiſs)* now ſeal me a bond for the re-payment.

L. Teaz. No, my note of hand will do as well.

[*Giving her hand.*

Sir Pet. Well, well, I muſt be ſatisfied with that—you ſhan't much longer reproach me for not having made you a proper ſettlement—I intend ſhortly to ſurprize you.

L. Teaz. Do you? You can't think, Sir Peter, how good humour becomes you—Now you look juſt as you did before I married you.

Sir Pet. Do I indeed?

L. Teaz. Don't you remember when you uſed to walk with me under the elms, and tell me ſtories of what a gallant you were in your youth, and aſked me if I could like an old fellow, who could deny me nothing.

Sir Pet. Aye, and you were ſo attentive and obliging to me then.

L. Teaz. Aye, to be ſure I was, and uſed to take your part againſt all my acquaintance ; and when my couſin Sophy uſed to laugh at me, for

C

Sir Oliv. Very true, as you fay, you muft know better than I; though I have it from very good authority—Have I not, Mofes?

Mofes. Moft undoubtedly.

Sir Oliv. But, Sir, as I underftand you want a few hundreds immediately, is there nothing that you would difpofe of?

Cha. How do you mean?

Sir Oliv. For inftance, now;. I have heard your father left behind him a quantity of maffy old plate.

Cha. Yes, but that is gone long ago—Mofes can inform you how, better than I can.

Sir Oliv. Good lack! all the family race cups and corporation bowls gone! *(Afide)* It was alfo fuppofed, that his library was one of the moft valuable and compleat.

Cha. Much too large and valuable for a private gentleman—for my part, I was always of a communicative difpofition, and thought it a pity to keep fo much knowledge to myfelf.

Sir Oliv. Mercy on me! knowledge that has run in the family like an heir-loom. *(Afide)* And pray, how may they have been difpofed of?

Cha. Oh! you muft afk the auctionier that—I don't believe even Mofes can direct you there.

Mofes. No—I never meddle with books.

Sir Oliv. The profligate! *(Afide)* And is there nothing you can difpofe of?

Cha. Nothing—unlefs you have a tafte for old family pictures. I have a whole room full of anceftors above ftairs.

Sir Oliv. Why fure you would not fell your relations!

Cha. Every foul of them to the beft bidder.

Sir Oliv. Not your great uncles and aunts.

Cha. Aye, and my grand-fathers and grand-mothers.

Sir Oliv. I'll never forgive him this. *(Afide)*
Why!—What!—Do you take me for Shylock in
the play, to raife money from me on your own
flefh and blood.

Cha. Nay, don't be in a paffion my little Premium—what is it to you, if you have your money's
worth?

Sir Oliv. That's very true, as you fay—well,
well, I believe I can difpofe of the family canvas.
I'll never forgive him this.   [*Afide.*

Enter CARELESS.

Car. Come, Charles, what the devil are you doing fo long with the broker?—We are waiting for
you.

Cha. Oh! Carelefs, you are juft come in time,
we are to have a fale above ftairs—I am going to
fell all my anceftors to little Premium.

Car. Burn your anceftors.

Cha. No, no, he may do that afterwards if he
will.—But Carelefs you fhall be auctionier.

Car. With all my heart, I handle a hammer as
well as a dice box——a going——a going.

Cha. Bravo!—And Mofes, you fhall be appraifer, if we want one.

Mofes. Yes, I'll be the appraifer.

Sir Oliv. Oh the profligate!   [*Aside.*

Cha. But what's the matter, my little Premï-um? You don't feem to relifh this bufinefs.

Sir Oliv. (Affecting to laugh) Oh, yes I do, vaft-ly—Ha, ha, ha, I——O the prodigal !

Cha. Very true ; for when a man wants money, who the devil can he make free with if he can't with his own relations.   [*Exit.*

Sir Oliv. (Following) I'll never forgive him.

[*Exeunt.*

ACT IV. SCENE I.

Enter CHARLES, Sir OLIVER, CARELESS, *and* MOSES.

CHARLES.

WALK in, gentlemen, walk in—here they are—the family of the Surfaces up to the Conqueft.

Sir Oliv. And, in my opinion, a goodly collection.

Cha. Aye, there they are, done in the true fpirit and ftyle of portrait painting, and not like your modern Raphael's, who will make your picture in-dependant of yourfelf—no, the great merit of thefe are, the inveterate likenefs they bear to the origi-nals. All ftiff and aukward as they were, and like nothing in human nature befides.

Sir Oliv. Oh, we fhall never fee fuch figures of men again.

Cha. I hope not—you fee, Mr. Premium, what a domeftic man I am ; here I fit of an evening fur-rounded by my anceftors —But come, let us pro-ceed to bufinefs—to your pulpit Mr. Auctionier—Oh, here's a great chair of my father's that feems fit for nothing elfe.

Car. The very thing—but what fhall I do for a hammer.

Cha. A hammer! *(looks round)* Let's fee, what have we here—Sir Richard, heir to Robert—a ge-nealogy in full, egad—here, Carelefs, you fhall have no common bit of mahogany—here's the family tree, and now you may knock down my anceftors with their own pedigree.

Sir Oliv. What an unnatural rogue he is !—An expoft facto parricide. *(Afide)*

Car. Gad, Charles, this is lucky, for it will not only ferve for a hammer, but a catalogue too if we fhould want it.

Cha. True—come, here's my great uncle, Sir Richard Ravelin, a marvellous good general in his day.—He ferved in all the Duke of Marlborough's wars, and got that cut over his eye at the battle of Malplaquet—he is not dreffed out in feathers like our modern captains, but enveloped in wig and re-gimentals, as a general fhould be—what fay you Mr. Premium ?

Mofes. Mr. Premium would have you fpeak.

Cha. Why, you fhall have him for ten pounds, and I'm fure that's cheap enough for a ftaff officer.

Sir Oliv. Heavens deliver me ! his great uncle Sir Richard going for ten pounds—*(Aside)*—well, Sir, I take him at that price.

Cha. Carelefs, knock down my uncle Richard.

Car. Going, going——a going——gone.

Cha. This is a maiden fifter of his, my great aunt Deborah, done by Kneller, thought to be one of his beft pictures, and efteemed a very formidable likenefs. There fhe fits, as a fhepherdefs feeding her flock—you fhall have her for five pounds ten. I'm fure the fheep are worth the money.

Sir Oliv. Ah, poor aunt Deborah ! a woman that fet fuch a value on herfelf, going for five pounds ten—*(Aside)*—Well, Sir, fhe's mine.

Cha. Knock down my aunt Deborah, Carelefs.

Car. Gone.

Cha. Here are two coufins of theirs—Mofes, thefe pictures were done when beaux wore perriwigs, and ladies their own hair.

Sir Oliv. Yes, truly—head dreffes feem to have been fomewhat lower in thofe days.

Cha. Here's a grandfather of my mother's, a judge well known on the weftern circuit. What will you give for him?

Mofes. Four guineas.

Cha. Four guineas ! why you don't bid the price of his wig. Premium, you have more refpect for the Wool Sack, do let me knock him down at fifteen.

Sir Oliv. By all means.

 *Gone.*

Cha. Here are two brothers, William and Walter Blunt, Efqrs. both members of parliament, and great fpeakers; and what's very extraordinary, I believe this is the firſt time they were ever bought or fold.

Sir Oliv. That's very extraordinary, indeed!— I'll take them at your own price, for the honour of parliament.

Cha. Well faid Premium.

Car. I'll knock them down at forty pounds— Going——going——gone.

Cha. Here's a jolly, portly fellow; I don't know what relation he is to the family, but he was formerly mayor of Norwich, let's knock him down at eight pounds.

Sir Oliv. No, I think fix is enough for a mayor.

Cha. Come, come, make it guineas, and I'll throw you the two aldermen into the bargain.

Sir Oliv. They are mine.

Cha. Carelefs, knock down the mayor and aldermen.

Car. Gone.

Cha. But hang it, we fhall be all day at this rate—Come, come, give me three hundred pounds, and take all on this fide the room in a lump—that will be the beft way.

Sir Oliv. Well, well, any thing to accommodate you; they are mine.—But there is one portrait you have always paffed over.

Car. What, that little ill-looking fellow over the fettee.

Sir Oliv. Yes, Sir, 'tis that I mean—but I don't think him fo ill-looking a fellow by any means.

Cha. That's the picture of my uncle Oliver—before he went abroad it was done, and is efteemed a very great likenefs.

Car. That your uncle Oliver ! Then in my opinion you will never be friends, for he is one of the moft ftern looking rogues I ever beheld—he has an unforgiving eye, and a damn'd difinheriting countenance.—Don't you think fo, little Premium ?

Sir Oliv. Upon my foul I do not, Sir—I think it as honeft a looking face as any in the room, dead or alive.—But I fuppofe your uncle Oliver goes with the reft of the lumber.

Cha. No, hang it, the old gentleman has been very good to me, and I'll keep his picture as long as I have a room to put it in.

Sir Oliv. The rogue's my nephew after all—I forgive him every thing. *(Afide)* But, Sir, I have fomehow taken a fancy to that picture.

Cha. I am forry for it, mafter broker, for you certainly won't have it.—What the devil, have you not got enough of the family ?

Sir Oliv. I forgive him every thing. *(Afide)* Look, Sir, I am a ftrange fort of a fellow, and when I take a thing in my head I don't value money : I'll give you as much for that as for all the reft.

Cha. Pray don't be troublefome—I tell you I won't part with it, and there's an end on't.

Sir Oliv. How like his father the dog is—I did not perceive it before, but I think I never faw fo ftrong a refemblance. *(Afide)* Well, Sir, here's a draft for your fum. *(Giving a bill)*

Cha. Why this bill is for eight hundred pounds.

Sir Oliv. You'll not let Sir Oliver go, then.

Cha. No, I tell you once for all.

Sir Oliv. Then never mind the difference, we'll balance that fome other time—but give me your hand, *(preffes it)* you are a damn'd honeft fellow, Charles—O Lord! I beg pardon, Sir, for being fo free.——Come along Mofes.

Cha. But hark'ye, Premium, you'll provide good lodgings for thefe gentlemen. *(Going)*

Sir Oliv. I'll fend for 'em in a day or two.

Cha. And pray let it be a genteel conveyance, for I affure you moft of 'em have been ufed to ride in their own carriages.

Sir Oliv. I will for all but Oliver.

Cha. For all but the honeft little Nabob.

Sir Oliv. You are fixed on that.

Cha. Peremptorily.

Sir Oliv. Ah the dear extravagant dog ! *(Afide)* Good day, Sir.—Come, Mofes.—Now let me fee who dare call him profligate.   [*Exit with* Mofes.

Car. Why Charles, this is the very prince of brokers.

Cha. I wonder where Mofes got acquainted with fo honeft a fellow.—But, Carelefs ftep into the company ; I'll wait on you prefently, I fee old *Rowley coming.*

Car. But hark'ye, Charles, don't let the fellow make you part with any of that money to difcharge mufty old debts. Tradefmen you know, are the moft impertinent people in the world.

Cha. True—and paying them would only be encouraging them.

Car. Well, fettle your bufinefs, and make what hafte you can.   [*Exit.*

Cha. Eight hundred pounds ! two-thirds of this are mine by right—five hundred and thirty odd pounds !—Gad, I never knew till now, that my anceftors were fuch valuable acquaintance.—Kind ladies and gentlemen, I am your very much obliged, and moft grateful humble fervant. *(Bowing to the pictures)*

Enter ROWLEY.

Ah ! old Rowley, you are juft come in time to take leave of your old acquaintance.

Row. Yes, Sir ; I heard they were going—but how can you fupport fuch fpirits under all your mis-fortunes ?

Cha. That's the caufe, Mafter Rowley—my mis-fortunes are fo many, that I can't afford to part with my fpirits.

Row. And can you really take leave of your an-ceftors with fo much unconcern.

Cha. Unconcern ! what, I fuppofe you are fur-prized that I am not more forrowful at lofing the company of fo many worthy friends. It is very diftreffing to be fure ; but you fee, they never move a mufcle, then why the devil fhould I ?

Row. Ah, dear Charles!—

Cha. But come, I have no time for trifling—here, take this bill and get it changed, and carry an hundred pounds to poor Stanley, or we fhall have fomebody call that has a better right to it.

Row. Ah, Sir, I wifh you would remember the proverb——

Cha. " *Be juſt before you are generous.*"—Why, fo I would if I could, but juſtice is an old, lame, hobbling beldam, and I can't get her to keep pace with generoſity for the foul of me.

Row. Do, dear Sir, reflect.

Cha. That's very true, as you fay—but Rowley, while I have, by heaven I'll give—fo damn your morality, and away to old Stanley with the money.

[*Exeunt.*

Enter Sir OLIVER *and* MOSES.

Mofes. Well, Sir, I think, as Sir Peter faid, you have feen Mr. Charles in all his glory—'tis great pity he's fo extravagant.

Sir Oliv. True, but he would not fell my picture.——

Mofes. And loves wine and women fo much.

Sir Oliv. But he would not fell my picture.——

Mofes. And games fo deep.

Sir Oliv. But he would not fell my picture.——Oh, here comes Rowley.

Enter ROWLEY.

Row. Well, Sir, I find you have made a purchafe.

Sir Oliv. Yes, our young rake has parted with his anceftors like old tapeftry.

Row. And he has commiffioned me to return you an hundred pounds of the purchafe money, but under your fictitious character of old Stanley. I faw a taylor and two hofiers dancing attendance, who I know, will go unpaid, and the hundred pounds would juft fatisfy them.

Sir Oliv. Well, well, I'll pay his debts and his benevolence too.—But now, I'm no more a broker, and you fhall introduce me to the elder brother as old Stanley.

Enter TRIP.

Trip. Gentlemen, I'm forry I was not in the way to fhew you out. Hark'ye Mofes.

[*Exit with* Mofes.

Sir Oliv. There's a fellow, now—will you believe it, that puppy intercepted the Jew on our coming, and wanted to raife money before he got to his mafter.

Row. Indeed!

Sir Oliv. And they are now planning an annuity bufinefs—Oh, Mafter Rowley, in my time fervants were content with the follies of their mafters, when they were wore a little threadbare; but now they have their vices, like their birth-day cloaths, with the glofs on.

[*Exeunt.*

SCENE II.

The Apartments of JOSEPH SURFACE.

Enter JOSEPH *and a* SERVANT.

Jof. No letter from Lady Teazle.

Ser. No, Sir.

Jof. I wonder ſhe did not write if ſhe could not come—I hope Sir Peter does not ſuſpeᴄt me——But Charles's diſſipation and extravagance are great points in my favour *(Knocking at the door)*—See if it is her.

Ser. 'Tis Lady Teazle, Sir; but ſhe always orders her chair to the Milliner's in the next ſtreet.

Jof. Then draw that ſcreen——my oppoſite neighbour is a maiden lady of ſo curious a temper—You need not wait. *(Exit Servant.)*—My Lady Teazle, I'm afraid, begins to ſuſpeᴄt my attachment to Maria; but ſhe muſt not be acquainted with the ſecret till I have her more in my power.

Enter Lady TEAZLE.

L. Teaz. What, ſentiment in ſoliloquy!—Have you been very impatient now? Nay, you look ſo grave—I aſſure you I came as ſoon as I could.

Jof. Oh, Madam, punᴄtuality is a ſpecies of conſtancy—a very unfaſhionable cuſtom amon̄ dies.

D

L. Teaz. Nay, now you wrong me ;⸗I'm fure you'd pity me if you knew my fituation—*(Both fit)*. — Sir Peter really grows fo peevifh, and fo ill-natured, there's no enduring him ; and then to fufpect me with Charles——

Jof. I'm glad my fcandalous friends keep up that report.   [*Afide.*

L. Teaz. For my part, I wifh Sir Peter to let Maria marry him—Wou'dn't you, Mr. Surface,

Jof. (Afide) Indeed I would not.—Oh, to be fure ; and then my dear Lady Teazle would be convinced how groundlefs her fufpicions were, of my having any thoughts of the filly girl.

L. Teaz. Then, there's my friend Lady Sneerwell has propagated malicious ftories about me—and what's very provoking, all too without the leaft foundation.

Jof. Ah ! there's the mifchief ;—for when a fcandalous ftory is believed againft me, there's no comfort like the confcioufnefs of having deferved it.

L. Teaz. And to be continually cenfured and fufpected, when I know the integrity of my own heart —it would almoft prompt me to give him fome grounds for it.

Jof. Certainly,—for when a hufband grows fufpicious, and withdraws his confidence from his wife, it then becomes a part of her duty to endeavour to out-wit him—You owe it to the natural privilege of your fex.

L. Teaz. Indeed !

Jof. Oh yes ; for your hufband fhould never be

deceived in you, and you ought to be frail in compliment to his difcernment.

L. Teaz. This is the neweft doctrine.

Jof. Very wholefome, believe me.

L. Teaz. So, the only way to prevent his fufpicions, is to give him caufe for them.

Jof. Certainly.

L. Teaz. But then, the confcioufnefs of my inno‧cence——

Jof. Ah, my dear Lady Teazle, 'tis that confci‧oufnefs of your innocence that ruins you.—What is it that makes you imprudent in your conduct, and carelefs of the cenfure of the world ? The confciouf‧nefs of your innocence—What is it makes you re‧gardlefs of forms, and inattentive to your hufband's peace ?—Why, the confcioufnefs of your innocence —Now, my dear Lady Teazle, if you could only be prevailed upon to make a trifling *faux pas*, you can't imagine how circumfpect you would grow.

L. Teaz. Do you think fo ?

Jof. Depend upon it.—Your cafe at prefent, my dear Lady Teazle, refembles that of a perfon in a plethora—you are abfolutely dying of too much health.

L. Teaz. Why, indeed if my undei ftanding could be convinced——

Jof. Your. underftanding !—Oh yes, your under‧ftanding *fhould* be convinced. Heaven forbid that I fhould perfuade you to any thing you thought wrong. No, no, I have too much honour for that.

L. Teaz. Don't you think you may as well leave honour out of the queſtion? *(Both riſe.)*

Joſ. Ah, I ſee, Lady Teazle, the effects of your country education ſtill remain.

L. Teaz. They do, indeed, and I begin to find myſelf imprudent ; and if I ſhould be brought to act wrong, it would be ſooner from Sir Peter's ill treatment of me, than from your honourable logic, I aſſure you.

Joſ. Then by this hand, which is unworthy of ―― *(Kneeling, a Servant enters)*—What do you want, you ſcoundrel?

Ser. I beg pardon, Sir—I thought you would not chuſe Sir Peter ſhould come up.

Joſ. Sir Peter !

L. Teaz. Sir Peter ! Oh, I'm undone !—What ſhall I do? Hide me ſomewhere, good Mr. Logic.

Joſ. Here, here, behind this ſcreen. *(She runs behind the ſcreen)* and now reach me a book. *(Sits down and reads.)*

Enter Sir Peter.

Sir Pet. Aye, there he is, ever improving himſelf —Mr. Surface, Mr. Surface.

Joſ. (Affecting to gape) Oh, Sir Peter I rejoice to ſee you—I was got over a ſleepy book here—I am vaſtly glad to ſee you—I thank you for this call—I believe you have not been here ſince I finiſhed my library—Books, books, you know, are the only thing I am a coxcomb in.

Sir Pet. Very true, indeed,—why even your

ſcreen is a ſource of knowledge—hung round with maps I ſee.

Joſ. Yes, I find great uſe in that ſcreen.

Sir Pet. Yes, yes, ſo you muſt when you want to find any thing in a hurry.

Joſ. Yes, or to hide any thing in a hurry.

[*Aſide.*

Sir Pet. But, my dear friend, I want to have ſome private talk with you.

Joſ. You need not wait.   [*Exit* Servant.

Sir Pet. Pray ſit down—*(Both ſit)*—My dear friend, I want to impart to you ſome of my diſtreſſes ——In ſhort, Lady Teazle's behaviour of late has given me very great uneaſineſs. She not only diſſipates and deſtroys my fortune, but 1 have ſtrong reaſons to believe ſhe has formed an attachment elſewhere.

Joſ. I am unhappy to hear it.

Sir Pet. Yes, and between you and me, I believe. I have diſcovered the perſon.

Joſ. You alarm me exceedingly.

Sir Pet. I knew you would ſympathize with me.

Joſ. Believe me, Sir Peter, ſuch a diſcovery would affect me—juſt as much as it does you.

Sir Pet. What a happineſs to have a friend we can truſt with our family ſecrets——Can't you gueſs who it is ?

Joſ. I hav'n't the moſt diſtant idea—It can't be Sir Benjamin Backbite.

Sir Pet. No, no.—What do you think of Charles ?

Jof. My brother! impoffible!——I can't think he would be capable of fuch bafenefs and ingratitude.

Sir Pet. Ah, the goodnefs of your own mind makes you flow to believe fuch villainy.

Jof. Very true, Sir Peter.—The man who is confcious of the integrity of his own heart, is ever flow to credit another's bafenefs.

Sir Pet. And that the fon of my old friend fhould practice againft the honour of my family.

Jof. Aye, there's the cafe, Sir Peter.—When ingratitude barbs the dart of injury, the wound feels double fmart.

Sir Pet. What noble fentiments!——He never ufed a fentiment, ungrateful boy! that I acted as guardian to, and who was brought up under my eye; and 1 never in my life refufed him—my advice.

Jof. I don't know, Sir Peter,——he may be fuch a man—if it be fo, he is no longer a brother of mine! I renounce him. I difclaim him——For the man who can break through the laws of hofpitality, and feduce the wife and daughter of his friend, deferves to be branded as a peft to fociety.

Sir Pet. And yet, Jofeph, if I was to make it public, I fhould be only fneered and laughed at.

Jof. Why, that's very true——No, no, you muft not make it public, people would talk——

Sir Pet. Talk,—they'd fay it was all my own fault; an old doating batchelor, to marry a young giddy girl. · They'd paragraph me in the newſpapers, and make ballads on me.

Joſ. And yet, Sir Peter, I can't think that my Lady Teazle's honour——

Sir Pet. Ah, my dear friend, what's the honour, oppoſed againſt the flattery of a handſome young fellow—But Joſeph, ſhe has been upbraiding me of late, that I have not made her a ſettlement; and I think, in our laſt quarrel, ſhe told me ſhe ſhould not be very ſorry if I was dead. Now, I have brought drafts of two deeds for your peruſal, and ſhe ſhall find, if I was to die, that I have not been inattentive to her welfare while living. By the one, ſhe will enjoy eight hundred pounds a year during my life; and by the other, the bulk of my fortune after my death.

Joſ. This conduct is truly generous.——I wiſh it mayn't corrupt my pupil.   [*Aſide.*

Sir Pet. But I would not have her as yet acquainted with the leaſt mark of my affection.

Joſ. Nor I—if I could help it.   [*Aſide.*

Sir Pet. And now I have unburthened myſelf to you, let us talk over your affair with Maria.

Joſ. Not a ſyllable upon the ſubject now. *(Alarmed.)*—Some other time; I am too much affected by your affairs, to think of my own. For, the man who can think of his own happineſs, while his friend is in diſtreſs, deſerves to be hunted as a monſter to ſociety.

Sir Pet. I am ſure of your affection for her.

Joſ. Let me intreat you, Sir Peter.——

Sir Pet. And though you are ſo averſe to Lady

Teazle's knowing it, I assure you she is not your ene-my, and I am sensibly chagrined you have made no further progress.

Jos. Sir Peter, I must not hear you———The man who——*(Enter Servant)* What do you want, sirrah ?

Ser. Your brother, Sir, is at the door talking to a gentleman ; he says he knows you are at home, that Sir Peter is with you, and he must see you.

Jos. I'm not at home.

Sir Pet. Yes, yes, you shall be at home.

Jos. (After some hesitation) Very well, let him come up.   [*Exit* Servant.

Sir Pet. Now, Joseph; I'll hide myself, and do you tax him about the affair with my Lady Teazle, and so draw the secret from him.

Jos. O fye ! Sir Peter———what join in a plot to trepan my brother !

Sir Pet. Oh aye, to serve your friend ;—besides, if he is innocent, as you say he is, it will give him an opportunity to clear himself, and make me very happy.   Hark, I hear him coming——Where shall I go ?——Behind this screen——What the devil ! here has been one listener already, for I'll swear I saw a petticoat,

Jos. (Affecting to laugh) It's very ridiculous——Ha ! ha ! ha !—a ridiculous affair indeed—ha ! ha ! ha !——Hark'ye, Sir Peter *(Pulling him aside)* tho' I hold a man of intrigue to be a most despicable cha-racter, yet you know it does not follow, that one is to be an absolute Joseph either.   Hark'ye, 'tis a little French Milliner, who calls upon me some-times, and hearing you were coming, and having some character to lose, she slipped behind the screen.

Sir Pet. A French Milliner! *(Smiling)* Cunning rogue! Joseph—Sly rogue—But zounds, she has overheard every thing that has passed about my wife.

Jos. Oh, never fear——take my word it will never go farther for her.

Sir Pet. Won't it?

Jos. No, depend upon it.

Sir Pet. Well, well, if it will go no farther—— But—where shall I hide myself?

Jos. Here, here, slip into the closet, and you may overhear every word.

L. Teaz. Can I steal away? *(Peeping.)*

Jos. Hush! hush! don't stir.

Sir Pet. Joseph tax him home. *(Peeping.)*

Jos. In, in, my dear Sir Peter.

L. Teaz. Can't you lock the closet door?

Jos. Not a word——you'll be discovered.

Sir Pet. Joseph, don't spare him.

Jos. For heaven's sake lie close.—A pretty situation I am in, to part man and wife in this manner.

[Aside.

Sir Pet. You're sure the little French Milliner won't blab?

Enter CHARLES.

Cha. Why, how now, brother; your fellow denied you, they said you were not at home.—What, have you had a jew or a wench with you?

Jos. Neither, brother, neither.

D 5

Cha. But where's Sir Peter? I thought he was with you.

Jof. He was, brother; but hearing you was coming, he left the houfe.

Cha. What, was the old fellow afraid I wanted to borrow money of him.

Jof. Borrow! no, brother; but I am forry to hear you have given that worthy man caufe for great uneafinefs.

Cha. Yes, I am told I do that to a great many worthy men—But how do you mean, brother?

Jof. Why, he thinks you have endeavoured to alienate the affeĉtions of Lady Teazle.

Cha. Who, I alienate the affeĉtions of Lady Teazle!————Upon my word he accufes me very unjuftly. What, has the old gentleman found out that he has got a young wife, or what is worfe, has the lady found out that fhe has got an old hufband?

Jof. For fhame, brother.

Cha. 'Tis true, I did once fufpeĉt her Ladyfhip had a partiality for me, but, upon my foul, I never gave her the leaft encouragement; for, you know, my attachment was to Maria.

Jof. This will make Sir Peter extremely happy——But if fhe had a partiality for you, fure you would not have been bafe enough——

Cha. Why, look ye, Jofeph, I hope I fhall never deliberately do a difhonourable aĉtion; but if a pretty woman fhould purpofely throw herfelf in my way, and that pretty woman fhould happen to be married to a man old enough to be her father———

Jof. What then ?

Cha. Why then, I believe I fhould——have occafion to borrow a little of your morality, brother. •

Jof. Oh fie, brother—The man who can jeft—

Cha. Oh, that's very true, as you were going to obferve.——But Jofeph, do you know that I am furprized at your fufpecting me with Lady Teazle. I thought you was always the favourite there.

Jof. Me !

Cha. Why yes, I have feen you exchange fuch fignificant glances.

Jof. 'Pfhaw !

Cha. Yes, I have; and don't you remember when I came in here, and caught you and her at———

Jof. I muft ftop him *(Afide.) (Stops his mouth)* Sir Peter has overheard every word that you have faid.

Cha. Sir Peter ! where is he ?—What, in the clofet—Foregad I'll have him out.

Jof. No, no. *(Stopping him.)*

Cha. I will—Sir Peter Teazle, come into court.

Enter Sir PETER.

What, my old guardian turn inquifitor, and take evidence incog.

Sir Pet. Give me your hand,—I own, my dear

boy, I have fufpected you wrongfully ; but you muft not be angry with Jofeph, it was all my plot, and I fhall think the better of you as long as I live for what I have overheard.

Cha. Then 'tis well you did not hear more. Is it not, Jofeph?

Sir Pet. What you would have retorted on Jofeph, would you?

Cha. And yet you might as well have fufpected him as me.   Might he not, Jofeph?

Enter SERVANT.

Ser. (Whifpering Jofeph)——Lady Sneerwell, Sir, is juft coming up, and fays fhe muft fee you.

Jof. Gentlemen, I muft beg your pardon, I have company waiting for me ; give me leave to conduct you down ftairs.

Cha. No, no, fpeak to them in another room ; I have not feen Sir Peter a great while, and I want to talk with him.

Jof. Well, I'll fend away the perfon and return immediately. Sir Peter, not a word of the little French Milliner.   [*Afide,* and *Exit.*

Sir Pet. Ah, Charles, what a pity it is you don't affociate more with your brother, we might then have fome hopes of your reformation ; he's a young man of fuch fentiments.—Ah, there's nothing in the world fo noble as a man of fentiment.

Cha. Oh, he's too moral by half; and fo apprehenfive of his good name, that, I dare fay, he would as soon let a prieft into his houfe as a wench.

Sir Pet. No, no, you accufe him wrongfully—Tho' Jofeph is not a rake, he is no faint.

Cha. Oh! a perfect anchorite—a young hermit.

Sir Pet. Hufh, hufh; don't abufe him, or he may chance to hear of it again.

Cha. Why you won't tell him, will you?

Sir Pet. No, no, but——I have a great mind to tell him *(Afide)—(Seems to hefitate)*—Hark'ye, Charles, have you a mind for a laugh at Jofeph?

Cha. I fhould like it of all things—let's have it.

Sir Pet. Gad I'll tell him—I'll be even with Jofeph for difcovering me in the clofet.——*(Afide.)*—Hark'ye Charles, he had a girl with him when I called.

Cha. Who, Jofeph! impoffible!

Sir Pet. Yes, a little French Milliner, *(takes him to the front)* and the beft of the joke is, fhe is now in the room.

Cha. The devil fhe is—Where?

Sir Pet. Hufh, hufh,—behind the fcreen.

Cha. I'll have her out.

Sir Pet. No, no, no, no.

Cha. Yes.

Sir Pet. No.

Cha. By the Lord I will—So now for't.

Both runs up to the fcreen—fcreen falls, at the fame time JOSEPH *enters.*

Cha. Lady Teazle, by all that's wonderful!

Sir Pet. Lady Teazle, by all that's horrible !

Cha. Sir Peter, this is the fmarteſt little French Milliner I ever faw.—But pray what's the meaning of all this? You ſeem to have been playing at hide-and-feek here, and for my part, I don't know who's in or who's out of the fecret.—Madam, will you pleafe to explain?—Not a word!—Brother, is it your pleafure to illuſtrate?—Morality dumb too!—Well, though I can make nothing of it, I fuppoſe you perfectly underſtand one another, good folks, and ſo I'll leave you. Brother, I am forry you have given that worthy man ſo much caufe for uneafinefs—Sir Peter, there's nothing in the world ſo noble as a man of ſentiment.— Ha, ha, ha! *[Exit.*

Joſ. Sir Peter, notwithſtanding appearances are againſt me—if—if you'll give me leave—I'll explain every thing to your fatisfaction.

Sir Pet. If you pleafe, Sir.

Joſ. Lady Teazle knowing my—Lady Teazle— I ſay—knowing my pretenfions—to your ward— Maria—and—Lady Teazle—I ſay, knowing the jealoufy of my—of your temper—ſhe called in here —in order that ſhe—that I might explain—what thefe pretenfions were—And—hearing you were coming—and—as I ſaid before—knowing the jealoufy of your temper—ſhe—my Lady Teazle—I ſay—went behind the fcreen——and—this is a full and clear account of the whole affair.

Sir Pet. A very clear account truly! and I dare ſay the lady will vouch for the truth of every word of it.

L. Teaz. (Advancing) For not one fyllable, Sir Peter.

Sir Pet. What the devil! don't you think it worth your while to agree in the lie ?

L. Teaz. There is not one word of truth in what that gentleman has been faying.

Jof. Zounds, madam, you won't ruin me.

L. Teaz. Stand out of the way, Mr. Hypocrite, I'll fpeak for myfelf.

Sir Pet. Aye, aye—let her alone—fhe'll make a better ftory of it than you did.

L. Teaz. I came here with no intention of liftening to his addreffes to Maria, and even ignorant of his pretenfions ; but feduced by his infidious arts, at leaft to liften to his addreffes, if not to facrifice his honour, as well as my own, to his unwarrantable defires.

Sir Pet. Now I believe the truth is coming indeed.

Jof. What! is the woman mad ?

L. Teaz. No, Sir, fhe has recovered her fenfes. Sir Peter, I cannot expect you will credit me; but the tendernefs you expreffed for me, when I am certain you did not know I was within hearing, has penetrated fo deep into my foul, that could I have efcaped the mortification of this difcovery, my future life fhould have convinced you of my fincere repentance. As for that fmooth-tongued hypocrite, who would have feduced the wife of his too credulous friend, while he pretended an honourable paffion for his ward, I now view him in fo defpicable a light,

that I fhall never again refpeꝗ myfelf for having lif-
tened to his addreſſes.   [*Exit.*

Jof. Sir Peter—Notwithſtanding all this—Heaven is my witnefs——

Sir Pet. That you are a villain——and fo I'll
leave you to your meditations——

Jof. Nay, Sir Peter, you muſt not leave me—
The man who fhuts his ears againſt conviꝗion—

Sid Pet. Oh, damn your fentiments——damn
your fentiments.——

ACT V. SCENE I.

Joseph Surface's *Apartment.*

Enter Joseph *and a* Servant.

Joseph.

Mr. Stanley!—why fhould you think I would fee
Mr. Stanley! you know well enough he comes in-
treating for fomething.

Serſ They let him in before I knew of it, and old
Rowley is with him.

Jof. 'Pſhaw, you blockhead; I am fo diſtraꝗed
with my own misfortunes, I am not in a humour to
fpeak to any one—but fhow the fellow up. *(Exit
Servant.)* Sure fortune never played a man of my
policy fuch a trick before—My charaꝗer ruined

with Sir Peter—my hopes of Maria loft—I'm in a
pretty humour to liften to poor relations truly—I
fhan't be able to beftow even a benevolent fentiment
on old Stanley. Oh, here he oomes; I'll retire,
and endeavour to put a little charity in my face however.   [*Exit.*

Enter Sir OLIVER *and* ROWLEY.

Sir Oliv. What, does he avoid us? That was
him, was it not?

Row. Yes, Sir; but his nerves are too weak to
bear the fight of a poor relation: I fhould have come
firft to break the matter to him.

Sir Oliv. A plague of his nerves——yet this is he
whom Sir Peter extols as a man of a moft benevolent
way of thinking.

Row. Yes—he has as much fpeculative benevolence as any man in the kingdom, though he is not
fo fenfual as to indulge himfelf in the exercife of it.

Sir Oliv. Yes, he has a ftring of fentiments, I fuppofe, at his fingers ends.

Row. And his favourite one is, *That charity begins
at home.*

Sir Oliv. And his, I prefume, is of that domeftic
fort, which never ftirs abroad at all.

Row. Well, Sir, I'll leave you to introduce yourfelf as old Stanley; I muft be here again to announce
you in your real charaƈter.

Sir Oliv. True—And you'll afterwards meet me at
Sir Peter's.

Row. Without lofing a moment.   [*Exit* Rowley.

Sir Oliv. Here he comes——I don't like the complaifance of his features.

Enter JOSEPH.

Jof. Sir, your moſt obedient ; I beg pardon for keeping you a moment——Mr. Stanley, I preſume.

Sir Oliv. At your ſervice, Sir.

Jof. Pray be ſeated, Mr. Stanley, I intreat you, Sir.

Sir Oliv. Dear Sir there's no occaſion. Too ceremonious by half. [*Aſide.*

Jof. Though I have not the pleaſure of your acquaintance, I am very glad to ſee you look ſo well.—— I think, Mr. Stanley, you was nearly related to my mother.

Sir Oliv. I was, Sir ; ſo nearly, that my preſent poverty I fear may do diſcredit to her wealthy children ; elſe I would not preſume to trouble you now.

Jof. Ah, Sir, don't mention that—For the man who is in diſtreſs has ever a right to claim kindred with the wealthy ; I am ſure I wiſh I was of that number, or that it was in my power to afford you even a ſmall relief.

Sir Oliv. If your uncle Sir Oliver was here I ſhould have a friend.

Jof. I wiſh he was, Sir, you ſhould not want an advocate with him, believe me.

Sir Oliv. I ſhould not need one ; my diſtreſſes would recommend me. But I imagined his boun-

ty had enabled you to be the agent of his cha-
rities.

Jof. Ah, Sir, you are miftaken; avarice, avarice, Mr. Stanley, is the vice of age; to be fure it
has been fpread abroad that he has been very bounti-
ful to me, but without the leaft foundation, though
I never chofe to contradict the report.

Sir Oliv. And has he never remitted you bullion,
rupees, or pagodas?

Jof. Oh, dear Sir, no fuch thing; I have indeed
received fome trifling prefents from him, fuch as
fhawls, avadavats, and Indian crackers; nothing
more, Sir.

Sir Oliv. There's gratitude for twelve thoufand,
pounds! *(Afide)* Shawls, avadavats, and Indian
crackers.

, *Jof.* Then there's my brother, Mr. Stanley; one
would fcarce believe what I have done for that unfortunate young man.

Sir Oliv. Not I for one. *(Afide)*

Jof. Oh, the fums I have lent him!—Well,
'twas an amiable weaknefs—I muft own I can't defend it, though it appears more blameable at prefent,
as it prevents me from ferving you, Mr. Stanley, as
my heart directs.

Sir Oliv. Diffembler—*(Afide)*—Then you cannot
affift me.

Jof. I am very unhappy to fay 'tis not in my
power at prefent; but you may depend upon
hearing from me when I can be of any fervice to
you.

Sir Oliv. Sweet Sir, you are too good.

Jof. Not at all, Sir; to pity without the power to relieve, is ftill more painful than to afk and be denied. Indeed, Mr. Stanley, you have deeply af-fected me. Sir, your moft devoted; I wifh you health and fpirits.

Sir Oliv. Your ever grateful and perpetual *(bowing low)* humble fervant.

Jof. I am extremely forry, Sir, for your misfor-tunes—Here, open the door—Mr. Stanley, your moft devoted.

Sir Oliv. Your moft obliged fervant. Charles, you are my heir.   . [*Afide* and *Exit.*

Jof. This is another of the evils that attend a man's having fo good a character—It fubjects him to the importunity of the neceffitous—The pure and fterling ore of charity, is a very expenfive article in the catalogue of a man's virtues; whereas, the fenti-mental French plate I ufe, anfwers the purpofe full as well, and pays no tax.   *(Going)*

Enter Rowley.

Row. Mr. Surface, your moft obedient; I wait on you from your uncle, who is juft arrived. *(Gives him a note.)*

Jof. How! Sir Oliver arrived!——Here, Mr. —————— call back Mr. Stanley.

Row. It's too late, Sir, I met him going out of the houfe.

Jof. Was ever any thing fo unfortunate! *(Afide)* —I hope my uncle has enjoyed good health and fpirits.

Row. Oh, very good, Sir; he bid me inform you he'll wait on you within this half hour.

Jof. Prefent him my kind love and duty, and affure him I'm quite impatient to fee him. *(Bowing)*

Row. I fhall, Sir.   '   .*[Exit* Rowley.

Jof. Pray do, Sir. *(Bows)*—This was the moft curfed piece of ill luck.   *[Exit* Jofeph.

SCENE II.

Sir PETER TEAZLE's *Houfe.*

Enter Mrs. CANDOUR *and* MAID.

Maid. Indeed, Madam, my lady will fee no one at prefent.

Mrs. Can. Did you tell her it was her friend Mrs. Candour?

Maid. I did, Madam, and fhe begs to be excufed.

Mrs. Can. Go again, for I am fure fhe muft be greatly diftreffed. *(Exit* Maid) How provoking to be kept waiting—I am not miftrefs of half the circumftances:—I fhall have the whole affair in the newfpapers, with the parties names at full length, before I have dropped the ftory at a dozen houfes.

Enter Sir BENJAMIN BACKBITE.

Mrs. Can. Oh, Sir Benjamin, I am glad you

are come; have you heard of Lady Teazle's affair?
Well, I never was fo furprized—and I am fo diftrefſ-
ed for the parties.

Sir Benj. Nay, I can't fay I pity Sir Peter, he
was always fo partial to Mr. Surface.

Mrs. Can. Mr. Surface! Why, it was Charles.

Sir Benj. Oh, no, madam, Mr. Surface was the
gallant.

Mrs. Can. No, Charles was the lover; and Mr.
Surface, to do him juſtice, was the caufe of the difcovery: he brought Sir Peter, and——

Sir Benj. Oh, my dear madam, no fuch thing;
for I had it from one——

Mrs. Can. Yes, and I had it from one, that had
it from one that knew——

Sir Benj. And I had it from one——

Mrs. Can. No fuch thing.——But here comes
my Lady Sneerwell, and perhaps ſhe may have heard
the particulars.

Enter Lady Sneerwell.

L. Sneer. Oh, dear Mrs. Candour, here is a fad
affair about our friend Lady Teazle.

Mrs. Can. Why, to be fure poor thing, I am
much concerned for her.

L. Sneer. I proteſt fo am I——though I muſt confefs ſhe was always too lively for me.

Mrs. Can. But ſhe had a great deal of good-nature.

Sir Benj. And had a very ready wit.

Mrs. Can. But do you know all the particulars?
(To Lady Sneerwell.)

Sir Benj. Yet who could have fufpected Mr. Surface ?

Mrs. Can. Charles you mean.

Sir Benj. No, Mr. Surface.

Mrs. Can. Oh, 'twas Charles.

L. Sneer. Charles !

Mrs. Can. Yes, Charles.

Sir Benj. I'll not pretend to difpute with you,
Mrs. Candour ; but be it as it may, I hope Sir Peter's wounds won't prove mortal.

Mrs. Can. Sir Peter's wounds ! what ! did they
fight, I never heard a word of that.

Sir Benj. No !——

Mrs. Can. No !——

L. Sneer. Nor I, a fyllable : Do, dear Sir Benjamin, tell us.

Sir Benj. Oh my dear madam, then you don't
know half the affair——Why—why—I'll tell you—
Sir Peter, you muft know, had a long time fufpected
Lady Teazle's vifits to Mr. Surface.

Mrs. Can. To Charles you mean.

Sir Benj. No, Mr. Surface—and upon going to
his houfe, and finding Lady Teazle there, Sir, fays
Sir Peter, you are a very ungrateful fellow.

Mrs. Can. Aye, that was Charles.

Sir Benj. Mr. Surface.——And old as I am, fays
he, I demand immediate fatisfaction : upon this,
they both drew their fwords, and to it they fell.

Mrs. Can. That muft be Charles, for it is very
unlikely that Mr. Surface fhould fight him in his own
houfe.

Sir Benj. 'Sdeath, madam, not at all. Lady

Teazle, upon feeing Sir Peter in fuch danger, ran out of the room in ftrong hyfterics, and was followed by Charles, calling out for hartfhorn and water. They fought, and Sir Peter received a wound in his right fide by the thruft of a fmall fword.

Enter CRABTREE.

Crab. Piftols! piftols! nephew.

Mrs. Can. Oh, Mr. Crabtree, I am glad you are come; now we fhall have the whole affair.

Sir Benj. No, no, it was a fmall fword, uncle.

Crab. Zounds, nephew, I fay it was a piftol.

Sir Benj. A thruft in *fecond* through the fmall guts.

Crab. A bullet lodged in the thorax.

Sir Benj. But give me leave, dear uncle it was a fmall fword.

Crab. I tell you it was a piftol——Won't you fuffer any body to know any thing but yourfelf.——It was a piftol, and Charles——

Mrs. Can. Aye! I knew it was Charles.

Sir Benj. Mr. Surface, uncle.

Crab. Why zounds, I fay it was Charles, muft no body fpeak but yourfelf. I'll tell you how the whole affair was.

L. Sneer. ⎱
Mrs. Can. ⎰ Aye do, do pray tell us.

Sir Benj. I fee my uncle knows nothing at all about the matter.

Crab. Mr. Surface, you muft know, Ladies, came late from Salt-hill, where he had been the evening *before* with a particular friend of his who had a fon at *Eton;* his piftols were left on the bureau, and unfortunately loaded, and on Sir Peter's taxing Charles——

Sir Benj. Mr. Surface you mean.

Crab. Do, pray nephew, hold your tongue, and let me fpeak fometimes—I fay, Ladies, upon his taking Charles to account, and taxing him with the bafeft ingratitude——

Sir Benj. Aye, Ladies, I told you Sir Peter taxed him with ingratitude.

Crab. They agreed each to take a piftol——They fired at the fame inftant——Charles's ball took place, and lodged in the thorax. Sir Peter's miffed, and what is very extraordinary, the ball grazed againft a little bronze Shakefpear that ftood over the chimney, flew off through the window at right angles, and wounded the poft man, who was juft come to the door with a double letter from Northamptonfhire.

Sir Benj. I heard nothing of all this I muft own. Ladies, my uncle's account is more circumftantial, though I believe mine is the true on.

L. Sneer. I am more interefted in this affair than they imagine, and muft have better information.

[*Afide, and Exit.*

Sir Benj. Lady Sneerwell's alarm is very eafily accounted for.

Crab. Why, yes; they do fay——but that's neither here nor there.

Mrs. Can. But, pray where is Sir Peter now ? I hope his wounds won't prove mortal.

Crab. He was carried home immediately, and

E

has given pofitive orders to be denied to every
body.

Sir Benj. And I believe Lady Teazle is attending
him.

Mrs. Can. I do believe fo too.

Crab. Certainly—l met one of the faculty as I
came in.

Sir Benj. Gad fo! and here he comes.

Crab. Yes, yes, that's the Doctor.

Mrs. Can. That certainly muſt be the phyfician—
Now we ſhall get information.

Enter Sir OLIVER SURFACE.

Dear Doctor how is your patient?

Sir Benj. I hope his wounds are not mortal.

Crab. Is he in a fair way of recovery?

Sir Benj. Pray, Doctor, was he not wounded by
a thruſt of a fword through the fmall guts?

Crab. Was it not by a bullet that lodged in the
thorax?

Sir Benj. Nay, pray anfwer me.

Crab. Dear, dear Doctor fpeak. *(All pulling
him.)*

Sir Oliv. Hey, hey, good people, are you all
mad?—Why, what the devil is the matter?—a
fword through the fmall guts, and a bullet lodged
in the thorax! What would you all be at?

Sir Benj. Then, perhaps, Sir, you are not a doctor.

Sir Oliv. If I am, Sir, I am to thank you for
my degree.

Crab. Only a particular friend, I fuppofe.

Sir Oliv. Nothing more, Sir.

Sir Benj. Then, I fuppofe, as you are a friend, you can be better able to give us fome account of his wounds.

Sir Oliv. Wounds!

Mrs. Can. What! havn't you heard he was wounded?—the faddeft accident.

Sir. Benj. A thruft with a fword through the fmall guts.

Crab. A bullet in the thorax.

Sir Oliv. Good people, fpeak one at a time, I be-feech' you—You both agree, that Sir Peter is dan-geroufly wounded.

Crab.
Sir Benj. } Aye, aye, we both agree in that.

Sir Oliv. Then I will be bold to fay, Sir Peter is one of the moft imprudent men in the world, for here he comes walking as if nothing had hap-pened.

Enter Sir PETER.

My good friend, you are certainly mad to walk about in this condition; you fhould go to bed, you that have had a fword through your fmall guts, and a bullet lodged in your thorax.

Sir Pet. A fword through my fmall guts, and a bullet lodged in my thorax.

Sir Oliv. Yes, thefe worthy people would have killed you without law or phyfic, and wanted to dub me a Doctor, in order to make me an accom-plice.

Sir Pet. What is all this?

E 2

Sir Benj. Sir Peter, we are all very glad to find the story of the duel is not true.

Crab. And exceedingly sorry about your other misfortunes.

Sir Pet. So, so, all over the town already. [*Aside.*

Mrs. Can. Though, as Sir Peter was so good a husband, I pity him sincerely.

Sir Pet. Plague of your pity.

Crab. As you continued so long a batchelor, you was certainly to blame to marry at all.

Sir Pet. Sir, I desire you will consider this is my own house.

Sir Benj. However you must not be offended at the jests you'll meet on this occasion.

Crab It is no uncommon case, that's one thing.

Sir Pet. I insist upon being master here: In plain terms I desire you'll leave my house immediately.

Mrs. Can. Well, well, Sir, we are going, and you may depend upon it, we shall make the best of the story. [*Exit.*

Sir Benj. And tell how hardly you have been treated.

Sir Pet. Leave my house directly. [*Exit* Sir Benjamin.

Crab. And how patiently you bear it. [*Exit* Crabtree.

Sir Pet. Leave my house, I say——Friends, furies, there is no bearing it !

Enter Rowley.

Sir Oliv. Well, Sir Peter, I have seen my Nephews.

4

Row. And, Sir Oliver is convinced, your judgment is right after all.

Sir Oliv. Aye, Joseph is the man.

Row. Such sentiments.

Sir Oliv. And acts up to the sentiments he professes.

Row. Oh, 'tis edification to hear him talk.

Sir Oliv. He is a pattern for the young men of the age.——But how comes it Sir Peter, that you don't join in his praises?

Sir Pet. Sir Oliver, we live in a damn'd wicked world, and the fewer we praise the better.

Sir Oliv. Right, right, my old friend—But was you always so moderate in your judgment?

Row. Do you say so, Sir Peter, you who was never mistaken in your life?

Sir Pet. Oh, plague of your jokes——I suppose you are acquainted with the whole affair.

Row. I am indeed, Sir.—I met Lady Teazle returning from Mr. Surface's so humbled, that she deign'd to beg even me to become her advocate.

Sir Pet. What! does Sir Oliver know it too?

Sir Oliv. Aye, aye, every circumstance.

Sir Pet. What! about the closet and the screen?

Sir Oliv. Yes, and the little French Milliner too —I never laughed more in my life.

Sir Pet. And a very pleasant jest it was.

Sir Oliv. This is your man of sentiment, Sir Peter.

Sir Pet. Oh, damn his sentiment.

Sir Oliv. You must have made a pretty appearance when Charles dragged you out of the closet.

Sir Pet. Yes, yes, that was very diverting.

Sir Oliv. And, egad Sir Peter, I fhould like to have feen your face when the fcreen was thrown down.

Sir Pet. My face when the fcreen was thrown down! oh yes!—There's no bearing this. [*Afide.*

Sir Oliv. Come, come, my old friend, don't be vexed, for I can't help laughing for the foul of me. Ha! ha! ha!

Sir Pet. Oh, laugh on—I am not vexed—no, no, it is the pleafanteft thing in the world. To be the ftanding jeft of all one's acquaintance, 'tis the happieft fituation imaginable.

Row. See, Sir, yonder's my Lady Teazle coming this way. and in tears, let me beg of you to be reconciled.

Sir Oliv. Well, well, I'll leave Rowley to mediate between you, and take my leave, but you muft make hafte after me to Mr. Surface's, where I go, if not to reclaim a libertine, at leaft to expofe hypocrify.

[*Exit.*

Sir Pet. I'll be with you at the difcovery; I fhould like to fee it, though it is a vile unlucky place for difcoveries. Rowley, *(looking out)* fhe is not coming this way.

Row. No, Sir, but fhe has left the room door open, and waits your coming.

Sir Pet. Well, certainly mortification is very becoming in a wife.—Don't you think I had beft let her pine a little longer.

Row. Oh, Sir, that's being too fevere.

Sir Pet. I don't think fo ; the letter I found from Charles, was evidently intended for her.

Row. Indeed, Sir Peter, you are much miftaken.

Sir Pet. If I was convinced of that—See, Mafter Rowley, fhe looks this way—What a remarkable elegant turn of the head fhe has—I have a good mind' to go to her.

Row. Do, dear Sir.

Sir Pet. But when it is known that we are reconciled, I fhall be laughed at more than ever.

Row. Let them laugh on, and retort their malice upon themfelves, by fhewing them you can be happy in fpite of their flander.

Sir Pet. Faith, and fo I will, Mafter Rowley, and my Lady Teazle and I may ftill be the happieft couple—in the country.

Row. O fye, Sir Peter, he that lays afide fufpicion—

Sir Pet. My dear Rowley, if you have any regard for me, never let me hear you utter any thing like a fentiment again ; I have had enough of that to laft me the remainder of my life.   [*Exeunt.*

SCENE III.

Joseph's *Library.*

Enter Joseph *and* Lady Sneerwell.

L. Sneer. Impoffible ! will not Sir Peter be in

diately reconciled to Charles, and no longer oppofe his union with Maria.

Jof. Can paffion mend it?

L. Sneer. No, nor cunning neither. I was a fool to league with fuch a blunderer.

Jof. Sure, my Lady Sneerwell, I am the greateft fufferer in this affair, and yet, you fee, I bear it with calmnefs.

L. Sneer. Becaufe the difappointment does not reach your heart; your intereft was only concerned. Had you felt for Maria, what I do for that unfortunate libertine your brother, you would not be diffuaded from taking every revenge in your power.

Jof. Why will you rail at me for the difappointment?

L. Sneer. Are you not the caufe? Had you not a fufficient field for your roguery in impofing upon Sir Peter, and fupplanting your brother, but you muft endeavour to feduce his wife? I hate fuch an avarice of crimes; 'tis an unfair monopoly, and never profpers.

Jof. Well, I own I am to blame—I have deviated from the direct rule of wrong. Yet, I cannot think circumftances are fo bad as your Ladyfhip apprehends.

L. Sneer. No!

Jof. You tell me you have made another trial of Snake, that he ftill proves fteady to our intereft, and that he is ready, if occafion requires, to fwear to a contract having paffed between Charles and your Ladyfhip.

L. Sneer. And what then?

Jof. Why, the letters which have been fo carefully circulated, will corroborate his evidence, and prove the truth of the affertion. But I expeᴄt my uncle every moment, and muft beg your Ladyfhip to retire into the next room.

L. Sneer. But if he fhould find you out.

Jof. I have no fear of that—Sir Peter won't tell for his own fake, and I fhall foon find out Sir Oliver's weak fide.

L. Sneer. Nay, I have no doubt of your abilities, only be conftant to one villainy at a time.

Jof. Well, I will, I will.—*(Exit* Lady Sneerwell)——It is confounded hard though, to be baited by one's confederates in wickednefs—*(knocking)* —Who have we got here? My uncle Oliver, I fuppofe—Oh, old Stanley again! How comes he here? He muft not ftay——

Enter Sɪʀ Oʟɪᴠᴇʀ.

I told you already, Mr. Stanley, that it was not in my power to relieve you.

Sir Oliv. But I hear, Sir, that Sir Oliver is arrived, and perhaps he might.

Jof. Well, Sir; you cannot ftay now, Sir; but any other time, Sir, you fhall certainly be relieved.

Sir Oliv. Oh, Sir Oliver and I muft be acquainted.

Jof. I muft infift upon your going. Indeed, Mr. Stanley you can't ftay.

Sir Oliv. Pofitively I muft fee Sir Oliver.

E 5

Jof. Then pofitively you fhan't ftay.

[*Pufhing him out.*

Enter CHARLES.

Cha. Hey day! what's the matter? Why, who the devil have we got here? What, my little Premium. Oh, brother, you muft not hurt my little broker. But, hark'ye, Jofeph, what, have you been borrowing money too?

Jof. Borrowing money! no brother——We expect my uncle Oliver here every minute, and Mr. Stanley infifts upon feeing him.

Cha. Stanley! Why his name is Premium.

Jof. No, no! 1 tell you his name is Stanley.

Cha. But 1 tell you again his name is Premium.

Jof. It don't fignify what his name is.

Cha. No more it don't, as you fay brother, for I fuppofe he goes by half an hundred names, befides. A. B. at the coffee houfes. But old Noll muft not come and catch my little broker here neither.

Jof. Mr. Stanley, I beg——

Cha. And I beg, Mr. Premium——

Jof. You muft go indeed, Mr. Stanley.

Cha. Aye, you muft go Mr. Premium.

[*Both pufhing him.*

Enter Sir PETER, Lady TEAZLE, MARIA *and* ROWLEY.

Sir Pet. What, my old friend Sir Oliver! what's the matter?—In the name of wonder were there ever two fuch ungracious nephews, to affault their uncle at his firft vifit.

L. Teaz. On my word, Sir, it was well we came to your refcue.

Jof. Charles !

Cha. Jofeph !

Jof. Now our ruin is complete.

Cha. Very !

Sir Pet. You find, Sir Oliver, your neceffitous character of old Stanley could not protect you.

Sir Oliv. No! nor Premium neither. The neceffities of the former could not extract a fhilling from that benevolent gentleman there ; and with the other I ftood a worfe chance than my anceftors, and had like to have been knocked down without being bid for. Sir Peter, my friend and Rowley, look upon that elder nephew of mine ; you both know what I have done for him, and how gladly I would have looked upon half my fortune as held only in truft for him. Judge then of my furprife and difappointment, at finding him deftitute of truth, charity, and gratitude.

Sir Pet. Sir Oliver, I fhould be as much furprifed as you, if I did not already know him to be artfully felfifh and hypocritical.

L. Teaz. And if he pleads not guilty to all this, let him call on me to fmifh his character.

Sir Pet. Then I believe we need not add more, for if he knows himfelf, it will be a fufficient punifhment for him, that he is known by the world.

Cha. If they talk this way to honefty, what will they fay to me by and by. [*Afide.*

Sir Oliv. As for that profligate there——
[*Pointing to Charles.*

Char. Aye, now comes my turn; the damn'd family pictures will ruin me.   [*Aside.*

Jof. Sir Oliver, will you honour me with a hearing?

Char. Now, if Joseph would make one of his long speeches, I should have time to recollect myself.   [*Aside.*

Sir Pet. I suppose you would undertake to justify yourself entirely.

Jof. I trust I could, Sir.

Sir Oliv. 'Pshaw; *(turns away from him)* and I suppose you could justify yourself too. *(To* Charles.)

Cha. Not that I know of, Sir.

Sir Oliv. What, my little Premium was let too much into the secret!

Cha. Why yes, Sir.; but they were family secrets, and should go no further.

Row. Come, come, Sir Oliver, I am sure you cannot look upon Charles's follies with anger.

Sir Oliv. No, nor with gravity neither.——Do you know, Sir Peter, the young rogue has been selling me his ancestors: I have bought judges and staff-officers by the foot, and maiden aunts as cheap as old china. *(During this speech Charles laughs behind his hat.)*

Cha. Why, that I have made free with the family canvas is true, my ancestors may rise in judgment against me, there's no denying it; but believe me when I tell you (and upon my soul I would not say it, if it was not so) if I don't appear mortified at the exposure of my follies, it is, because I feel at this

moment the warmeſt ſatisfaction, at ſeeing you, my
liberal benefactor. *(Embraces him.)*

Sir Oliv. Charles, I forgive you ; give me your
hand again, the little ill-looking fellow over the ſet-
tee has made your peace for you.

Cha. Then, Sir, my gratitude to the originaľ is
ſtill increaſed.

L. Teaz. Sir Oliver, here is another with whom
I dare ſay Charles is no leſs anxious to be reconciled.

Sir Oliv. I have heard of that attachment before,
and with the Lady's leave—if I conſtrue right that
bluſh—

Sir Pet. Well, child, ſpeak for yourſelf.

Maria. I have little more to ſay, than that I
wiſh' him happy, and for any influence I might
once have had over his affections, I moſt willingly reſign them to one who has a better claim to
them.

Sir Pet. Hey, what's the matter now? while
he was a rake and a profligate, you would hear of
nobody elſe ; and now that he is likely to reform,
you won't have him. What's the meaning of all
this?

Maria. His own heart, and Lady Sneerwell, can
beſt inform you.

Cha. Lady Sneerwell!

Joſ. I am very ſorry, brother, I am obliged to
ſpeak on this point, but juſtice demands it from me ;
and Lady Sneerwell's wrongs can no longer be concealed.

Enter Lady Sɴᴇᴇʀᴡᴇʟʟ.

Sir Pet. Another French Milliner!—I believe he has one in every room in the houfe.

L. Sneer. Ungrateful Charles! well you may feem confounded and furprifed at the indelicate fituation to which your perfidy has reduced me.

Cha. Pray uncle is this another of your plots, for,, as I live, this is the firft I ever heard of it.

Jof. There is but one witnefs, I believe, neceffary to the bufinefs.

Sir Pet. And that witnefs is Mr. Snake—You were perfectly in the right in bringing him with you. Let him appear.

Row. Defire Mr. Snake to walk in.—It is rather unlucky, Madam, that he fhould be brought to con-front, and not fupport your Ladyfhip.

Enter Sɴᴀᴋᴇ.

L. Sneer. I am furprifed! what, fpeak villain! have you too confpired againft me?

Snake. I beg your Ladyfhip ten thoufand par-dons; I muft own you paid me very liberally for the lying queftions, but I have unfortunately been offer-ed double for fpeaking the truth.

Sir Pet. Plot and counterplot—I give your lady-fhip much joy of your negociation.

L. Sneer. May the torments of defpair and difap-pointment light upon you all. *(Going.)*

L. Teaz. Hold, Lady Sneerwell; before you go, give me leave to return you thanks, for the trouble

you and this gentleman took, in writing letters in
my name to Charles, and anſwering them yourſelf;
—and, at the ſame time, I muſt beg you will preſent
my compliments to the ſcandalous college, of which
you are preſident, and inform them, that Lady Teazle, licentiate, returns the diploma they granted her,
as ſhe leaves off practice, and kills characters no
longer.

L. Sneer. You too, Madam! Provoking inſolent!
may your huſband live theſe fifty years.   [*Exit.*

L. Teaz. Oh Lord, what a malicious creature
it is!

Sir Pet. Not for her laſt wiſh I hope.

L. Teaz. Oh, no, no, no.

Sir Pet. Well, Sir——What have you to ſay for
yourſelf? (*To* Joſeph)

Joſ. Sir, I am ſo confounded that Lady Sneerwell
ſhould impoſe upon us all, by ſuborning Mr. Snake,
that I know not what to ſay——but——left her malice ſhould prompt her to injure my brother——I had
better follow her.   [*Exit.*

Sir Pet. Moral to the laſt.

Sir Oliv. Marry her, Joſeph, marry her if you
can—Oil and vinegar—You'll do very well together.

Row. Mr. Snake, I believe, we have no further
occaſion for you.

Snake. Before I go, I muſt beg pardon of theſe
good ladies and gentlemen, for whatever trouble I
have been the humble inſtrument of cauſing.

Sir Pet. You have made amends by your open con-
feſſion.

In the lone ruſtic hall for ever pounded,
With dogs, cats, rats, and ſqualling brats ſurrounded!
With humble curates can I now retire ?
(While good Sir Peter boozes with the 'ſquire)
And at back-gammon mortify my ſoul,
That pants for Loo, or flutters at a vole !
Seven's the main !—dear ſound !—thou muſt expire,
Loſt at hot-cockles round a Chriſtmas fire !
The tranſient hour of faſhion too ſoon ſpent,
" *Farewell the tranquil mind, farewell content !*
" *Farewell the plumed head—the cuſhion'd tete,*
" *That takes the cuſhion from its proper ſeat !*
" *The ſpirit ſtirring drum !—card drums I mean—*
" *Spadille, odd Trick, Pam, Baſto, King and Queen !*
" *And you, ye knockers, that with brazen throat,*
" *The welcome viſitor's approach denote,*
" *Farewell !—All quality of high renown,*
" *Pride, pomp and circumſtance of glorious town,*
" *Farewell !—your revels I partake no more,*
" *And Lady Teazle's occupation's o'er !"*
—All this I told our bard, he ſmil'd, and ſaid, 'twas
                clear,
I ought to play deep tragedy next year :
Mean while he drew wiſe morals from his play,
And in theſe ſolemn periods ſtalk'd away :
" *Bleſt were the fair, like you her faults who ſtopt,*
" *And clos'd her follies when the curtain dropt !*
" *No more in vice or error to engage,*
" *Or play the fool at large on life's great ſtage !"*

THE

C R I T I C;

OR,

A TRAGEDY REHEARSED.

–

DRAMATIC PIECE,

IN THREE ACTS.

BY R. B. SHERIDAN, ESQ.

ADAPTED FOR

THEATRICAL REPRESENTATION,

AS PERFORMED AT THE

THEATRE-ROYAL,

DRURY-LANE.

REGULATED FROM THE PROMPT-BOOK.

By Permiſſion of the Managers.

DUBLIN :

PRINTED BY *WILLIAM PORTER,*

FOR WILLIAM JONES, NO. 86, DAME-STREET.

M DCC XCIII.

TO MRS. GREVILLE.

MADAM,

IN requesting your permission to address the following pages to you, which as they aim themselves to be critical, require every protection and allowance that approving taste or friendly prejudice can give them, I yet ventured to mention no other motive than the gratification of private friendship and esteem. Had I suggested a hope that your implied approbation would give a sanction to their defects, your particular reserve, and dislike to the reputation of critical taste, as well as of poetical talent, would have made you refuse the protection of your name to such a purpose. However, I am not so ungrateful as now to attempt to combat this disposition in you. I shall not here presume to argue that the present state of poetry claims and expects every assistance that taste and example can afford it: nor endeavour to prove that a fastidious concealment of the most elegant productions of judgment and fancy is an ill return for the possession of those endowments.—Con nue to deceive yourself in the idea that you ar *only to be eminently admired and regarded for the valuable qualities that attach private friendfhips, and the graceful talents that adorn converfation. Enough of what you have written, has ftolen into full public notice to anfwer my purpofe; and you will, perhaps, be the only perfon, converfant in elegant literature, who fhall read this addrefs, and not perceive, that by publifhing your particular approbation of the following drama, I have a more interefted object than to boaft the true refpect and regard with which*

I have the honour to be,

. MADAM,

Your very fincere,

And obedient humble fervant,

R. B. SHERIDAN.

PROLOGUE.

BY THE HONORABLE

RICHARD FITZPATRICK.

THE Sister Muses, whom these realms obey,
Who o'er the Drama hold divided sway,
Sometimes, by evil counsellors, 'tis said
Like earth-born potentates have been misled :
In those gay days of wickedness and wit,
When Villiers criticiz'd what Dryden writ,
The Tragic Queen, to please a tasteless crowd,
Had learned to bellow, rant, and roar so loud,
That frighten'd Nature, her best friend before,
The blust'ring beldam's company forswore.
Her comic Sister, who had wit 'tis true,
With all her merits, had her failings too ;
And would sometimes in mirthful moments use
A style too flippant for a well-bred Muse.
Then female modesty abash'd, began
To seek the friendly refuge of the fan,
A while behind that slight entrenchment stood
'Till driv'n from thence, she left the stage for good.
In our more pious, and far chaster times !
These sure no longer are the Muse's crimes !
But some complain, that, former faults to shun,
The reformation to extremes has run.
The frantic hero's wild delirium past,
Now insipidity succeeds bombast ;

F

So flow Melpomene's cold numbers creep,
Here dullness seems her drowsy court to keep,
And we, are scarce awake, whilst you are fast asleep.

Thalia, once so ill-behav'd and rude,
Reform'd; is now become an arrant prude,
Retailing nightly to the yawning pit,
The purest morals, undefil'd by wit!
Our Author offers in these motley scenes,
A slight remonstrance to the Drama's queens,
Nor let the goddesses be over nice;
Free spoken subjects give the best advice.
Although not quite a novice in his trade,
His cause to-night requires no common aid.
To this, a friendly, just, and pow'rful court,
I come Ambassador to beg support.
Can he undaunted, brave the critic's rage?
In civil broils, with brother bards engage?
Ho'd forth their errors to the public eye,
Nay more, e'en News-papers themselves defy?
Say, must his single arm encounter all?
By numbers vanquish'd, e'en the brave may fall;
And though no leader should success distrust,
Whose troops are willing, and whose cause is just;
To bid such hosts of angry foes defiance,
His chief dependance must be, your alliance.

F 2

Men.

DANGLE, - - - - -	Mr. Dodd.
SNEER, - - - - -	Mr. Palmer.
Sir FRETFUL PLAGIARY, - -	Mr. Parfons.
Signor PASTICCIO RITORNELLO, -	Mr. Delpini.
INTERPRETER, - - - -	Mr. Baddeley.
UNDER PROMPTER, - - -	Mr. Phillimore.
PUFF, - - - - -	Mr. King.

Women.

Mrs. DANGLE, - - - -	Mrs. Hopkins.
ITALIAN GIRLS, - - - -	{ Mifs Field, and t { Mifs Abrams.

CHARACTERS OF THE TRAGEDY.

Men.

LORD BURLEIGH, - - - -	Mr. Moody.
GOVERNOR of TILBURY FORT, -	Mr. Wrighten.
EARL of LEICESTER, - - -	Mr. Farren,
Sir WALTER RALEIGH, - -	Mr. Burton.
Sir CHRISTOPHER HATTON, - -	Mr. Waldrop.
MASTER of the HORSE, - -	Mr. Kenny.
BEEFEATER, - - - -	Mr. Wright.
JUSTICE, - - - - -	Mr Packer.
SON, - - - - -	Mr. Lamash.
CONSTABLE, - - - -	Mr Fawcett.
THAMES, - - - - -	Mr. Gawdry.
Don FEROLO WHISKERANDOS, -	Mr. Bannifter, j

Women.

1ft NIECE, - - - - -	Mifs Collet.
2d NIECE, - - - - -	Mifs Kirby.
JUSTICE'S LADY, - - - -	Mrs. Johnfton.
CONFIDANT, - - - -	Mrs. Bradfhaw
TILBURINA, - - - -	Mifs Pope.

Guards, Conftables, Servants, Chorus, Rivers, Attendan
&c. &c.

THE

C R I T I C.

ACT I. SCENE I.

Mr. and Mrs. DANGLE *at Breakfaſt, and reading
Newſpapers.*

Dangle (reading.)

" BRUTUS to Lord North."—" Letter the ſecond,
" on the State of the Army."—'Pſhaw ! " To the
" firſt L— daſh D. of the A— daſh Y."—" Ge-
" nuine Extract of a Letter from St. Kitt's."—
" Coxheath Intelligence."—" It is now confident-
" ly aſſerted that Sir Charles Hardy."—'Pſhew !
—Nothing but about the fleet, and the nation !—
and I hate all politics but theatrical politics.—
Where's the Morning Chronicle ?

Mrs. Dan. Yes, that's your gazette.

Dan. So, here we have it.——

" *Theatrical intelligence extraordinary,*"——" We
" hear there is a new tragedy in rehearſal at Drury-
" Lane Theatre, call'd the Spaniſh Armada, ſaid

" to be written by Mr. Puff, a gentleman well known
" in the theatrical world ; if we may allow ourselves
" to give credit to the report of the performers,
" who, truth to fay, are in general but indifferent
'' judges, this piece abounds with the moft ftriking
" and received beauties of modern compofition."—
So! I am very glad my friend Puff's tragedy is in
fuch forwardnefs.—Mrs. Dangle, my dear, you will
be very glad to hear that Puff's tragedy——

Mrs. Dan. Lord, Mr. Dangle, why will you
plague me about fuch nonfenfe?—Now the plays are
begun I fhall have no peace.—Isn't it fufficient to
make yourfelf ridiculous by your paffion for the theatre, without continually teazing me to join you?
Why can't you ride your hobby-horfe without de-
fiiing to place me on a pillion behind you, Mr.
Dangle?

Dan. Nay, my dear, I was only going to read—

Mrs. Dan. No, no; you never will read any
thing that's worth liftening to:—you hate to hear
about your country ; there are letters every day with
Roman fignatures, demonftrating the certainty of an
invafion, and proving that the nation is utterly undone—But you never will read any thing to entertain
one.

Dan. What has a woman to do with politics, Mrs.
Dangle?

Mrs. Dan. And what have you to do with the
theatre, Mr. Dangle? Why fhould you affect the
character of a Critic? I have no patience with you !—
haven't you made yourfelf the jeft of all your acquaint-
ance by your interference in matters where you have

no bufinefs? Are not you call'd a theatrical Quid-
nunc, and a mock Mæcenas to fecond-hand authors?

Dan. True; my power with the Managers is pretty notorious; but is it no credit to have applications
from all quarters for my intereft?—From lords to recommend fidlers, from ladies to get boxes, from authors to get anfwers, and from actors to get engagements.

Mrs. Dan. Yes, truly; you have contrived to get
a fhare in all the plague and trouble of theatrical
property, without the profit, or even the credit of
the abufe that attends it.

Dan. I am fure, Mrs. Dángle, you are no lofer
by it, however; you have all the advantages of it:
—mightn't you, laft winter, have had the reading of
the new Pantomime a fortnight previous to its performance? And doesn't Mr. Fofbrook let you take
places for a play before it is advertis'd, and fet you
down for a Box for every new piece through the feafon? And didn't my friend, Mr. Smatter, dedicate
his laft Farce to you at my particular requeft, Mrs.
Dangle?

Mrs. Dan. Yes; but wasn't the Farce damn'd,
Mr. Dangle? And to be fure it is extremely pleafant
to have one's houfe made the motley rendezvous of all
the lackeys of literature!—The very high change of
trading authors and jobbing critics!—Yes, my draw-
ing room is an abfolute regifter-office for candidate
actors, and poets without character;—then to be continually alarmed with Miffes and Ma'ams piping hif-
teric changes on Juliets and Dorindas, Pollys and

ftaff's Page, and are about as near the ftandard of the original.

Sir Fret. Ha!——

Sneer. —In fhort, that even the fineft paffages you fteal are of no fervice to you; for the poverty of your own language prevents their affimilating; fo that they lie on the furface like lumps of marl on a barren moor, encumbering what it is not in their power to fertilize!——

Sir Fret. (After great agitation.)——Now another perfon would be vex'd at this.

Sneer. Oh! but I wou'dn't have told you, only to divert you.

Sir Fret. I know it—I *am* diverted,—Ha! ha! ha!—not the leaft invention!—Ha! ha! ha! very good!—very good!

Sneer. Yes—no genius! Ha! ha! ha!

Dan. A fevere rogue! Ha! ha! ha! But you are quite right, Sir Fretful, never to read fuch non-fenfe.

Sir Fret. To be fure—for if there is any thing to one's praife, it is a foolifh vanity to be gratified at it, and if it is abufe,—why one is always fure to hear of it from one damn'd good natur'd friend or another!

Enter SERVANT.

Ser. Sir, there is an Italian gentleman, with a French interpreter, and three young ladies, and a dozen muficians, who fay they are fent by Lady Rondeau and Mrs. Fuge.

Dan. Gadfo! they come by appointment. Dear Mrs. Dangle, do let them know I'll fee them directly.

Mrs. Dan. You know, Mr. Dangle, I·fhan't underftand a word they fay.

Dan. But you hear there's an interpreter.

Mrs. Dan. Well, I'll try to endure their complaifance till you come.   [*Exit.*

Ser. And Mr. Puff, Sir, has fent word' that the
laft rehearfal is to be this morning, and that he'll
call on you prefently.

Dan. That's true—I fhall certainly be at home.
(Exit Servant.) Now, Sir Fretful, if you have a
mind to have juftice done you in the way of anfwer
—Egad, Mr. Puff's your man.

Sir Fret. 'Pfhaw! Sir, why fhould I wifh to have
it anfwered, when I tell you I am pleafed at it?

Dan. True, I had forgot that.—But I hope you
are not fretted at what Mr. Sneer——

Sir Fret. —Zounds! no, Mr. Dangle, don't I
tell you thefe things never fret me in the leaft.

Dan. Nay, I only thought——

Sir Fret. —And let me tell you, Mr. Dangle, 'tis
damn'd affronting in you, to fuppofe that I am hurt,
when I tell you I am not.

Sneer. But why fo warm, Sir Fretful?

Sir Fret. Gadflife! Mr. Sneer, you are as abfurd
as Dangle; how often muft I repeat it to you, that
nothing can vex me, but your fuppofing it poffible
for me to mind the damn'd nonfenfe you have been repeating to me!—and let me tell you, if you continue
to believe this, you muft mean to infult me, gentlemen—and then your difrefpect will affect me no more
than the newfpaper criticifms—and I fhall treat it—

with exactly the fame calm indifference and philofophic contempt—and fo your fervant.   [*Exit.*

Sneer. Ha! ha! ha! Poor Sir Fretful! Now will
he go and vent his philofophy in anonymous abufe of
all modern critics and authors—But, Dangle, you
muft get your friend Puff to take me to the rehearfal
of his tragedy.

Dan. I'll anfwer for't, he'll thank you for defiring
it.   But come and help me to judge of this mufical
family; they are recommended by people of confequence, I affure you.

Sneer. I am at your difpofal the whole morning—
but I thought you had been a decided critic in mufic,
as well as in literature.

Dan. So I am—but I have a bad ear.—Efaith,
Sneer, tho', I am afraid we were a little too fevere
on Sir Fretful—tho' he is my friend. ·

Sneer. Why, 'tis certain, that unneceffarily to
mortify the vanity of any writer, is a cruelty which
mere dulnefs never can deferve; but where a bafe
and perfonal malignity ufurps the place of literary
emulation, the aggreffor deferves neither quarters nor
pity.

Dan. That's true egad!—tho' he's my friend!

SCENE II.

A Drawing-room, Harpsichord, &c. Italian Family, French Interpreter, Mrs. Dangle and Servants discovered.

Interp. Je dis madame, ja'i l'honneur to *introduce* & de vous demander votre protection pour le Signor Pasticcio Retornello & pour sa charmante famille.

Sig. Past. Ah! Vosignoria noi vi preghiamo di favoritevi colla vostra protezione.

1st Daugh. Vosignoria fatevi questi grazzie.

2d Daugh. Si Signora.

Interp. Madame—*me interpret.*—C'est à dire—in English—quils vous prient de leur faire l'honneur—

Mrs. Dan. —I say again, gentlemen, I don't understand a word you say.

Sig. Past. Questo Signore spiegheró.

Interp. Oui—*me interpret.*—nous avons les lettres de recommendation pour Monsieur Dangle de——

Mrs. Dan. —Upon my word, Sir, I don't understand you.

Sig. Past. La Contessa Rondeau e nostra padrona.

3d Daugh. Si, padre, & mi Ladi Fuge.

Interp. O!—*me interpret.*—Madame, ils disent— in English—Qu'ils ont l'honneur d'etre proteges de ces Demes.—*You understand?*

Mrs. Dan. No, Sir——no understand!

Enter DANGLE *and* SNEER.

Interp. Ah voici Monsieur Dangle!

All Italians. A! Signor Dangle!

Mrs. Dan. Mr. Dangle, here are two very civ
gentlemen trying to make themselves underftooi
and I don't know which is the interpreter.

Dan. Ebien!

Interp. Monsieur Dangle—le grand bruit
de vos talents pour la critique & de votre intereft avec Meffieurs les Directeurs a tous les
Theatres.

Sig. Paft. Vofignoria fiete fi famofo par la
voftra conofcenfa e voftra intereffa colla le Di-
rettore da—

Dan. Egad I think the Interpreter is the harde
to be underftood of the two!

Sneer. Why, I thought, Dangle, you had bee
an admirable linguift!

Dan. So I am, if they would not talk fo damn'
faft.

Sneer. Well, I'll explain that—the lefs time w
lofe in hearing them the better—for that I fuppof
is what they are brought here for.

[Sneer *fpeaks to Sig.* Paft.—*They fing trios, &*
Dangle *beating out of time.* Servant *enters an*
whifpers Dangle.]

Dan. Shew him up. *(Exit* Servant.) Bravo! ad
mirable! braviffimo! admirabliffimo!—Ah! Sneer
where will you find fuch as thefe vo'ces in Eng
land?

Sneer. Not eafily.

Dan. But Puff is coming.—Signor and little Signora's—obligatiffimo !—Spofa Signora Danglena—Mrs. Dangle, fhall I beg you to offer them fome refrefhments, and take their addrefs in the next room.

[*Exit* Mrs. Dangle *with the* Italians *and* Interpreter *ceremonioufly.*

Re-enter SERVANT.

Ser. Mr. Puff, Sir !

Dar. My dear Puff !

Enter Puff.

Puff. My dear Dangle, how is it with you ?

Dan. Mr. Sneer, give me leave to introduce Mr. Puff to you.

Puff. Mr. Sneer is this ? Sir, he is a gentleman whom I have long panted for the honour of knowing —a gentleman whofe critical talents and tranfcendant judgment——

Sneer. —Dear Sir——

Dan. Nay, don't be modeft, Sneer, my friend Puff only talks to you in the ftile of his profeffion.

Sneer. His profeffion !

Puff. Yes, Sir ; I make no fecret of the trade I follow—among friends and brother authors, Dangle knows I love to be frank on the fubjcct, and to advertife myfelf *viva voce.*—I am, Sir, a Practitioner in Panegyric, or to fpeak more plainly—a Profeffor of the Art of Puffing, at your fervice—or any body elfe's.

G

Sneer. Sir, you are very obliging!—I believe, Mr. Puff, I have often admired your talents in the daily prints.

Puff. Yes, Sir, I flatter myfelf I do as much bufinefs in that way as any fix of the fraternity in town—Devilifh hard work all the fummer—Friend Dangle! never work'd harder!—But harkee—the Winter Managers were a little fore I believe.

Dan. No—I believe they took it all in good part.

Puff. Aye!—then that muft have been affectation in them, for egad, there were fome of the attacks which there was no laughing at!

Sneer. Aye, the humorous ones.—But I fhould think Mr. Puff, that Authors would in general be able to do this fort of work for themfelves.

Puff. Why yes—but in a clumfy way.—Befides, we look on that as an encroachment, and fo take the oppofite fide.—I dare fay now, you conceive half the very civil paragraphs and advertifements you fee, to be written by the parties concerned, or their friends? —No fuch thing—Nine out of ten, manufactured by me in the way of bufinefs.

Sneer. Indeed!—

Puff. Even the Auctioneers now—the Auctioneers I fay, tho' the rogues have lately got fome credit for their language—not an article of the merit their's! —take them out of their pulpits, and they are as dull as Catalogues.——No, Sir;—'twas I firft enrich'd their ftyle—'twas I firft taught them to crowd their advertifements with panegyrical fuperlatives, each epithet rifing above the other—like the Bidders in r own Auction-rooms! From me they learn'd to

inlay their phrafeology with variegated chips of exo-
tic metaphor: by _me_ too their inventive faculties
were called forth.—Yes, Sir, by _me_ they were inftructed to clothe ideal walls with gratuitous fruits—
to infinuate obfequious rivulets into vifionary groves
—to teach courteous fhrubs to nod their approbation
of the grateful 'foil! or, on emergencies, to raife
upftart oaks, where there never had been an acorn;
to create a delightful vicinage without the affiftance
of a neighbour; or fix the temple of Hygeia in the
fens of Lincolnfhire!

Dan. I am fure you have done them infinite fervice; for now, when a gentleman is ruined, he parts
with his houfe with fome credit.

Sneer. Service! if they had any gratitude, they
would erect a ftatue to him, they would figure him
as a prefiding Mercury, the god of traffic and fiction,
with a hammer in his hand inftead of a caduceus.—
But pray, Mr. Puff, what firft put you on exercifing
your talents in this way?

Puff. Egad, Sir—fheer neceffity—the proper parent of an art fo nearly allied to invention: you muft
know, Mr. Sneer, that from the firft time I tried my
hand at an advertifement, my fuccefs was fuch, that
for fometime after, I led a moft extraordinary life indeed!

Sneer. How, pray?

Puff. Sir, I fupported myfelf two years entirely
by my misfortunes.

Sneer. By your misfortunes!

Puff. Yes, Sir, affifted by long ficknefs, and

tainly don't fall off, I affure you—No, no, it don't
fall off.

Dan. Now, Mrs. Dangle, didn't you fay it ftruck
you in the fame light?

Mrs. Dan. No, indeed, I did not—I did not fee
a fault in any part of the play from the beginning to
the end.

Sir Fret. Upon my foul the women are the beft
judges after all!

Mrs. Dan. Or if I made any objection, I am fure
it was to nothing in the piece; but that I was afraid
it was, on the whole, a little too long.

Sir Fret. Pray, Madam, do you fpeak as to dura-
tion of time; or do you mean that the ftory is tedi-
oufly fpun out?

Mrs. Dan. O Lud, no—I fpeak only with re-
ference to the ufual length of acting plays.

Sir Fret. Then I am very happy—very happy indeed—becaufe the play is a fhort play, a remarkably
fhort play;—I fhould not venture to differ with a lady
on a point of tafte; but, on thefe occafions, the
watch, you know, is the Critic.

Mrs. Dan. Then, I fuppofe, it muft have been
Mr. Dangle's drawling manner of reading it to me.

Sir Fret. Oh, if Mr. Dangle read it, that's quite
another affair!—But I affure you, Mr. Dangle, the
firft meeting you can fpare me three hours and an half,
I'll undertake to read you the whole from beginning to
end, with the Prologue and Epilogue, and allow
time for the mufic between the acts.

Mrs. Dan. Dangle, to fave it on the large with.

Sir Fret. which you may be fure

Dan. Egad, Sneer, you will be quite an adept in the bufinefs.

Puff. Now, Sir, the Puff Collateral is much ufed as an appendage to advertifements, and may take the form of anecdote.—Yefterday as the celebrated George Bon-mot was fauntering down St. James's ſtreet, he met the lively Lady Mary Myrtle, coming out of the Park—' Good God, Lady Mary, I'm furprifed to meet you in a white jacket—for I expected never to have feen you, but in a full-trimmed uniform and a light-horfeman's cap!'—' Heavens, George, where could you have learn'd that?'—' Why, replied the wit, I juſt faw a print of you, in a new publication called the Camp Magazine, which, by the bye, is a devilifh clever thing—and is fold at No. 3, on the right hand of the way, two doors from the printing-office, the corner of Ivy-lane, Paternofter-row, price only one fhilling!'

Sneer. Very ingenious indeed!

Puff. But the Puff Collufive is the neweſt of any; for it acts in the difguife of determined hoftility.— It is much ufed by bold bookfellers and enterprifing poets—An indignant correfpondent obferves—that the new poem called Beelzebub's Cotillion, or Proferpine's Fete Champetre, is one of the moſt unjuſtifiable performances he ever read! The feverity with which certain characters are handled is quite fhocking! And as there are many defcriptions in it too warmly coloured for female delicacy, the fhameful avidity with which this piece is bought by all people of fafhion, is a reproach on the taſte of the times, and a *difgrace* to the delicacy of the age!—Here you fee the two ftrongeft inducements are held forth.—Firft, that nobody ought to read it ;—and fecondly, that every body buys it : on the ftrength of which, the publifher boldly prints the tenth edition, before he had fold ten of the firft ; and then eftablifhes it by threatening himfelf with the pillory, or abfolutely in- dicting himfelf for Scan. Mag. !

Dan. Ha ! ha ! ha !—'gad, I know it is fo.

Puff. As to the Puff Oblique, or Puff by Impli- cation, it is too various and extenfive to be illuftrat- ed by an inftance ;—it attracts in titles and prefumes in patents ; it lurks in the *limitation* of a fubfcription, and invites in the affurance of croud and incommoda- tion at public places ; it delights to draw forth con- cealed merit, with a moft difinterefted affiduity ; and fometimes wears a countenance of fmiling cenfure and tender reproach.—It has a wonderful memory for Parliamentary Debates, and will often give the whole fpeech of a favoured member with the moft flattering accuracy. But, above all, it is a great dealer in reports and fuppofitions. It has the earlieft intelligence of intended preferments that will reflect *honour* on the *patrons ;* and embryo promotions of modeft gentlemen—who know nothing of the matter themfelves. It can hint a ribband for implied fer- vices, in the air of a common report ; and with the carelefnefs of a cafual paragraph, fuggeft officers into commands—to which they have no pretenfion but their wifhes. This, Sir, is the laft principal clafs of the Art of Puffing—An art which I hope you will now a- gree with me, is of the higheft dignity—yielding a ta- *blature of benevolence* and public fpirit ; befriending

G 5

cafe in point, to the time in which an author writes,
if he knows his own intereſt, he will take advantage
of it ; fo, Sir, I call my tragedy The Spaniſh Armada ; and have laid the ſcene before Tilbury Fort.

Sneer. A moſt happy thought certainly !

Dan. Egad it was—I told you fo —But pray now,
I don't underſtand how you have contrived to introduce any love into it.

Puff. Love !—Oh, nothing ſo eafy ; for it is a received point among poets, that where hiſtory gives
you a good heroic out-line for a play, you may fill
up with a little love at your own diſcretion : in doing
which, nine times out of ten, you only make up a
deficiency in the private hiſtory of the times. Now,
I rather think I have done this with ſome ſuccefs.

Sneer. No fcandal about Queen Elizabeth, I
hope ?

Puff. O Lud ! no, no—I only ſuppofe the Governor of Tilbury Fort's daughter to be in love with
the fon of the Spaniſh Admiral.

Sneer. Oh, is that all ?

Dan. Excellent, Efaith !—I fee it at once.—But
won't this appear rather improbable ?

Puff. To be fure it will—but what the plague ! a
play is not to ſhew occurrences that happen every day,
but things juſt fo ſtrange, that tho' they never *did*,
they might happen.

Sneer. Certainly, nothing is unnatural, that is not
phyſically impoſſible.

Puff. Very true—and for that matter Don Ferolo
Whiſkerandos—for that's the lover's name, might
have been over here in the train of the Spaniſh Ar-

baffador ; or Tilburina, for that is the lady's name, might have been in love with him, from having heard his character, or feen his picture ; or from knowing that he was the laft man in the world fhe ought to be in love with—or for any other good female reafon.— However, Sir, the fact is, that though fhe is but a Knight's daughter, egad ! fhe is in love like any Princefs !

Dan. Poor young lady ! I feel for her already ; for I can conceive how great the conflict muft be between her paffion and her duty; her love for her country, and her love for Don Ferolo Whifker-andos !

Puff. O amazing !—her poor fufceptible heart is fwayed to and fro, by contending paffions like—

Enter UNDER PROMPTER.

Und. Prompt. Sir, the fcene is fet, and every thing is ready to begin, if you pleafe.—

Puff. 'Egad ; then we'll lofe no time.

Und. Prompt. Tho' I believe, Sir, you will find it very fhort, for all the performers have profited by the kind permiffion you granted them.

Puff. Hey ! what !

Und. Prompt. You know, Sir, you gave them leave to cut out or omit whatever they found heavy or unneceffary to the plot ; and I muft own they have taken very liberal advantage of your indulgence.

Puff. Well, well.—They are in general very good judges ; and I know I am luxuriant.—Now, Mr. Hopkins, as foon as you pleafe.

Und. Prompt. *(To the Mufic.)* Gentlemen, will you play a few bars of fomething, juft to—

Puff. Aye, that's right—for as we have the fcenes, and dreffes, egad, we'll go to't, as if it was the firft night's performance ;—but you need not mind ftopping between the acts.   [*Exit* Under Prompter.

(Orcheſtra play. Then the Bell rings.)

Soh! ftand clear gentlemen.—Now you know there will be a cry of down!—down!—hats off!! filence!—Then up curtain—and let us fee what our painters have done for us.

SCENE II.

The Curtain riſes and diſcovers Tilbury Fort.

Two Centinels aſleep.

Dan. Tilbury Fort!—very fine indeed!

Puff. Now, what do you think I open with?

Sneer. Faith, I can't guefs—

Puff. A clock.—Hark!—*(clock ſtrikes.)* I open with a clock ftriking, to beget an awful attention in the audience—it alfo marks the time, which is four o'clock in the morning, and faves a defcription of the rifing fun, and a great deal about gilding the eaftern hemifphere.

Dan. But pray, are the centinels to be afleep?

Puff. Faft as watchmen.

Sneer. Isn't that odd though at fuch an alarming crifis?

Puff. To be fure it is—but fmaller things muſt give way to a ſtriking ſcene at the opening ; that's a rule.—And the cafe is, that two great men are coming to this very ſpot to begin the piece ; now, it is not to be fuppofed they would open their lips, if thefe fellows were watching them ; fo, egad, I muſt either have ſent them off their poſts, or ſet them aſleep.

Sneer. O, that accounts for it !—But tell us, who are thefe coming ?—

Puff. Thefe are they—Sir Walter Raleigh, and Sir Chriſtopher Hatton.—You'll know Sir Chriſto-pher, by his turning out his toes—famous you know for his dancing. I like to preſerve all the little traits of charaƈter.—Now attend.

Enter Sir WALTER RALEIGH *and* Sir CHRISTOPHER
HATTON.

" *Sir Chriſ.* ——True,, gallant Raleigh !—
Dan. What, they had been talking before ?
Puff. O, yes ; all the way as they came along.—I beg pardon gentlemen *(to the Aƈtors)* but thefe are particular friends of mine, whofe remarks may be of great fervice to us.—Don't mind interrupting them whenever any thing ſtrikes you.
						[*To* Sneer *and* Dangle.
" *Sir Chriſ.* ——True, gallant Raleigh !
" But O, thou champion of thy country's fame,
" There *is* a queſtion which I yet muſt aſk ;
" A queſtion, which I never aſk'd before—
" What mean thefe mighty armaments ?
" *This general muſter ?* and this throng of chiefs?

Sneer. Pray, Mr. Puff, how came Sir Chriſtopher Hatton never to aſk that queſtion before ?

Puff. What, before the Play began ? how the plague could he ?

Dan. That's true, efaith !

Puff. But you will hear what he thinks of the matter.

" *Sir Chriſ.* Alas, my noble friend, when I be-
        " hold
" Yon tented plains in martial ſymmetry
" Array'd.——When I count o'er yon glittering
        " lines
" Of creſted warriors, where the proud ſteeds,
        " neigh,
" And valor-breathing trumpet's ſhrill appeal,
" Reſponſive vibrate on my liſt'ning ear ;
" When virgin majeſty herſelf I view,
" Like her protecting Pallas veil'd in ſteel,
" With graceful confidence exhort to arms !'
" When briefly all I hear or ſee bears ſtamp
" Of martial vigilance, and ſtern defence,
" I cannot but ſurmiſe.——Forgive, my friend,
" If the conjecture's raſh——I cannot but
" Surmiſe.——The ſtate ſome danger apprehends !"

Sneer. A very cautious conjecture that.

Puff. Yes, that's his character ; not to give an opinion, but on ſecure grounds—now then.

" *Sir Wal.* O, moſt accompliſhed Chriſtopher.——

Puff. He calls him by his chriſtian name, to ſhew that they are on the moſt familiar terms.

" *Sir Wal.* O, moſt accompliſh'd Chriſtopher, I
        find

" Thy ftaunch fagacity ftill tracks the future,.
" In the frefh print of the o'ertaken paft.
  Puff. Figurative!
  " *Sir Wal.* Thy fears are juft.
  " *Sir Chrif.* —But where ? whence ? when ? and
    " what
" The danger is——Methinks I fain would learn.
  " *Sir Wal.* You know, my friend, fcarce two re-
    " volving funs,
" And three revolving moons, have clofed their
    " courfe,
" Since haughty Philip, in defpight of peace,
" With hoftile hand hath ftruck at England's trade.
  " *Sir Chrif.* ——I know it well.
  " *Sir Wal.* Philip you know is proud, Iberia's
    " king!
  " *Sir Chrif.* He is.
  " *Sir Wal.* ——His fubjects in bafe bigotry
" And Catholic oppreffion held—while we
" You know, the Proteftant perfuafion hold.
  " *Sir Chrif.* We do.
  " *Sir Wal.* You know, befide——his boafted ar-
    " mament,
" The fam'd Armada——by the Pope baptized,
" With purpofe to invade thefe realms——
  " *Sir Chrif.*   ——————Is failed,
" Our laft advices fo report.
  " *Sir Wal.* While the Iberian Admiral's chief
    " hope,
" His darling fon——
  " *Sir Chrif.* ————Ferolo Whifkerandos hight——

" *Sir Wal.* The fame—by chance a pris'ner hath,
 " been ta'en;
" And in this fort of Tilbury——

 " *Sir Chrif.* ————————Is' now
" Confin'd—'tis true, and oft from yon tall turrets top
" I've mark'd the youthful Spaniard's haughty mien
" Unconquer'd, tho' in chains !

 " *Sir Wal.* ————————You alfo know——

Dan. —Mr. Puff, as he *knows* all this, why does
Sir Walter go on telling him ?.

Puff. But the audience are not fuppofed to know
any thing of the matter,· are they ?

Sneer. True, but I think you manage ill : for
there certainly appears no reafon why Sir Walter
fhould be fo communicative.

Puff. For, egad now, that is one of the moft ungrateful obfervations I ever heard—for the lefs inducement he has to tell all this, the more I think,
you ought to be oblig'd to him ; for I am fure you'd,
know nothing of the matter without it.

Dan. That's very true, upon my word.

Puff. But you will find he was *not* going on.

 " *Sir Chrif.* Enough, enough—'tis plain—and I
  " no more
" Am in amazement loft !——

Puff. Here, now you fee, Sir Chriftopher did not
in fact afk any one queftion for· his own information.

Sneer. No indeed :—his has been a moft difinterefted curiofity !

Dan. Really, I find, we are very much oblig'd to
them both.

Puff. To be fure you are. Now then for the Commander in Chief, the Earl of Leicefter! who, you know, was no favourite but of the Queen's.—We left off—' in amazement loft!'—

" *Sir Chrif.* ——Am in amazement loft.——
" But, fee where noble Leicefter comes! fupreme
" In honours and command.
" *Sir Wal.* ——And yet methinks,
" At fuch a time, fo perilous, fo fear'd,
" That ftaff might well become an abler grafp.
" *Sir Chrif.* And fo by heav'n! think I; but
" foft, he's here!

Puff. Aye, they envy him.

Sneer. But who are thefe with him?

Puff. O! very valiant knights; one is the Governor of the Fort, the other the mafter of the horfe.— And now, I think you fhall hear fome better language: I was obliged to be plain and intelligible in the firft fcene, becaufe there was fo much matter of fact in it; but now, efaith, you have trope, figure, and metaphor, as plenty as noun-fubftantives.

Enter Earl *of* LEICESTER, *the Governor, and others.*

" *E. of Leic.* How's this my friends! is't thus
" your new fledg'd zeal
" And plumed valour moulds in roofted floth?
" Why dimly glimmers that heroic flame,
" Whofe red'ning blaze by patriot fpirit fed,
" Should be the beacon of a kindling realm? ·
" Can the quick current of a patriot heart,
" *Thus* ftagnate in a cold and weedy converfe,.

" Or freeze in tidelefs inactivity ?

" No ! rather let the fountain of your valour

" Spring thro' each ftream of enterprize,

" Each petty channel of conducive daring,

" Till the full torrent of your foaming wrath

" O'erwhelm the flats of funk hoftility !

   Puff. There it is—follow'd up !

   " *Sir Wal.* No more ! the frefh'ning breath of thy

     " rebuke

" Hath fill'd the fwelling canvafs of our fouls !

" And thus, tho' fate fhould cut the cable of

               [All take hands.

" Our topmoft hopes, in friendfhip's clofing line

" We'll grapple with defpair, and if we fall,

" We'll fall in Glory's wake !'

   " *E. of Leic.* There fpoke Old England's genius!'

" Then, are we all refolv'd?

   " *All.* We are——all refolv'd.

   " *E. of Leic.* To conquer——or be free ?

   " *All.* To conquer, or be free.

   " *E. of Leic.* All ?

   " *All.* All.

   Dan. *Nem. con.* egad !

   Puff. O yes, where they *do* agree on the ftage,. their unanimity is wonderful !

   " *E. of Leic.* Then, let's embrace—and now——

   Sneer. What the plague, is he going to pray ?

   Puff. Yes, hufh !—in great emergencies, there is nothing like a prayer !

   " *E. of Leic.* O mighty Mars !

   Dan. But why fhould he pray to Mars ?

   Puff. Hufh !

" *E. of Leic.* ———If in thy homage bred,
" Each point of difcipline I've ftill obferv'd ;
" Nor but by due promotion, and the right
" Of fervice, to the rank of Major-General
" Have ris'n ; affift thy votary now !
   " *Gov.* Yet do not rife——hear me !
   " *Maft. of Horfe.* And me !
   " *Knight.* And me !
   " *Sir Wal.* And me !
   " *Sir Chrif.* And me !
   Puff. Now, pray all together.
   " *All.* Behold thy votaries fubmiffive beg,
" That thou will deign to grant them all they afk ;
" Affift them to accomplifh all their ends,
" And fanctify whatever means they ufe
" To gain them !
   Sneer. A very orthodox quintetto !
   Puff. Vaftly well, gentlemen.—Is that well ma-
naged or not ? Have you fuch a prayer as that on
the ftage ?
   Sneer. Not exactly.
   E. of Leic. *(To* Puff.) But, Sir, you hav'nt fet-
tled how we are to get off here.
   Puff. You could not go off kneeling, could you ?
   Sir Wal. *(To* Puff.) O no, Sir ! impoffible !
   Puff. It would have a good effect efaith, if you
could ! exeunt praying !—Yes, and would vary the
eftablifhed mode of fpringing off with a glance at the
pit.
   Sneer. O never mind, fo as you get them off, I'll
anfwer for it the audience wont care how.

Puff. Well then, repeat the laſt line ſtanding, and go off the old way.

" *All.* And ſanctify whatever means we uſe to
" gain them.   [*Exeunt.*

Dan. Bravo ! a fine exit.

Sneer. Well, really Mr. Puff.——

Puff. Stay a moment.——

The CENTINELS *get up.*

" 1ſt *Cent.* All this ſhall to Lord Burleigh's ear.

" 2d *Cent.* 'Tis meet it ſhould.

[*Exeunt* Centinels.

Dan. Hey !—why, I thought thoſe fellows had been aſleep ?

Puff. Only a pretence, there's the art of it ; they were ſpies of Lord Burleigh's.

Sneer. —But isn't it odd, they were never taken notice of, not even by the commander in chief.

Puff. O Lud, Sir, if people who want to liſten, or overhear, were not always conniv'd at in a Tragedy, there would be no carrying on any plot in the world.

Dan. That's certain !

Puff. But take care, my dear Dangle, the morning gun is going to fire.   [*Cannon fires.*

Dan. Well, that will have a fine effect.

Puff. I think ſo, and helps to realize the ſcene.——

[*Cannon twice.*

What the plague !—*three* morning guns !—there never is but one !—aye, this is always the way at the Theatre—give theſe fellows a good thing, and they

never know when to have done with it. You have
no more cannon to fire ?

Prompt. *(From within)* No, Sir.

Puff. Now then, for soft mufic.

Sneer. Pray what's that for ?

Puff. It fhews that Tilburina is coming ; nothing
introduces you a heroine like foft mufic.—Here fhe
comes.

Dan. And her confidant, I fuppofe ?

Puff. To be fure : here they are—inconfolable to
the minuet in Ariadne ! *(Soft mufic.)*

Enter TILBURINA *and* CONFIDANT.

" *Tilb.* Now has the whifpering breath of gentle
   " morn
" Bad Nature's voice, and Nature's beauty rife ;
" While orient Phœbus with unborrow'd hues,
" Cloaths the wak'd lovelinefs which all night flept
" In heav'nly drapery ! Darknefs is fled.
" Now flowers unfold their beauties to the fun,
" And blufhing, kifs the beam he fends to wake
   " them.
" The ftrip'd carnation, and the guarded rofe,
" The vulgar wall-flow'r, and fmart gillyflower,
" The polyanthus mean—the dapper daizy,
" Sweet William, and fweet marjorum——and all
" The tribe of fingle and of double pinks !
" Now too, the feather'd warblers tune their notes
" Around, and charm the lift'ning grove.—The
   " lark !
" The linnet ! chafinch ! bullfinch ! goldfinch !
   " greenfinch !

" ——But O to me, no joy can they afford !
" Nor rofe, nor wall-flow'r, nor fmart gillyflower,
" Nor polyanthus mean, nor dapper daizy,
" Nor William fweet, nor marjoium——nor lark,
" Linnet, nor all the finches of the grove !
   Puff. Your white handkerchief, Madam——
   Tilb. I thought, Sir, I wasn't to ufe that 'till,
' heart rending woe.'
   Puff. O yes, Madam—at ' the finches of the
grove,' if you pleafe.
   " *Tilb.* ——————Nor lark,
" Linnet, nor all the finches of the grove ! [*Weeps.*
   Puff. Vaftly well, Madam !
   Dan. Vaftly well indeed !
   " *Tilb.* For, O too fure, heart rending woe is
     " now
" The lot of wretched Tilburina !
   Dan. O !—'tis too much.
   Sneer. Oh !——it is indeed.
   " *Conf.* Be comforted, fweet Lady——for who
     " knows,
" But Heav'n has yet fome milk-white day in ftore.
   " *Tilb.* Alas, my gentle Nora,
" Thy tender youth, as yet hath never mourn'd
" Love's fatal dart.—Elfe wouldft thou know, that
     " when
" The foul is funk in comfortlefs defpair,
" It cannot tafte of merryment !
   Dan. That's certain.
   " *Conf.* But fee where your ftern father comes ;
" It is not meet that he fhould find you thus.

Puff. Hey, what the plague!—what a cut is here!—why, what is become of the defcription of her firft meeting with Don Whifkerandos? his gallant behaviour in the fea fight, and the fimile of the canary bird?

Tilb. Indeed, Sir, you'll find they will not be mifs'd.

Puff. Very well.—Very well!

Tilb. The cue, Ma'am, if you pleafe.

" *Conf.* It is not meet that he fhould find you
" thus.

" *Tilb.* Thou counfel'ft right, but 'tis no eafy
" tafk
" For barefac'd grief to wear a mafk of joy.

Enter GOVERNOR.

" *Gov.* How's this—in tears?——O Tilburina,
" fhame!
" Is this a time for maudling tendernefs,
" And Cupid's baby woes?——haft thou not heard
" That haughty Spain's Pope-confecrated fleet
" Advances to our fhores, while England's fate,
" Like a clipp'd guinea, trembles in the fcale!
" *Tilb.* Then, is the crifis of *my* fate at hand!
" I fee the fleets approach——I fee——

Puff. Now, pray gentlemen, mind.—This is one of the moft ufeful figures we tragedy writers have, by which a hero or heroine, in confideration of their being often obliged to overlook things that *are* on the ftage, is allow'd to hear and fee a number of things that are not.

Sneer. Yes—a kind of poetical fecond-fight!

H

Puff. Yes—now then, Madam.

" *Tilb.* ——————I fee their decks

" Are clear'd !——I fee the fignal made !

" The line is form'd !——a cable's length afunder !

" I fee the frigates ftation'd in the rear ;

" And now, I hear the thunder of the guns !

" I hear the victors fhouts——I alfo hear

" The vanquifh'd groan !—and now 'tis fmoke—

     " and now

" I fee the loofe fails fhiver in the wind ?

" I fee——I fee——what foon you'll fee——

     " *Gov.* Hold daughter ! peace ! this love hath

         " turn'd thy brain :

" The Spanifh fleet thou *canft* not fee—becaufe

" ——It is not yet in fight !

Dan. Egad, tho', the governor feems to make no allowance for this poetical figure you talk of.

Puff. No, a plain matter-of-fact man—that's his character.

     " *Tilb.* But will you then refufe his offer?

     " *Gov.* I muft—I will—I can—I ought—I do.

     " *Tilb.* Think what a noble price.

     " *Gov.* No more——you urge in vain.

     " *Tilb.* His liberty is all he afks.

Snecr. All *who* afks Mr. Puff? Who is—

Puff. Egad, Sir, I can't tell.—Here has been fuch cutting and flafhing, I don't know where they have got to myfelf.

     " *Tilb.* Indeed, Sir, you will find it will connect very well.

     " ——And your reward fecure.

Puff. O—if they had'nt been fo devilifh free with

their cutting here, you would have found that Don Whiſkerandos has been tampering for his liberty, and has perſuaded Tilburina to make this propoſal to her father—and now pray obſerve the conciſeneſs with which the argument is conducted. Egad, the *pro & con* goes as ſmart as hits in a fencing match. It is indeed a ſort of ſmall-ſword logic, which we have borrowed from the French.

" *Tilb.* A retreat in Spain!

" *Gov.* Outlawry here !

" *Tilb.* Your daughter's prayer !

" *Gov.* Your father's oath !

" *Tilb.* My lover !

" *Gov.* My country !

" *Tilb.* Tilburina !

" *Gov.* England !

" *Tilb.* A title !

" *Gov.* Honor !

" *Tilb.* A penſion !

" *Gov.* Conſcience !

" *Tilb.* A thouſand pounds !

" *Gov.* Hah ! thou haſt touch'd me nearly !

Puff. There you ſee——ſhe threw in *Tilburina*, Quick, parry cart with *England !*—Hah ! thruſt in teirce a title !—parried by honor.—Hah ! a penſion over the arm !—but by by conſcience.—Then flank-onade with a thouſand pounds—and a palpable hit egad !

" *Tilb.* Canſt thou——

" Reject the *ſuppliant*, and the *daughter* too ?

" *Gov.* No more; I wou'd not hear thee plead

" *in vain,*

H 2

" The *father* softens—but the *governor*

" Is fix'd ! [*Exit.*

Dan. Aye, that antithefis of perfons—is a moft
eftablifh'd figure.

" *Tilb.* Tis well——hence then fond hopes—fond
" paffion hence ;

" Duty, behold I am all over thine.——

" *Whifk.* (*Without.*) Where is my love—my——

" *Tilb.* Ha !

" *Whifk.* (*Entering.*) My beauteous enemy——

Puff. O dear, Ma'am, you muft ftart a great deal
more than that ; confider you had juft determined in
favour of duty—when in a moment the found of his
voice revives your paffion—overthrows your refolution—deftroys your obedience.—If you don't exprefs
all that in your ftart—you do nothing at all.

Tilb. Well, we'll try again !

Dan. Speaking from within, has always a fine
effect.

Sneer. Very.

" *Whifk.* My conquering Tilburina ! How ! is't
" thus

" We meet ? why are thy looks averfe ? what means

" That falling tear——that frown of boding woe?

" Hah ! now indeed I am a prifoner !

" Yes, now I feel the galling weight of thefe

" Difgraceful chains——which, cruel Tilburina !

" Thy doating captive gloried in before.——

" But thou art falfe, and Whifkerandos is undone !

" *Tilb.* O no ; how little doft thou know thy
" Tilburina !

" *Whisk.* · Art thou then true ? Begone cares,
　" doubts, and fears,
" I make you all a prefent to the winds ;
"' And if the winds reject you——try the waves.

Puff. The wind you know, is the eftablifhed re-
ceiver of all ftolen fighs, and caft off griefs and appre-
henfions.

　" *Tilb.* Yet muft we part ?——ftern duty feals·
　" our doom :
" Though here I call yon confcious clouds to wit-
　" nefs,-
" Could I purfue the bias of my foul,
" All friends, all right of parents, I'd difclàim,
" And thou, my Whifkerandos, fhould'ft be father
" And mother, brother, coufin, uncle, aunt,
" And friend to me !

　" *Whisk.* O matchlefs excellence !——and muft
　" we part ?
" Well, if——we muft——we muft—and in that
　" cafe, ·
" The lefs is faid the better.

Puff. Hey day ! here's a cut !—What, are all the
mutual proteftations out ?

Tilb. Now, pray Sir, don't interrupt us juft here,
you ruin our feelings.

Puff. Your feelings !——but zounds, *my* feelings,
Ma'am !

Sneer. No ; pray don't interrupt them.
　" *Whisk.* One laft embrace.——
　" *Tilb.* Now——farewell, for ever.
　" *Whisk.* For ever !
　" *Tilb.* Aye, for ever.　　　　　[Goi...

Puff. S'death and fury!—Gadflife! Sir! Madam! if you go out without the parting look, you might as well dance out—Here, here!

Conf. But pray, Sir, how am *I* to get off here?

Puff. Yes, phaw! what the devil fignifies how you get off! edge away at the top, or where you will—*(Pufhes the Confidant off.)* Now, Ma'am, you fee——

Tilb. We underftand you, Sir.

           " Aye, for ever."

" *Both.* Ohh!——   [*Turning back and exeunt.*
                           [*Scene clofes.*

Dan. O charming!

Puff. Hey!—'tis pretty well I believe—you fee I don't attempt to ftrike out any thing new—but I take it I improve on the eftablifhed modes.

Sneer. You do indeed.—But pray is not Queen Elizabeth to appear?

Puff. No, not once—but fhe is to be talk'd of for ever; fo that, egad, you'll think a hundred times that fhe is on the point of coming in.

Sneer. Hang it, I think its a pity to keep *her* in the green room all night.

Puff. O no, that always has a fine effect—it keeps up expectation.

Dan. But are we not to have a battle?

Puff. Yes, yes, you will have a battle at laft, but, egad, it's not to be by land—but by fea—and that is the only quite new thing in the piece.

Dan. What, Drake at the Armada, hey?

Puff. Yes, efaith—fire-fhips and all—then we fhall

end with the proceffion.——Hey! that will do I think.

Sneer. No doubt on't.

Puff. Come, we muft not lofe time—fo now for the Under Plot.

Sneer. What the plague, have you another plot?

Puff. O Lord, yes—ever while you live, have two plots to your tragedy.—The grand point in managing them, is only to let your under plot have as little connexion with your main plot as poffible.—I flatter myfelf nothing can be more diftinct than mine, for as in my chief plot, the characters are all great people—I have laid my under plot in low life—and as the former is to end in deep diftrefs, I make the other end as happy as a farce.—Now Mr. Hopkins, as foon as you pleafe.

Enter UNDER PROMPTER.

Und. Prompt. Sir, the carpenter fays it is impoffible you can go to the Park fcene yet.

Puff. The Park fcene! No—I mean the defcription fcene here, in the wood.

Und. Prompt. Sir, the performers have cut it out.

Puff. Cut it out!

Und. Prompt. Yes, Sir.

Puff. What! the whole account of Queen Elizabeth?

Und. Prompt. Yes, Sir.

Puff. And the defcription of her horfe and fide-faddle?

Und. Prompt. Yes, Sir.

Puff. So, fo, this is very fine indeed! Mr. Hopkins, how the plague could you fuffer this?

Hopk. *(From within.)* Sir, indeed the pruning knife—

Puff. The pruning knife—zounds the axe! why, here has been fuch lopping and topping, I fhan't have the bare trunk of my play left prefently.—Very well, Sir—the performers muft do as they pleafe, but upon my foul, I'll print it every word.

Sneer. That I would indeed.

Puff. Very well—Sir—then we muft go on— zounds! I would not have parted with the defcription of the horfe!—Well, Sir, go on—Sir, it waa one of the fineft and moft laboured things—Very well, Sir, let them go on—there you had him and his accoutrements from the bit to the crupper—very well, Sir, we muft go to the Park fcene.

Und. Prompt. Sir, there is the point, the carpenters fay, that unlefs there is fome bufinefs put in here before the drop, they fhan't have time to clear away the fort, or fink Gravefend and the river.

Puff. So! this is a pretty dilemma truly!—Gentlemen—you muft excufe me, thefe fellows will never be ready, unlefs I go and look after them myfelf.

Sneer. O dear Sir—thefe little things will happen—

Puff. To cut out this fcene!—but I'll print it— egad, I'll print it every word! 　.　　[*Exeunt.*

ACT III. SCENE I.

Before the Curtain.

Enter Puff, Sneer, *and* Dangle.

Puff.

W<small>ELL</small>, we are ready—now then for the juſtices.
[*Curtain riſes; Juſtices, Conſtables, &c. diſcovered.*]

Sneer. This, I ſuppoſe, is a fort of fenate ſcene.

Puff. To be ſure—there has not been one yet.

Dan. It is the under plot, isn't it?

Puff. Yes. What, gentlemen, do you mean to
go at once to the diſcovery ſcene?

Juſt. If you pleaſe, Sir.

Puff. O very well—harkee, I don't chuſe to ſay
any thing more, but efaith, they have mangled my
play in a moſt ſhocking manner!

Dan. It's a great pity!

Puff. Now then, Mr. Juſtice, if you pleaſe.

" *Juſt.* Are all the volunteers without?

" *Conſt.*   ————————They are.

" Some ten in fetters, and ſome twenty drunk.

" *Juſt.* Attends the youth, whoſe moſt opprobri-
     " ous fame

" And clear convicted crimes have ſtampt him ſol-
     " dier?

" *Conſt.* He waits your pleaſure ; eager to repay
" The bleſt reprieve that ſends him to the fields

" Of glory, there to raife his branded hand
" In honor's caufe.
   " *Juft.*   'Tis well——'tis Juftice arms him !
" O ! may he now defend his country's laws
" With half the fpirit he has broke them all !
" If 'tis your worfhip's pleafure, bid him enter.
   " *Conft.* I fly, the herald of your will.

                        [*Exit* Conftable.

Puff. Quick, Sir !—

Sneer. But, Mr. Puff, I think not only the Juftice, but the clown feems to talk in as high a ftyle as the firft hero among them.

Puff. Heaven forbid they fhould not in a free country !—Sir, I am not for making flavifh diftinc-tions, and giving all the fine language to the upper fort of people.

Dan. That's very noble in you indeed.

Enter Juftice's LADY.

Puff. Now pray mark this fcene,
   " *Lady.* Forgive this interruption, good my love ;
" But as I juft now paft, a pris'ner youth
" Whom rude hands hither lead, ftrange bodings
        " feiz'd
" My fluttering heart, and to myfelf I faid,
" An if our Tom had liv'd, he'd furely been
" This ftripling's height !
   " *Juft.* Ha ! fure fome powerful fympathy directs
" Us both——

Enter Son *and* Constable.

" *Juſt.* What is thy name ?

" *Son.* My name's Tom Jenkins—*alias,* have I

   " none—

" Tho' orphan'd, and without a friend !

" *Juſt.* Thy parents?

" *Son.* My father dwelt in Rocheſter——and was,

" As I have heard——a fiſhmonger——no more.

Puff. What, Sir, do you leave out the account of your birth, parentage and education ?

Son. They have ſettled it ſo, Sir, here.

Puff. Oh ! oh !

" *Lady.* How loudly nature whiſpers to my heart!

" Had he no other name ?

" *Son.*   ——I've ſeen a bill

" Of his, ſign'd *Tomkins,* creditor.

" *Juſt.* This does indeed confirm each circumſtance

" The gypſey told !——Prepare !

" *Son.* I do.

" *Juſt.* No orphan, nor without a friend ar't

   " thou——

" *I* am thy father, *here's* thy mother, *there*

" Thy uncle——this thy firſt couſin, and thoſe

" Are all your near relations !

" *Moth.* O ecſtacy of bliſs !

" *Son.* O moſt unlook'd for happineſs !

" *Juſt.* O wonderful event !

     [*They faint alternately in each others arms.*

Puff. There, you ſee relationſhip, like murder, will out.

Juſt. Now let's revive——elſe were this joy too
" much !
" But come——and we'll unfold the reſt within,
" And thou my boy muſt needs want reſt and food,
" Hence may each orphan hope, as chance directs,
" To find a father—where he leaſt expects !

[*Exeunt.*

Puff. What do you think of that ?

Dan. One of the fineſt diſcovery-ſcenes I ever ſaw.
—Why, this under-plot would have made a tragedy
itſelf.

Sneer. Aye, or a comedy either.

Puff. And keeps quite clear you ſee of the other.

Enter SCENEMAN, *taking away the Seats.*

Puff. The ſcene remains, does it ?

Sceneman. Yes, Sir.

Puff. You are to leave one chair you know—But
it is always awkward in a tragedy, to have you fellows
coming in in your playhouſe liveries to remove things
—I wiſh that could be managed better.—So now for
my myſterious yeoman.

Enter a BEEFEATER.

" *Beefeater.* Perdition catch my ſoul but *I* do love
" thee.

Sneer. Haven't I heard that line before ?

Puff. No, I fancy not—Where pray ?

Dan. Yes, I think there is ſomething like it in
Othello.

Puff. Gad ! now you put me in mind on't, I be-

4

lieve there is—but that's of no confequence—all that
can be faid is, that two people happened to hit on
the fame thought—And Shakefpeare made ufe of it
firft, that's all.

Sneer. Very true.

Puff. Now, Sir, your foliloquy—but fpeak more
to the pit, if you pleafe—the foliloquy always to the
pit—that's a rule.

" *Beefeater.* Tho' hopelefs love finds comfort in
" defpair,

" It never can endure a rival's blifs !'

" But foft——I am obferv'd.   [*Exit* Beefeater.

Dan. That's a very fhort foliloquy.

Puff. Yes—but it would have been a great deal
longer if he had not been obferved.

Sneer. A moft fentimental Beefeater that, Mr.
Puff.

Puff. Harkee—I would not have you be too fure
that he is a Beefeater.

Sneer. What ! a hero in difguife ?

Puff. No matter—I only give you a hint—But
now for my principal character—Here he comes—
Lord Burleigh in perfon ! Pray, gentlemen, ftep
this way—foftly—I only hope the Lord High Trea-
furer is perfect—if he is but perfect !

[*Enter* BURLEIGH, *goes flowly to a chair and fits.*]

Sneer. Mr. Puff !

Puff. Hufh !—vaftly well, Sir ! vaftly well, a
moft interefting gravity !

Dan. What, isn't he to fpeak at all ?

Puff. Egad, I thought you'd afk me that—yes

is a very likely thing—that a Minifter in his fituation, with the whole affairs of the nation on his head, fhould have time to talk !—but hufh ! or you'll put him out.

Sneer. Put him out ! how the plague can that be, if he's not going to fay any thing ?

Puff. There's a reafon !—why, his part is to *think*, and how the plague ! do you imagine he can *think* if you keep talking ?

Dan. That's very true, upon my word !

[Burleigh *comes forward, fhakes his head and exit.*]

Sneer. He is very perfect indeed—Now, pray what did he mean by that ?

Puff. You don't take it ?

Sneer. No ; I don't upon my foul.

Puff. Why, by that fhake of the head, he gave you to underftand that even tho' they had more juftice in their caufe and wifdom in their meafures—yet, if there was not a greater fpirit fhown on the part of the people—the country would at laft fall a facrifice to the hoftile ambition of the Spanifh monarchy.

Sneer. The devil !—did he mean all that by fhaking his head ?

Puff. Every word of it—if he fhook his head as I taught him.

Dan. Ah ! there is certainly a vaft deal to be done on the ftage by dumb fhew, and expreffion of face, and a judicious author knows how much he may truft to it.

Sneer. O, here are fome of our old acquaintance.

Enter HATTON *and* RALEIGH;

" *Sir Chrif.* My niece, and *your* niece too !
" By heav'n there's witchcraft in't——He could not
" elfe
" Have gain'd their hearts——But fee where they
" approach ;
" Some horrid purpofe low'ring on their brows !
" *Sir Wal.* Let us withdraw and mark them.
[*They withdraw.*

Sneer. What is all this ?

Puff. Ah ! here has been more pruning !—but
the fact is, thefe two young ladies are alfo in love
with Don Whifkerandos.—Now, gentlemen, this
fcene goes entirely for what we call Situation and
Stage Effect, by which the greateft applaufe may be
obtained, without the affiftance of language, fentiment or character: pray mark !

Enter the TWO NIECES.

" 1*ft Niece.* Ellena here !
" She is his fcorn as much as I—that is
" Some comfort ftill !

Puff. O dear Madam, you are not to fay that to
her face !—*afide*, Ma'am, *afide.*—The whole fcene is
to be *afide.*

" 1*ft Niece.* She is his fcorn as much as I—that is
" Some comfort ftill ! [*Afide.*
" 2*d Niece.* I know he prizes not Pollina's love,
" But Tilburina lords it o'er his heart. [*Afide.*

" *1ſt Niece.* But ſee the proud deſtroyer of my
" peace.

" Revenge is all the good I've left.   [*Aſide.*

" *2d Niece.* He comes, the falſe diſturber of my
" quiet.

" Now vengeance do thy worſt——   [*Aſide.*

Enter WHISKERANDOS.

" *Whiſk.* O hateful liberty—if thus in vain·
" · I ſeek my Tilburina !

" *Both Nieces.* And ever ſhalt !

" *Sir Chriſtopher and Sir Walter come forward.*
" Hold ! we will avenge you.

" *Whiſk.* Hold *you*——or ſee your nieces bleed !

[*The two nieces draw their two daggers to ſtrike
Whiſkerandos, the two Uncles at the inſtant with
their two ſwords drawn, catch their two nieces,
arms, and turn the points of their ſwords to
Whiſkerandos, who immediately draws two
daggers, and holds them to the two nieces' bo-
ſoms.*]

Puff. There's ſituation for you!—there's an heroic group !—You ſee the ladies can't ſtab Whiſkerandos—he durſt not ſtrike them for fear of their uncles—the uncles durſt not kill him, becauſe of their
nieces—I have them all at a dead lock !—for every
one of them is afraid to let go firſt.

Sneer. Why, then they muſt ſtand there for ever.

Puff. So they would, if I hadn't a very fine contrivance for't—Now mind——

Enter BEEFEATER *with his Halberd.*

" *Beefeater.* In the Queen's name I charge you
" all to drop
" Your fwords and daggers !
           [*They drop their fwords and daggers.*
Sneer. That is a contrivance indeed.
Puff. Aye—in the Queen's name.
" *Sir Chrif.* Come niece !
" *Sir Ral.* Come niece !
           [*Exeunt with the two nieces.*
" *Whifk.* What's he, who bids us thus renounce
" our guard ?
" *Beefeater.* Thou muft do more, renounce thy
" löve !
" *Whifk.* Thou lieft——bafe Beefeater !
" *Beefeater.* ——Ha! Hell ! the lie !
" By heav'n thou'ft rous'd the lion in my heart !
" Off yeoman's habit !—bafe difguife !—off ! off !
   [*Difcovers himfelf, by throwing off his upper drefs,
     and appearing in a very fine waiftcoat.*]
" Am I' a Beefeater now ?
" Or beams my creft as terrible as when
" In Bifcay's Bay I' took thy captive floop._
Puff. There, egad ! he comes out to be the very
Captain of the privateer who had taken Whifkeran-
dos prifoner—and was himfelf an old lover of Til-
burina's.
Dan. Admirably manag'd indeed.
Puff. Now ftand out of their way.
" *Whifk.* I thank thee fortune ! that haft thus be-
" ftow'd

" A weapon to chaftife this infolent.

            [*Takes up one of the fwords.*

" *Beefeater.* I take thy challenge, Spaniard, and
     " I thank

" Thee fortune too !—   [*Takes up the other fword.*

Dan. That's excellently contrived !—it feems as
if the two uncles had left their fwords on purpofe for
them.

Puff. No, egad, they could not help leaving
them.

    " *Whifk.* Vengeance and Tilburina !

    " *Beefeater.*   ——Exactly fo———

     [*They fight, and after the ufual number of wounds
       given, Whifkerandos falls.*]

    " *Whifk.* O curfed parry !——that laft thruft in
     " tierce

" Was fatal——Captain, thou haft fenced well !

" And Whifkerandos quits this buftling fcene

" For all eter———

    " *Beefeater.* —nity—He would have added, but
     " ftern death

" Cut fhort his being, and the noun at once !

Puff. O, my dear Sir, you are too flow, now
mind me.—Sir, fhall I trouble you to die again ?

    " *Whifk.* And Whifkerandos quits this buftling
     " fcene

" For all eter———

    " *Beefeater.* ——nity—He would have added—

Puff. No, Sir—that's not it—once more if you
pleafe—

Whifk. I wifh, Sir—you would practife this without me——I can't ftay dying here all night.

Puff. Very well, we'll go over it by and bye——
I muſt humour theſe gentlemen !

[*Exit* Whiſkerandos.

" *Beefeater.* Farewell——brave Spaniard ! and
　" when next——

Puff. Dear Sir, you needn't ſpeak that ſpeech as
the body has walked off.

Beefeater. That's true, Sir——then I'll join the
fleet.

Puff. If you pleaſe.　　　　[*Exit* Beefeater.
Now who comes on ?

Enter GOVERNOR, *with his hair properly diſordered.*

" *Gov.* A hemiſphere of evil planets reign !
" And every planet ſheds contagious phrenſy !
" My Spaniſh priſoner is ſlain ! my daughter,
" Meeting the dead corſe borne along——has gone
" Diſtract !　　　　[*A loud flouriſh of trumpets.*
　　" But hark ! I am ſummon'd to the fort,
" Perhaps the fleets have met ! amazing criſis !
" O Tilburina ! from thy aged father's beard
" Thou'ſt pluck'd the few brown hairs which time
　　" had left !　　　　[*Exit* Governor.

Sneer. Poor gentleman !

Puff. Yes—and no one to blame but his daughter!

Dan. And the planets——

Puff. True—Now enter Tilburina !—

Sneer. Egad, the buſineſs comes on quick here.

Puff. Yes, Sir—now ſhe comes in ſtark mad in
white ſatin.

Sneer. Why in white ſatin ?

Puff. O' Lord, Sir, when a heroine goes mad, she always goes into white satin—don't she, Dangle?

Dan. Always—it's a rule.

Puff. Yes—here it is——*(looking at the book.)* ' Enter Tilburina stark mad in white satin, and her confidant stark mad in white linen.'

Enter TILBURINA *and* CONFIDANT *mad, according to custom.*

Sneer. But what the deuce is the confidant to be mad too?

Puff. To be sure she is, the confidant is always to do whatever her mistress does; weep when she weeps, smile when she smiles, go mad when she goes mad. ——Now, Madam Confidant—but—keep your madness in the back ground, if you please.

" *Tilb.* The wind whistles——the moon rises——
     " see

" They have kill'd my squirrel in his cage!
" Is this a grashopper!——Ha! no, it is my
" Whiskerandos——you shall not keep him——
" I know you have him in your pocket——
" An oyster may be cros'd in love!——Who says
" A whale's a bird?—Ha! did you call, my love?
" ——He's here! He's there!—He's every where!
" Ah me! He's no where!   [*Exit* Tilburina.

Puff. There, do you ever desire to see any body madder than that?

Sneer. Never while I live!

Puff. You observed how she mangled the metre?

Dan. Yes—egad, it was the firſt thing made me ſuſpeſt ſhe was out of her ſenſes.

Sneer. And pray what becomes of her?

Puff. She is gone to throw herſelf into the ſea to be ſure—and that brings us at once to the ſcene of aſtion, and ſo to my cataſtrophe—my ſea fight, I mean.

Sneer. What, you bring that in at laſt?

Puff. Yes—yes—you know my play is *called* the *Spaniſh Armada*, otherwiſe, egad, 1 have no occaſion for the battle at all —Now then for my magnifi-cence!—my battle!—my noiſe!—and my proceſſi-on!—You are all ready?

Prompt. (*Within.*) Yes, Sir.

Puff. Is the Thames dreſt?

Enter THAMES, *with two Attendants.*

Thames. Here I am, Sir.

Puff. Very well indeed—See, gentlemen, there's a river for you!—This is blending a little of the maſque with my tragedy—a new fancy you know—and very uſeful in my caſe; for as there *muſt be a pro-ceſſion*, I ſuppoſe Thames and all his tributary rivers to compliment Britannia with a fete in honour of the viſtory.

Sneer. But pray, who are theſe gentlemen in green with him?

Puff. Thoſe?—thoſe are his banks.

Sneer. His banks?

Puff. Yes, one crown'd with alders, and the other with a villa!—you take the alluſions?—but hey!

what the plague! you have got both your banks on one fide—Here, Sir, come round—Ever while you live, Thames, go between your banks. *(Bell rings.)* —There, foh! now for't!—Stand afide, my dear friends—away Thames!

> [*Exit* Thames *between his banks.*
> [*Flourifh of drums—trumpets—cannon, &c. &c. Scene changes to the fea—the fleets engage—the mufic plays ' Britannia ftrike home.'—Spanifh fleet deftroy'd by fire-fhips, &c.—Englifh fleet advances—mufic plays ' Rule Britannia.'— The proceffion of all the Englifh rivers and their tributaries with their emblems, &c. begins with Handel's water mufic—ends with a chorus, to the march in Judas Maccabæus.—During this fcene, Puff directs and applauds every thing—— then*]

Puff. Well, pretty well—but not quite perfect— fo ladies and gentlemen, if you pleafe, we'll rehearfe this piece again to-morrow.

THE

R I V A L S.

COMEDY.

BY R. B. SHERIDAN, ESQ.

ADAPTED FOR

THEATRICAL REPRESENTATION,

AS PERFORMED AT THE

THEATRE-ROYAL,

DRURY-LANE.

REGULATED FROM THE PROMPT-BOOK.

By Permission of the Managers.

-DUBLIN :

PRINTED BY WILLIAM PORTER,

FOR WILLIAM JONES, NO. 86; DAME-STREET.

M DCC XCIII.

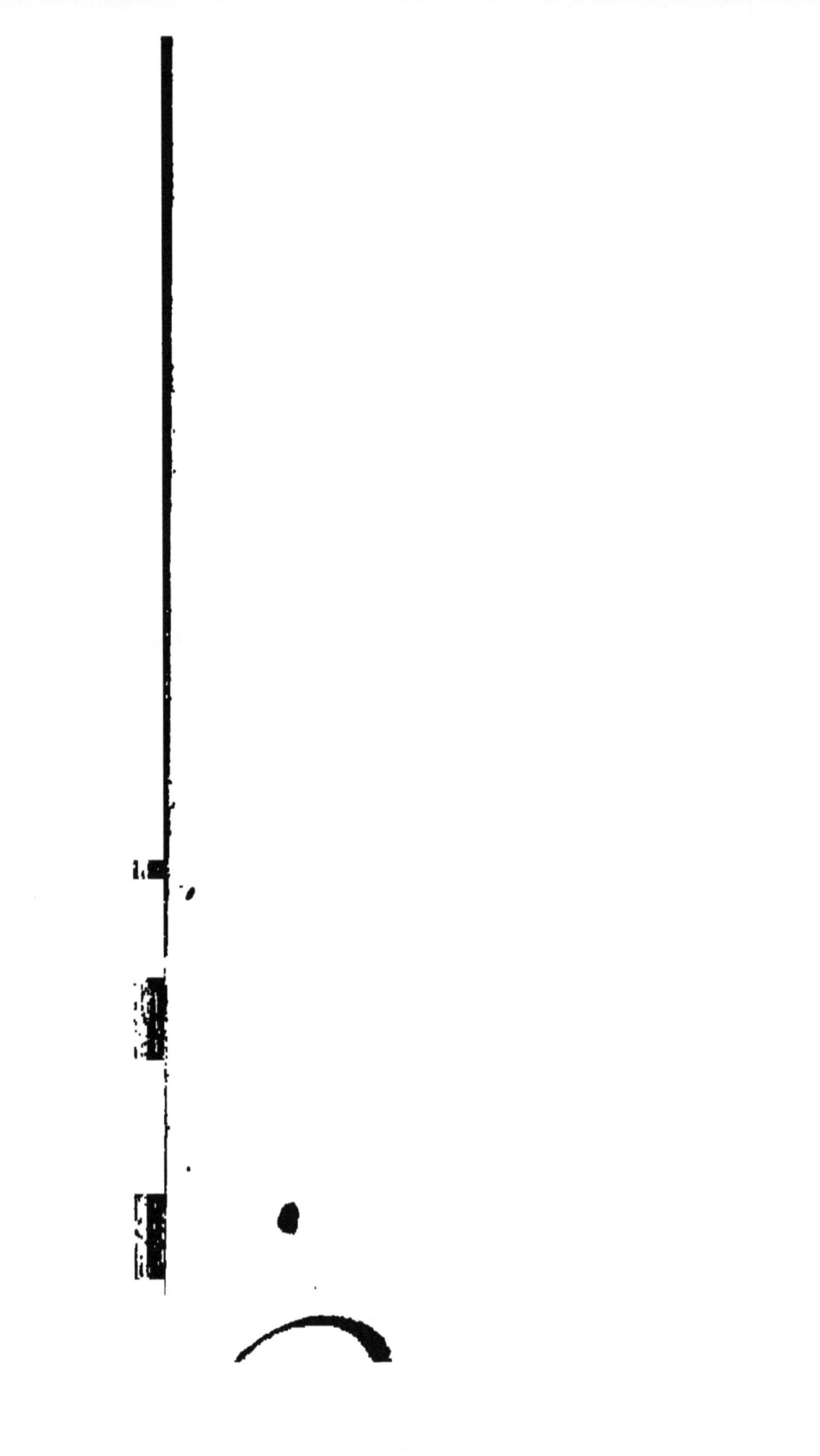

PROLOGUE.

BY THE AUTHOR.

SPOKEN BY

MR. WOODWARD AND MR. QUICK.

*Enter Serjeant at Law, and Attorney following,
and giving a Paper.*

Serj.

*WHAT's here—a vile cramp hand! I cannot see
Without my spectacles. Att. He means his fee.
Nay, Mr. Serjeant, good Sir, try again.*
                              [Gives Money.
Serj. The scrawl improves [more] *O come, 'tis pret-
   ty plain.
Hey! how's this?—Dibble!—sure it cannot be!
A Poet's Brief! A Poet and a Fee!*
   *Att. Yea Sir!—though you without Reward, I
   know,
Would gladly plead the Muses cause*—(Serj.) *So—So!
And if the Fee offends—your wrath should fall
On me*—(Serj.) *Dear Dibble no offence at all—*
   *Att. Some Sons of Phœbus—in the Courts we meet,
   Serj. And fifty sons of Phœbus in the Fleet!
   Att. Nor pleads he worse, who with a decent sprig
Of Bays—adorns his legal waste of wig.*
   *Serj. Full-bottom'd Heroes thus, on signs, unfurl
A leaf of laurel—in a grove of curl!*

I

Must we displace her? And instead advance
The Goddess of the woeful countenance—
The sentimental Muse!—Her emblems view
The Pilgrim's progress, and a sprig of rue!
View her—too chaste to look like flesh and blood—
Primly portray'd on emblematic wood!
There fix'd in usurpation shou'd she stand,
She'll snatch the dagger from her sister's hand:
And having made her votaries weep a flood
Good Heav'n! she'll end her *Comedies in blood—*
Bid Harry Woodward *break poor* Dunstall's *crown!*
Imprison Quick—*and knock* Ned Shuter *down;*
While sed Barsanti—*weeping o'er the scene,*
Shall stab herself—or poison Mrs. Green.———
     Such dire encroachments to prevent in time,
Demands the Critic's voice—the Poet's rhyme.
Can our light scenes add strength to holy laws!
Such puny patronage but hurts the cause:
Fair Virtue scorns our feeble aid to ask;
And moral Truth disdains the Trickster's mask.
For here their fav'rite stands*, whose brow—severe
And sad—claims Youth's respect, and Pity's tear;
Who—when oppress'd by foes her worth creates—
Can point a poignard at the Guilt she hates.

* Pointing to Tragedy.

EPILOGUE.

BY THE AUTHOR.

SPOKEN BY MRS. BULKLEY.

LADIES for You—*I heard our Poet say—*
He'd try to coax some Moral *from his Play* :
' *One moral's plain—cried I—without more fuss* ;
' *Man's social happiness all rests on Us—*
' *Thro' all the Drama—whether damn'd or not—*
' Love *gilds the* Scene, *and* Women *guide the* plot.
' *From ev'ry rank—obedience is our due—*
' *D'ye doubt ?—The world's great stage shall prove it*
  ' *true.*

The Cit—well skill'd to shun domestic strife—
Will sup abroad ;—but first—he'll ask his wife :
John Trot, *his friend for once, will do the same,*
But then—he'll just step home to tell his dame —

The surly 'Squire—*at noon resolves to rule,*
*And half the day—*Zounds ! *Madam is a fool* !
Convinc'd at night—the vanquish'd Victor says,
Ah ! *Kate* ! you women have such coaxing ways !—

The jolly Toper *chides each tardy blade—*
Till reeling Bacchus calls on Love for aid :
Then with each Toast, *he sees fair bumpers swim,*
And kisses Chloe on the sparkling Brim!

Nay, I have heard that Statesmen—great and wise—
Will sometimes counsel with a Lady's eyes ;
The servile suitors—watch her various face,
She smiles preferment—or she frowns disgrace,
Curtsies a pension here—there nods a place.

Nor with less awe, in scenes of humbler life,
Is view'd *the* mistress, *or is* heard *the* wife.
The poorest Peasant of the poorest soil,
The child of Poverty, and heir to Toil—
Early from radiant Love's impartial light,
Steals one small spark, to cheer his world of night :
Dear spark !—that oft thro' winter's chilling woes,
Is all the warmth his little cottage knows !
The wand'ring Tar*—who, not for years, has press'd*
The widow'd partner of his day of rest—
On the cold dock—far from her arms remov'd—
Still hums the ditty which his Susan lov'd :
And while around the cadence rude is blown,
The Boatswain whistles in a softer tone.

The Soldier, *fairly proud of wounds and toil,*
Pants for the triumph *of his Nancy's smile ;*
But ere the battle, should he list' her cries,
The Lover trembles—and the Hero dies !
That heart, by war and honour steel'd to fear,
Droops on a sigh, and sickens at a tear !

But Ye more cautious—ye nice judging few,
Who give to Beauty only Beauty's due,
Tho' friends to Love—Ye view with deep regret
Our conquests marr'd—and triumphs incomplete,

'*Till polish'd Wit more lasting charms disclose,*
And Judgment fix the darts which Beauty throws!
—In female breasts did Sense and Merit rule,
The Lover's mind would ask no other school;
Sham'd into sense—the Scholars of our eyes,
Our Beaux from Gallantry *would soon be wise;*
Would gladly light their homage to improve,
The Lamp of Knowledge at the Torch of Love!

Men.

Sir Anthony Absolute,	-	-	Mr. Shuter.
Captain Absolute,	-	-	Mr. Woodward.
Faulkland,	-	-	Mr. Lewis.
Acres,	-	-	Mr. Quick.
Sir Lucius O'Trigger,		-	Mr. Clinch
Fag,	-	-	Mr Lee-Lewes.
David,	-	-	Mr. Dunstal.
Coachman,	-	-	Mr. Fearon.

Women.

Mrs. Malaprop,	-	-	Mrs. Green.
Lydia Languish,	-	-	Miss Barsanti.
Julia,	-	-	Mrs. Bulkley.
Lucy,	-	-	Mrs. Lessingham.

Maid, Boy, Servants, &c.

Scene, *Bath.*

Time of Action, within One Day.

THE

R I V A L S.

ACT I. SCENE I.

A Street in Bath.

Coachman *croſſes the Stage.——Enter* Fag, *looking after him.*

Fag.

What !—Thomas !—Sure 'tis he ?——What !— Thomas !—Thomas !

Coachman. Hey ! Odd's life !—Mr. Fag !—give us your hand, my old fellow ſervant.

Fag. Excuſe my glove, Thomas !—I'm dev'liſh glad to ſee you, my lad : why, my prince of charioteers, you look as hearty !—but who the deuce thought of ſeeing you in Bath ?

Coachman. Sure, Maſter, Madam Julia, Harry, Mrs. Kate, and the poſtillion be all come.

Fag. Indeed !

Coachman. Aye ! Maſter thought another fit of the gout was coming to make him a viſit :—ſo he'd

I 5

a mind to gi't the flip, and whip ! we were all off at an hour's warning.

Fag. Aye, aye ! hafty in every thing, or it would not be Sir Anthony Abfolute !

Coachman. But tell us, Mr. Fag, how does young Mafter ? Odd ! Sir Anthony will ftare to fee the Captain here !

Fag. I do not ferve Captain Abfolute now.—

Coachman. Why fure !

Fag. At prefent l am employed by Enfign Beverley.

Coachman. I doubt, Mr. Fag, you ha'n't changed for the better.

Fag. I have not changed, Thomas.

Coachman. No ! why didn't you fay you had left young Mafter ?

Fag. No—Well, honeft Thomas, I muft puzzle you no farther ;—briefly then—Captain Abfolute and Enfign Beverley are one and the fame perfon.

Coachman. The devil they are !

Fag. So it is indeed, Thomas ; and the *Enfign—*half of my Mafter being on guard at prefent—the *Captain* has nothing to do with me.

Coachman. So, fo !—what, this is fome freak, I warrant !—Do tell us, Mr. Fag, the meaning o't—you know I ha' trufted you.

Fag. You'll be fecret, Thomas ?

Coachman. As a coach-horfe.

Fag. Why then the caufe of all this is—*Love—Love,* Thomas, who (as you may get read to you) has been a mafquerader ever fince the days of Jupiter.

Coachman. Aye, aye;—I gueffed there was a lady in the cafe:—but pray, why does your Mafter pafs only for *Enfign?*—now if he had fhamm'd *General* indeed———　　　　　　　　　　　　　　　ſ

. *Fag.* Ah! Thomas, there lies the myftery o'the matter.—Hark'ee, Thomas, my Mafter is in love with a lady of a very fingular tafte: a lady who likes him better as a *half-pay Enfign*, than if fhe knew he was fon and heir to Sir Anthony Abfolute, a baronet of three thoufand a-year.

Coachman. That is an odd tafte indeed!—but has fhe got the ftuff, Mr. Fag; is fhe rich, hey?

Fag. Rich!—why, I believe fhe owns half the ftocks!—Z—ds! Thomas, fhe could pay the national debt as eafily as I could my wafherwoman!— She has a lap dog that eats out of gold—fhe feeds her parrot with fmall pearls—and all her thread-papers are made of bank notes!

Coachman. Bravo!—faith!—Odd! I warrant fhe has a fet of thoufands at leaft:—but does fhe draw kindly with the Captain?

Fag. As fond as pigeons.

Coachman. May one hear her name?

Fag. Mifs Lydia Languifh—But there is an old tough aunt in the way;—though by the bye— fhe has never feen my Mafter—for he got. acquainted with Mifs while on a vifit in Gloucefterfhire.

Coachman. Well—I wifh they were once harneffed together in matrimony.——But pray, Mr.

·˙Fag, what kind of a place is this Bath?—I ha'
heard a deal of it—here's a mort o'merry-making—
hey?

Fag. Pretty well, Thomas, pretty well—'tis a
good lounge; in the morning we go to the pump-
room (though neither my master nor I drink the wa-
ters); after breakfast we saunter on the parades or
play a game at billiards; at night we dance: but
d—n the place, I'm tired of it: their regular hours
ft ipify me—not a fiddle nor a card after eleven!—
however, Mr. Faulkland's gentleman and I keep it
up a little in private parties;—I'll introduce you
there, Thomas—you'll like him much.

Coachman. Sure I know Mr. Du-Peign—you know
his Master is to marry Madam Julia.

Fag. I had forgot—But Thomas you must polish
a little—indeed you must.———Here now—this
wig!—what the devil do you do with a *wig*, Thomas?—none of the London whips of any degree of
Ton wear *wigs* now.

Coachman. More's the pity! more's the pity, I·
say—Odd's life! when I heard how the lawyers and
doctors had took to their own hair, I thought how
'twould go next:—Odd rabbit it! when the fashion
had got foot on the Bar, I guess'd 'twould mount to
the Box!—but 'tis all out of character, believe me,
Mr. Fag: and look'ee, I'll never gi' up mine—the
lawyers and doctors may do as they will.

Fag. Well, Thomas, we'll not quarrel about that.

Coachman. Why, bless you, the gentlemen of the
professions ben't all of a mind—for in our village
now tho'ff *Jack Gauge* the exciseman has ta'en to his

carrots, there's little Dick the farrier swears he'll never forsake his bob, tho' all the college should appear with their own heads!

Fag. Indeed! well said Dick! but hold—mark! mark! Thomas.

Coachman. Zooks! 'tis the Captain—Is that the lady with him?

Fag. No! no! that is Madam Lucy—my Master's mistress's maid.—They lodge at that house—but I must after him to tell him the news.

Coachman. Odd! he's giving her money!——well, Mr. Fag——

Fag. Good bye, Thomas.—I have an appointment in Gyde's Porch this evening at eight; meet me there, and we'll make a little party.

[*Exeunt severally.*

SCENE II.

A Dressing-room in Mrs. Malaprop's *Lodgings.*

LYDIA *sitting on a sopha, with a book in her hand.—* LUCY, *as just returned from a message.*

Lucy. Indeed, Ma'am, I travers'd half the town in search of it:—I don't believe there's a circulating library in Bath, I ha'nt been at.

Lydia. And could not you get ' The Reward of Constancy?'

Lucy. No indeed, Ma'am.

Lydia. Nor ' The Fatal Connection?'

Lucy. No indeed, Ma'am.

Lydia. Nor ' The Miftakes of the Héart ?'

Lucy. Ma'am, as ill-luck would have it, Mr. Bull faid Mifs Sukey Saunter had juft fetch'd it away.

Lydia. Heigh-ho !—Did you enquire for ' The Delicate Diftrefs ?'

Lucy.——Or ' The Memoirs of Lady Woodford ?' Yes indeed, Ma'am.—I afk'd every where for it ; and I might have brought it from Mr. Frederick's, but Lady Slattern Lounger, who had juft fent it home, had fo foiled and dog's-ear'd it, it wa'n't fit for a chriftian to read.

Lydia. Heigh-ho !—Yes, I always know when Lady Slattern has been before me.—She has a moft obfetving thumb ; and I believe cherifhes her nails for the convenience of making marginal notes.—— Well, child, what *have* you brought me ?

Lucy. Oh ! here Ma'am.

> [*Taking books from under her cloak, and from her pockets.*]

This is ' The Gordian Knot'—and this ' Peregrine Pickle.' Here are ' The Tears of Senfibility,' and ' Humphry Clinker.' This is ' The Memoirs of a Lady of Quality, written by herfelf,'—and here the fecond volume of ' The Sentimental Journey.'

Lydia. Heigh-ho !—What are thofe books by the glafs ?

Lucy. The great one is only ' The whole Duty of Man,' where I prefs a few blonds, Ma'am.

Lydia. Very well—give me the *fal volatile.*

Lucy. Is it in a blue cover, Ma'am?

Lydia. My fmelling-bottle, you fimpleton !

Lucy. O, the drops!—here Ma'am.

Lydia. Hold!—here's fome one coming—quick, fee who it is.———   [*Exit* Lucy.

Surely I heard my coufin Julia's voice.!

[*Re-enter* Lucy.

Lucy. Lud! Ma'am, here is Mifs Melville.

Lydia. Is it poffible ?———

Enter JULIA.

Lydia. My deareft Julia, how delighted am I! *(Embrace)* How unexpected was this happinefs !

Julia. True, Lydia——and our pleafure is the greater ;—but what has been the matter ?—you were denied to me at firft !

Lydia. Ah, Julia, I have a thoufand things to tell you!—but firft inform me, what has conjur'd you to Bath ?—Is Sir Anthony here ?

Julia. He is—we are arrived within this hour— and I fuppofe he will be here to wait on Mrs. Malaprop as foon as he is drefs'd.

Lydia. Then before we are interrupted, let me impart to you fome of my diftrefs!—I know your gentle nature will fympathize with me, tho' your prudence may condemn me!—My letters have inform'd you of my whole connection with Beverley ; —but I have loft him, Julia!——my aunt has dif-cover'd our intercourfe by a note fhe intercepted, and has confined me ever fince !—Yet, would you believe it ? fhe has fallen abfolutely in love with a tall Irifh Baronet fhe met one night fince we have been here, at Lady Macfhuffle's rout.

Julia. You jeft, Lydia!

Lydia. No, upon my word.—She really carries on a kind of correfpondence with him, under a feigned name though, till fhe chufes to be known to him;—but it is a *Delia* or a *Celia,* I affure you.

Julia. Then, furely, fhe is now more indulgent to her niece.

Lydia. Quite the contrary. Since fhe has dif-covered her own frailty, fhe is become more fufpi-cious of mine. Then I muft inform you of another plague!—That odious *Acres* is to be in Bath to-day; fo that I proteft I fhall be teafed out of all fpirits!

Julia. Come, come, Lydia, hope for the beft—Sir Anthony fhall ufe his intereft with Mrs. Mala-prop.

Lydia. But you have not heard the worft. Un-fortunately I had quarrell'd with my poor Beverley, juft before my aunt made the difcovery, and I have not feen him fince to make it up.

Julia. What was his offence?

Lydia. Nothing at all!—But, I don't know how it was, as often as we had been together, we had never had a quarrel!—And fomehow, I was afraid he would never give me an opportunity.—So, laft Thurfday, I wrote a letter to myfelf, to inform my-felf that Beverley was at that time paying his ad-dreffes to another woman.—I figned it, *your Friend unknown,* fhew'd it to Beverley, charg'd him with his falfehood, put myfelf in a violent paffion, and vow'd *I'd* never fee him more.

Julia. And you let him depart fo, and have not feen him fince ?

Lydia. 'Twas the next day my aunt found the matter out; I intended only to have teafed him three days and a half, and now I've loft him for ever.

Julia. If he is as deferving and fincere as you have reprefented him to me, he will never give you up fo. Yet confider, Lydia, you tell me he is but an Enfign, and you have thirty thoufand pounds !

Lydia. But you know I lofe moft of my fortune if I marry without my aunt's confent, till of age ; and that-is what I have determin'd to do, ever fince I knew the penalty.—Nor could I love the man, who would wifh to wait a day for the alternative.

Julia. Nay, this is caprice !

Lydia. What, does Julia tax me with caprice ? ——I thought her lover Faulkland had enured her to it.

Julia. I do not love even *his* faults.

Lydia. But a-propos—you have fent to him, I fuppofe ?

Julia. Not yet, upon my word—nor has he the leaft idea of my being in Bath.——Sir Anthony's refolution was fo fudden, I could not inform him of it.

Lydia. Well, Julia, you are your own miftrefs, (though under the protection of Sir Anthony) yet have you, for this long year, been a flave to the caprice, the whim, the jealoufy of this ungrateful Faulkland, who will ever delay affuming the right

of a hufband, while you fuffer him to be equally im-
perious as a lover.

Julia. Nay, you are wrong entirely.—We were
contracted before my father's death.—That, and
fome confequent embarraffments, have delay'd what
I know to be my Faulkland's moft ardent wifh.——
He is too generous to trifle on fuch a point.—And
for his character you wrong him there too.—No,
Lydia, he is too proud, too noble to be jealous; if
he is captious, 'tis without diffembling; if fretful,
without rudenefs.—Unus'd to the fopperies of love,
he is negligent of the little duties expected from a
lover—but being unhackney'd in the paffion, his affection is ardent and fincere! and as it engroffes his
whole foul, he expects every thought and emotion
of his miftrefs to move in unifon with his.——Yet,
though his pride calls for this. full return—his humi-
lity makes him undervalue thofe qualities in him,
which would entitle him to it; and not feeling why
he fhould be lov'd to the degree he wifhes, he ftill
fufpects that he is not lov'd enough:—This temper,
I muft own, has coft me many unhappy hours; but I
have learn'd to think myfelf his debtor, for thofe
imperfections which arife from the ardour of his attachment.

Lydia. Well, I cannot blame you for defending
him.——But tell me candidly, Julia, had he never
fav'd your life, do you think you fhould have been
attach'd to him as you are?—Believe me, the rude
blaft that overfet your boat was a profperous gale of
love to him.

Julia. Gratitude may have ftrength'ned my attachment to Mr. Faulkland, but I lov'd him before he had prefervd me; yet furely that alone were an obligation fufficient——

Lydia. Obligation !——Why a water-fpaniel would have done as much !—Well, I fhould never think of giving my heart to a man becaufe he could fwim !

Julia. Come, Lydia, you are too inconfiderate.

Lydia. Nay, I do but jeft.—What's here ?

Enter Lucy, *in a hurry.*

Lucy. O Ma'am, here is Sir Anthony Abfolute juft come home with your aunt.

Lydia. They'll not come here.—Lúcy do you watch.   [*Exit* Lucy.

Julia. Yet I muft go.——Sir Anthony does not know I am here, and if we meet, he'll detain me, to fhew me the town.—I'll take another opportunity of paying my refpects to Mrs. Malaprop, when fhe fhall treat me, as long as fhe choofes, with her felect words fo ingenioufly *mifapplied,* without being *mifpronounced.*

Re-enter Lucy.

Lucy. O Lud ! Ma'am, they are both coming up ftairs.

Lydia. Well, I'll not detain you, Coz.—Adieu, my dear Julia ; I'm fure you are in hafte to fend to Faulkland.——There—through my room you'll find another ftair-cafe.

Julia. Adieu.—*(Embrace.)*   [*Exit* Julia.

Lydia. Here, my dear Lucy, hide thefe books. —Quick, quick.—Fling *Peregrine Pickle* under the toilet—throw *Roderick Random* into the clofet—put *The Innocent Adultery* into *The Whole Duty of Man* —thruft *Lord Aimworth* under the fopha—cram *Ovid* behind the bolfter—there—put *The Man of Feeling* into your pocket—fo, fo, now lay *Mrs. Chapone* in fight, and leave *Fordyce's Sermons* open on the table.

Lucy. O burn it, Ma'am, the hair-dreffer has torn away as far as *Proper Pride.*

Lydia. Never mind—open at *Sobriety.*—Fling me *Lord Chefterfield's Letters.*—Now for 'em.

Enter Mrs. MALAPROP *and* Sir ANTHONY ABSO-LUTE.

Mrs. Mal. There, Sir Anthony, there fits the deliberate Simpleton, who wants to difgrace her family, and lavifh herfelf on a fellow not worth a fhilling.

Lydia. Madam, I thought you once————

Mrs. Mal. You thought, Mifs!—I don't know any bufinefs you have to think at all.—Thought does not become a young woman. But the point we would requeft of you is, that you will promife to forget this fellow—to illiterate him, I fay, quite from your memory.

Lydia. Ah, Madam! our memories are independent of our wills.—It is not fo eafy to forget.

Mrs. Mal. But 1 fay it is, Mifs; there is nothing on earth fo eafy as to *forget*, if a perfon choofes to let about it.—I'm fure I have as much forgot your "poor dear uncle as if he had never exifted—and I thought it my duty fo to do; and let me tell you, Lydia, thefe violent memories don't become a young woman.

Sir Anth. Why, fure fhe wont pretend to remember what fhe's order'd not !—aye, this comes of her reading !

Lydia. What crime, Madam, have I committed to be treated thus ?

Mrs. Mal. Now don't attempt to extirpate your-felf from the matter ; you know I have proof controvertible of it.—But tell me, will you promife to do as you're bid ?——Will you take a hufband of your friend's choofing?

Lydia. Madam, I muft tell you plainly, that had I no preference for any one elfe, the choice you have made would be my averfion.

Mrs. Mal. What bufinefs have you, Mifs, with *preference* and *averfion ?* They don't become a young woman ; and you ought to know, that as both always wear off, 'tis fafeft in matrimony to begin with a little *averfion.* I am fure I hated your poor dear uncle before marriage as if he'd been a black-a-moor—and yet, Mifs, you are fenfible what a wife 1 made !—and when it pleas'd heaven to re-leafe me from him, 'tis unknown what tears I fhed ! —But fuppofe we were going to give you another choice, will you promife us to give up this Bever-ley ?

Lydia. Could I belie my thoughts fo far, as to give that promife, my actions would certainly as far -belie *my words.*

Mrs. Mal. Take yourſelf to your room.——You are fit company for nothing but your own ill-humours.

Lydia. Willingly, Ma'am—I cannot change for the worſe.   [*Exit* Lydia.

Mrs. Mal. There's a little intricate huſſy for you !

Sir Anth. It is not to be wonder'd at, Ma'am— all this is the natural conſequence of teaching girls to read.—Had I a thouſand daughters, by heaven ! I'd as ſoon have them taught the black art as their alphabet !

Mrs. Mal. Nay, nay, Sir Anthony, you are an abſolute miſanthropy.

Sir Anth. In my way hither, Mrs. Malaprop, I obſerved your niece's maid coming forth from a circulating library !—She had a book in each hand— they were half-bound volumes, with marble covers ! —From that moment I gueſs'd how full of duty I ſhould ſee her miſtreſs !

Mrs. Mal. Thoſe are vile places, indeed !

Sir Anth. Madam, a circulating library in a town is, as an ever-green tree of diabolical knowledge !— It bloſſoms through the year !—And depend on it, Mrs. Malaprop, that they who are ſo fond of handling the leaves, will long for the fruit at laſt.

Mrs. Mal. Fie, fie, Sir Anthony, you ſurely ſpeak laconically.

Sir Anth. Why, Mrs. Malaprop, in moderation, now, what would you have a woman know ?

Mrs. Mal. Obſerve me, Sir Anthony—I would by no means wiſh a daughter of mine to be a progreſs

of learning; I don't think, fo much learning becomes a young woman ; for inftance—I would never
let her meddle with Greek, or Hebrew, or Algebra,
or Simony, or Fluxions, or Paradoxes, or fuch in-
flammatory branches of learning—neither would it
be neceffary for her to handle any of your mathema-
tical, aftronomical, diabolical inftruments :—But,
Sir Anthony, I would fend her, at nine years old,
to a boarding-fchool, in order to learn a little ingenuity and artifice.—Then, Sir, fhe fhould have a fu-
percilious knowledge in accounts ;—and as fhe grew
up, I would have her inftructed in geometry, that
fhe might know fomething of the contagious coun-
tries ;—but above all, Sir Anthony, fhe fhould be
miftrefs of orthodoxy, that fhe might not mif-fpell,
and mif-pronounce words fo fhamefully as girls ufually do ; and likewife that fhe might reprehend the
true meaning of what fhe is faying.——This, Sir
Anthony, is what I would have a woman know;
—and I don't think there is a fuperftitious article
in it.

   Sir Anth. Well, well, Mrs. Malaprop, I will difpute the point no further with you; though I muft
confefs, that you are a truly moderate and polite
arguer, for almoft every third word you fay is on my
fide of the queftion.—But, Mrs. Malaprop, to the
more important point in debate—you fay, you have
no objection to my propofal.

   Mrs. Mal. None, I affure you.—I am under no
pofitive engagement with Mr. Acres, and as Lydia
is fo obftinate againft him, perhaps your fon may
have better fuccefs.

Sir Anth. Well, Madam, I will write for the boy directly.——He knows not a fyllable of this yet, though I have for fome time had the propofal in my head. He is at prefent with his regiment.

Mrs. Mal. We have never feen your fon, Sir Anthony; but I hope no objection on his fide.

Sir Anth. Objection!—let him object if he dare! —No, no, Mrs. Malaprop, Jack knows that the leaft demur puts me in a frenzy directly.—My pro- cefs was always very fimple—in their younger days 'twas ' Jack do this;'—if he demurr'd—I knock'd him down—and if he grumbled at that—I always fent him out of the room.

Mrs. Mal. Aye, and the propereft way, o'my confcience!— nothing is fo conciliating to young people as feverity.—Well, Sir Anthony, I fhall give Mr. Acres his difcharge, and prepare Lydia to re- ceive your fon's invocations ;—and I hope you will reprefent *her* to the Captain as an object not altoge- ther illegible.

Sir Anth. Madam, I will handle the fubject pru- dently.—Well, I muft leave you—and let me beg you, Mrs. Malaprop, to enforce this matter roundly to the girl;—take my advice—keep a tight hand— if fhe rejects this propofal—clap her under lock and key :—and if you were juft to let the fervants forget to bring her dinner for three or four days, you can't conceive how fhe'd come about ! [*Exit* Sir Anth.

Mrs. Mal. Well, at any rate I fhall be glad to get her from under my intuition.—She has fome- how difcovered my partiality for Sir Lucius O'Trig- ger—fure, Lucy can't have betray'd me !—No, the girl is fuch a fimpleton, I fhould have made her confefs it.—Lucy!—Lucy!—*(calls.)* Had fhe been one of your artificial ones, I fhould never have trufted her.

Enter LUCY.

Lucy. Did you call, Ma'am?

Mrs. Mal. Yes, girl.—Did you fee Sir Lucius while you was out?

Lucy. No, indeed, Ma'am, not a glimpfe of him.

Mrs. Mal. You are fure, Lucy, that you never mention'd————

Lucy. O Gemini! I'd fooner cut my tongue out.

Mrs. Mal. Well, don't let your fimplicity be impos'd on.

Lucy. No, Ma'am.

Mrs. Mal. So, come to me prefently, and I'll give you another letter to Sir Lucius:—but mind, Lucy—if ever you betray what you are intrufted with—(unlefs it be other people's fecrets to me) you forfeit my malevolence for ever:—and your being a fimpleton fhall be no excufe for your locality.

[*Exit* Mrs. Mal.

Lucy. Ha! ha! ha!—So, my dear *fimplicity*, let me give you a little refpite—*(altering her manner)*—let girls in my ftation be as fond as they pleafe of appearing expert, and knowing in their trufts;—commend me to a mafk of *fillinefs*, and a pair of fharp eyes for my own intereft under it!—Let me fee to what account have I turn'd my *fimplicity* lately—

[*looks at a paper.*

For *abetting Mifs Lydia Languifh* in a defign of run

ning away with an *Enſign!*—in money—*ſundry times*—
twelve pounds twelve—*gowns five*—*hats, ruffles, caps,*
&c. &c.—*numberleſs!*—*From the ſaid Enſign, within*
this laſt month, *ſix guineas and a half.*—About a quarter's pay!—Item, *from Mrs. Malaprop, for betray-
ing the young people to her*—when I found matters
were likely to be diſcovered—*two guineas, and a
black paduſoy.*—Item, *from Mr. Acres, for carrying
divers letters*—which I never deliver'd—*two guineas,
and a pair of buckles.*—Item, *from Sir Lucius O'Trigger—three crowns—two gold pocket-pieces—and a ſilver
ſnuff-box!*—Well done, *ſimplicity!*—yet I was forced
to make my Hibernian believe, that he was correſ-
ponding, not with the *Aunt,* but with the *Niece:*
for though not over rich, I found he had too much
pride and delicacy to ſacrifice the feelings of a gentleman to the neceſſities of his fortune. [*Exit.*

ACT II. SCENE I.

Captain Abſolute's *Lodgings.*

Captain ABSOLUTE *and* FAG.

FAG.

Sir, while I was there, Sir Anthony came in: I
told him, you had ſent me to inquire after his
health, and to know if he was at leiſure to ſee
you.

Abf. And what did he fay, on hearing I was at Bath?

Fag. Sir, in my life I never faw an elderly gentleman more aftonifhed! He ftarted back two or three paces, rapt out a dozen interjectoral oaths, and afked, what the devil had brought you here?

Abf. Well, Sir, and what did you fay?

Fag. O, I lied, Sir—I forget the precife lie, but you may depend on't, he got no truth from me. Yet, with fubmiffion, for fear of blunders in future, I fhould be glad to fix what *has* brought us to Bath : in order that we may lie a little confiftently.—Sir Anthony's fervants were curious, Sir, very curious indeed.

Abf. You have faid nothing to them——?

Fag. O, not a word, Sir—not a word.——Mr. Thomas, indeed, the coachman (whom I take to be the difcreeteft of whips)—

Abf. S'death!—you rafcal! you have not trufted him!

Fag. O, *no*, Sir—no—no—not a fyllable, upon my veracity!—He was, indeed, a little inquifitive; but I was fly, Sir—devilifh fly!—My Mafter (faid I) honeft Thomas (you know, Sir, one fays *honeft* to one's inferiors) is come to Bath to *recruit*—Yes, Sir—I faid, *to recruit*—and whether for men, money, or conftitution, you know, Sir, is nothing to him, nor any one elfe.

Abf. Well—*recruit* will do—let it be fo—

Fag. O, Sir, recruit will do furprifingly—indeed, to give the thing an air, I told Thomas, that your *Honour* had already inlifted, five difbanded

chairmen, feven minority waiters, and thirteen billi*
ard markers.

Abf. You blockhead, never fay more than is neceffary.

Fag. I beg pardon, 'Sir—I beg pardon——But,
with fubmiffion, a lie is nothing unlefs one fupports
it.——Sir, whenever I draw on my invention for a
good current lie, 1 always forge indorfements as well
as the bill.

Abf. Well, take care you don't hurt your credit,
by offering too much fecurity.——Is Mr. Faulkland
returned?

Fag. He is above, Sir, changing his drefs.

Abf. Can you tell whether he has been informed
of Sir Anthony's and Mifs Melville's arrival?

Fag. I fancy not, Sir; he has feen no one fince
he came in, but his gentleman, who was with him
at Briftol.——I think, Sir, I hear Mr. Faulkland
coming down———

Abf. Go tell him, I am here.

Fag. Yes, Sir—*(going)* I beg pardon, Sir, but
fhould Sir Anthony call, you will do me the favour to remember, that we are *recruiting*, -if you
pleafe.

Abf. Well, well..

Fag. And in tendernefs to my charaĉter, if your
Honour could bring in the chairmen and waiters, I
fhall efteem it as an obligation;—for though I never
fcruple a lie to ferve my Mafter, yet it hurts one's
confcience to be found out.   [*Exit.*

Abf. Now for my whimfical friend——if he does

not know·that his miſtreſs is here, I'll teaſe him a little before I tell him——

Enter FAULKLAND.

Faulkland, you're welcome to Bath again; you are punctual in your return.

Faulk. Yes; I had·nothing to detain me, when I had finiſhed the buſineſs I went on. Well, what news ſince l left you? How ſtand matters between you and Lydia?

Abſ. Faith, much as they were; l have not ſeen her ſince our quarrel; ·however I expect to be recalled every hour.

Faulk. Why don't you perſuade·her·to·go off with you at once?

Abſ. What, and loſe two-thirds of her fortune? You forget that, my friend.——No, no, I could have brought her to·that long ago.

Faulk. Nay then, you trifle too long—if you are ſure of *her*, propoſe to the aunt *in your own charac-ter*, and write to Sir Anthony for his conſent.

Abſ. Softly, foftly, for though I·am convinced my little Lydia would elope with me·as Enſign Beverley, yet am I by no means certain that· ſhe would take me with the impediment of our friend's conſent, a regular humdrum wedding, and the reverſion of a good fortune on my ſide; no, no, I muſt prepare her gradually for the diſcovery, and make myſelf neceſſary to her, before I riſk it.——Well, but Faulkland, you'll dine with us to-day at the Hotel?

Faulk. Indeed I cannot : I am not in spirits to be of such a party.

Abf. By Heavens! I shall forswear your company. You are the most teasing, captious, incorrigible lover!—Do, love like a man.

Faull. I own I am unfit for company.

Abf. Am not *I* a lover; aye, and a romantic one too? Yet do I carry every where with me such a confounded farrago of doubts, fears, hopes, wishes, and all the flimsy furniture of a country Mifs's brain!

Faulk. Ah! Jack, your heart and foul are not, like mine, fixed immutably on one only object.——You throw for a large ftake, but losing—you could ftake, and throw again :—but I have set my fum of happinefs on this caft, and not to fucceed, were to be ftript of all.

Abf. But for Heaven's fake! what grounds for apprehenfion can your whimfical brain conjure up at prefent?

Faulk. What grounds for apprehenfion did you say? Heavens! are there not a thoufand! I fear for her fpirits—her health—her life—My abfence may fret her; her anxiety for my return, her fears for me, may opprefs her gentle temper. And for her health—does not every hour bring me caufe to be alarmed? If it rains, fome fhower may even then have chilled her delicate frame!—If the wind be keen, fome rude blaft may have affected her! The heat of noon, the dews of the evening, may endanger the life of her, for whom only I value mine. O! Jack, when delicate and feeling fouls are feparated, there is

not a feature in the fky, not a movement of the ele-
ments; not an afpiration of the breeze, but hints
fome caufe for a lover's apprehenfion !

Abf. Aye, but we may chufe whether we will take
the hint or not.——So then, Faulkland, if you were
convinced that Julia were well and in fpirits, you
would be entirely content.

Faulk. I fhould be happy beyond meafure—I am
anxious only for that.

Abf. Then to cure your anxiety at once—Mifs
Melville is in perfect health, and is at this moment
in Bath.

Faulk. Nay, Jack—don't trifle with me.

Abf. She is arrived here with my father within this
hour.

Faulk. Can you be ferious?

Abf. I thought you knew Sir Anthony better
than to be furprifed at a fudden whim of this kind.—
Serioufly then, it is as I tell you—upon my honour.

Faulk. My dear friend!——Hollo, Du Peigne!
my hat—my dear Jack—now nothing on earth can
give me a moment's uneafinefs.

Enter FAG.

Fag. Sir, Mr. Acres, juft arrived, is below.

Abf. Stay, Faulkland, this Acres lives within a
mile of Sir Anthony, and he fhall tell you how your
miftrefs has been ever fince you left her.—Fag, fhew
the gentleman up.   [*Exit* Fag.

Faulk. What, is he much acquainted in the family ?

Abf. O very intimate : I infift on your not going; befides, his character will divert you.

Faulk. Well, I fhould like to afk him a few quef- tions.

Abf. He is likewife a rival of mine—that is of my *other felf's*, for he does not think his friend Captain Abfolute ever faw the lady in queftion ;—— and it is ridiculous enough to hear him complain to me of *one Beverley*, a concealed fculking rival, who——

Faulk. Hufh !—He's here.

Enter ACRES.

Acres. Hah ! my dear friend, noble captain, and honeft Jack, how do'ft thou ? juft arrived faith, as you fee.—Sir, your humble fervant. Warm work on the roads, Jack—Odds whips and wheels ! I've travelled like a Comet, with a tail of duft all the way as long as the Mall.

Abf. Ah ! Bob, you are indeed an excentric Planet, but we know your attraction hither—give me leave to introduce Mr. Faulkland to you ; Mr. Faulkland, Mr. Acres.

Acres. Sir, I am moft heartily glad to fee you : Sir, I folicit your connections.—Hey Jack, what this is Mr. Faulkland, who——

Abf. Aye, Bob, Mifs Melville's Mr. Faulkland.

Acres. Od'fo ! fhe and your father can be but juft arrived before me—I fuppofe you have feen *hem.*—Ah ! Mr. Faulkland, you are indeed a happy man.

Faulk. I have not feen Mifs Melville yet, Sir—I hope fhe enjoyed full health and fpirits in Devonfhire.

Acres. Never knew her better in my life, Sir—never better.—Odd's Blufhes and Blooms! fhe has been as healthy as the German Spa.

Faulk. Indeed!—I did hear that fhe had been a little indifpofed.

Acres. Falfe, falfe, Sir—only faid to vex you: quite the reverfe I affure you.

Faulk. There, Jack, you fee fhe has the advantage of me; I had almoft fretted myfelf ill.

Abf. Now are you angry with your miftrefs for not having been fick.

Faulk. No, no, you mifunderftand me:—yet furely a little trifling indifpofition is not an unnatural confequence of abfence from thofe we love.—Now confefs—isn't there fomething unkind in this violent, robuft, unfeeling health?

Abf. O, it was very unkind of her to be well in your abfence, to be fure!

Acres. Good apartments, Jack.

Faulk. Well Sir, but you was faying that Mifs Melville has been fo *exceedingly* well—what then, fhe has been merry and gay I fuppofe?—Always in fpirits—hey?

Acres. Merry, Odds Crickets! fhe has been the bell and fpirit of the company wherever fhe has been —fo lively and entertaining! fo full of wit and humour!

Faulk. There, Jack, there.—O, by my foul!

there is an innate levity in woman, that nothing can overcome.—What! happy and I away!

Abf. Have done :—how foolifh this is! juft now you were only apprehenfive for your miftrefs's *fpirits.*

Faulk. Why Jack, have I been the joy and fpirit of the company?

Abf. No indeed, you have not.

Faulk. Have I been lively and entertaining?

Abf. O upon my word, I acquit you.

Faulk. Have I been full of wit and humour?

Abf. No, faith, to do you juftice, you have been confoundedly ftupid indeed.

Acres. What's the matter with the gentleman?

Abf. He is only expreffing his great fatisfaction at hearing that Julia has been fo well and happy—that's all—hey, Faulkland?

Faulk. Oh! I am rejoiced to hear it—yes, yes, fhe has a *happy* difpofition!

Acres. That fhe has indeed—then fhe is fo accomplifhed—fo fweet a voice—fo expert at her harpfichord—fuch a miftrefs of flat and fharp, fquallante, rumblante, and quiverante!—there was this time month—Odds Minnums and Crotchets! how fhe did chirup at Mrs. Piano's Concert.

Faulk. There again, what fay you to this? you fee fhe has been all mirth and fong—not a thought of me.

Abf. Pho, man, is not mufic the food of love?

Faulk. Well, well, it may be fo.—Pray Mr.—— what's his d—d name!—Do you remember what *fongs* Mifs Melville fung?

Acres. Not I indeed.

Abf. Stay now, they were fome pretty, melancholy, purling ftream airs, I warrant ; perhaps you may recollect ;—did fhe fing—' *When abfent from my foul's delight ?'*

Acres. No, that wa'n't it.

Abf. Or,——' *Go, gentle Gales !'*——" *Go, gentle Gales !"* (fings.)

Acres. O no! nothing like it.—Odds ! now I re-collect one of them—' *My heart's my own, my will is free.'* (fings.)

Faulk. Fool! fool that I am ! to fix all my happinefs on fuch a trifler ! S'death ! to make herfelf the pipe and ballad-monger of a circle ! to footh her light heart with catches and glees !—What can you fay to this, Sir ?

Abf. Why, that I fhould be glad to hear my miftrefs had been fo merry, *Sir.*

Faulk. Nay, nay, nay—I am not forry that fhe has been happy—no, no, I am glad of that—I would not have had her fad or fick—yet furely a fympathetic heart would have fhewn itfelf even in the choice of a fong—fhe might have been temperately healthy, and fomehow, plaintively gay ;—but fhe has been dancing too, I doubt not !

Acres. What does the gentleman fay about dancing ?

Abf. He fays the lady we fpeak of dances as well as fhe fings.

Acres. Aye truly, does fhe—there was at our laft race ball——

Faulk. Hell and the devil ! There ! there—I told

u fo! I told you fo! Oh! fhe thrives in my ab-
nce!—Dancing!—but her whole feelings have
:en in oppofition with mine?—l have been anxious,
.lent, penfive, fedentary—my days have been hours
)f care, my nights of watchfulnefs.——She has been
all Health! Spirit! Laugh! Song! Dance!——
Oh! d—n'd, d—n'd levity!

Abf. For Heaven's fake! Faulkland, don't expofe yourfelf fo ——Suppofe fhe has danced, what
then?——does not the ceremony of fociety often
oblige—

Faulk. Well, well, I'll contain myfelf—perhaps
as you fay—for form fake ——What, Mr. Acres,
you were praifing Mifs Melville's manner of dancing
a *minuet*—hey?

Acres. O, I dare infure her for that—but what I
was going to fpeak of was her *country dancing :*——
Odds fwimmings! fhe has fuch an air with her!—.

Faulk. Now difappointment on her!—defend this,
Abfolute, why don't you defend this?——Country-
dances! jiggs, and reels! am I to blame now? A
Minuet I could have forgiven—I fhould not have
minded that—I fay I fhould not have regarded a Minuet—but *Country-dances!* Z——ds! had fhe made
one in a *Cotillion*—I believe I could have forgiven
even that—but to be monkey-led for a night!—to
run the gauntlet thro' a ftring of amorous palming
puppies!—to fhew paces like a managed filly!——O
Jack, there never can be but *one* man in the world,
whom a truly modeft and delicate woman ought to
pair with in a *Country-dance*; and even then, the

reſt of the couples ſhould be her great uncles and aunts!

Abſ. Aye, to be ſure!—grand-fathers and grand-mothers!

Faulk. If there be but one vicious mind in the Set, 'twill ſpread like a contagion—the action of their pulſe beats to the laſcivious movement of the jigg—their quivering, warm breath'd ſighs impregnate the very air—the atmoſphere becomes electrical to love, and each amorous ſpark darts thro' every link of the chain!—I muſt leave you—I own I am ſomewhat flurried—and that confounded booby has perceived it.

[*Going.*

Abſ. Nay, but ſtay Faulkland, and thank Mr. Acres for his good news.

Faulk. D—n his news! ⸱ [*Exit* Faulkland.

Abſ. Ha! ha! ha! poor Faulkland five minutes ſince—" nothing on earth could give him a moment's uneaſineſs!"

Acres. The gentleman wa'nt angry at my praiſing his miſtreſs, was he?

Abſ. A little jealous, I believe, Bob.

Acres. You don't ſay ſo? Ha! ha! jealous of me—that's a good joke.

Abſ. There's nothing ſtrange in that, Bob; let me tell you, that ſprightly grace and inſinuating manner of your's will do ſome miſchief among the girls here.

Acres. Ah! you joke—ha! ha! miſchief! ha! ha! but you know I am not my own property, my dear Lydia has foreſtalled me.——She could never abide me in the country, becauſe I uſed to dreſs ſo

badly—but odds frogs and tambours! I shan't take
matters so here—now ancient Madam has no voice
in it—I'll make my old clothes know who's master—
I shall straitway cashier the hunting-frock—and ren-
der my leather breeches incapable—My hair has been
in training for some time.

Abs. Indeed!

Acres. Aye—and tho'ff the side-curls are a little
restive, my hind-part takes to it very kindly.

Abs. O, you'll polish, I doubt not.

Acres. Absolutely I propose so—then if I can find
out this Ensign Beverley, odds triggers and flints! I'll
make him know the difference o't.

Abs. Spoke like a man—but pray, Bob, 1 observe
you have got an odd kind of a new method of swearing——

Acres. Ha! ha! you've taken notice of it—'tis
genteel, isn't it?—I didn't invent it myself though;
but a commander in our militia—a great scholar, I
assure you—says that there is no meaning in the common oaths, and that nothing but their antiquity
makes them respectable;—because, he says, the an-
cients would never stick to an oath or two, but would
say, By Jove! or by Bacchus! or by Mars! or by
Venus! or by Pallas! according to the sentiment—
so that to swear with propriety, says my little Major,
the ' oath should be an echo to the sense;' and this
we call the *oath referential,* or *sentimental swearing*—
ha! ha! ha! 'tis genteel, isn't it?

Abs. Very genteel, and very new indeed—and I
dare say will supplant all other figures of impreca-
tion.

Acres. Aye, aye, the beſt terms will grow obſo-
lete——Damns have had their day.

Enter FAG.

Fag. Sir, there is a gentleman below, deſires to
ſee you—ſhall I ſhew him into the parlour?

Abſ. Aye—you may.

Acres. Well, I muſt be gone——

Abſ. Stay; who is it, Fag?

Fag. Your father, Sir.

Abſ. You puppy, why didn't you ſhew him up
directly?   [*Exit* Fag.

Acres. You have buſineſs with Sir Anthony.——
I expect a meſſage from Mrs. Malaprop at my lodgings—I have ſent alſo to my dear friend Sir Lucius
O'Trigger.——Adieu, Jack, we muſt meet at
night, when you ſhall give me a dozen bumpers to
little Lydia.

Abſ. That I will with all my heart. [*Exit* Acres.
Now for a parental lecture—I hope he has heard
nothing of the buſineſs that has brought me here.—
I wiſh the gout had held him faſt in Devonſhire,
with all my ſoul!

Enter SIR ANTHONY.

Sir, I am delighted to ſee you here; and looking
ſo well!—your ſudden arrival at Bath made me apprehenſive for your health.

Sir Anth. Very apprehenſive, I dare ſay, Jack.—
What, you are recruiting here, hey?

Abſ. Yes, Sir, I am on duty.

Sir Anth. Well, Jack, I am glad to fee you, tho'
I did not expeët it, for I was going to write to you
on a little matter of bufinefs.—Jack, I have been
confidering that I grow old and infirm, and fhall pro-
bably not trouble you long.

Abf. Pardon me, Sir, I never faw you look more
ftrong and hearty; and I pray frequently that you
may continue fo.

Sir Anth. I hope your prayers may be heard with
all my heart. Well then, Jack, I have been confidering that I am fo ftrong and hearty, I may continue to plague you a long time.—Now, Jack, I am,
fenfible that the income of your commiffion, and what
I have hitherto allowed you, is but a fmall pittance
for a lad of your fpirit.

Abf. Sir, you are very good.

Sir Anth. And it is my wifh, while yet I live, to
have my Boy make fome figure in the world.—I have
refolved, therefore, to fix you at once in a noble independence.

Abf. Sir, your kindnefs overpowers me—fuch generofity makes the gratitude of reafon more lively
than the fenfations even of filial affeëtion.

Sir Anth. I am glad you are fo fenfible of my attention—and you fhall be mafter of a large eftate in a
few weeks.

Abf. Let my future life, Sir, fpeak my gratitude:
I cannot exprefs the fenfe I have of your munificence.
——Yet, Sir, I prefume you would not wifh me to
quit the army?

Sir Anth. O, that fhall be as your wife choofes.

Abf. My wife, Sir!

Sir Anth. Aye, aye, fettle that between you—fet tle that between you?

Abf. A wife, Sir, did you fay?

Sir Anth. Aye, a wife—why; did not I. mention her before?

Abf. Not- a word of her, Sir..

Sir Anth, Odd fo!—I muftn't forget. *her* tho'—. Yes, Jack,. the independence I was talking of is by a marriage—the fortune is faddled with a wife—but I fuppofe that makes no difference..

Abf. Sir! Sir!—you amaze me!

Sir Anth. Why, what the devil's the matter with the fool? Juft now you were all gratitude and duty.

Abf. I was, Sir—you talked to me of independence and a. fortune, 'but not a word of a-wife..

Sir Anth. Why—what difference does that make? Odd's life, Sir! if you have the eftate, you muft take it with the live ftock on it, as it ftands.

Abf. If my happinefs is to be the price, I muft, beg leave to decline the purchafe.——Pray, Sir, who is the lady?

Sir Anth. What's that to you, Sir?——Come,. give me your promife to love,. and to marry her di-rectly.

Abf. Sure,. Sir, this is not very reafonable, to fummon my affections for a lady I know nothing of!

Sir Anth. I am fure, Sir, 'tis more unreafonable in. you to *object* to a lady you know nothing of.

Abf. Then, Sir, I muft tell you plainly, that my

inclinations are fix'd on another—my heart is engaged to an Angel.

Sir Anth. Then pray let it fend an excufe.——
It is very forry—but *bufinefs* prevents its waiting on
her.

Abf. But my vows are pledged to her.

Sir Anth. Let her foreclofe, Jack ; let her foreclofe ; they are not worth redeeming ; befides, you
have the Angel's vows in exchange, I fuppofe; fo
there can be no lofs there.

Abf. You muft excufe me, Sir, if I tell you, once
for all, that in this point I cannot obey you.

Sir Anth. Hark'ee Jack ;—I have heard you for
fome time with patience—I have been cool—quite
cool ;—but take care—you know I am compliance
itfelf—when I am not thwarted ;—no one more eafily led—when I have my own way ;—but don't put
me in a phrenzy.

Abf. Sir, I muft repeat it—in this I cannot obey
you.

Sir Anth. Now, d—n me ! if ever I call you *Jack*
again while I live !

Abf. Nay, Sir, but hear me.

Sir Anth. Sir, I wont hear a word—not a word !
not one word ! fo give me your promife by a nod—
and I'll tell you what, Jack—I mean, you Dog—if
you don't by——

Abf. What, Sir, promife to link myfelf to fome
mafs of uglinefs ! to——

Sir Anth. Z——ds ! firrah ! the lady fhall be as
ugly as I choofe : fhe fhall have a hump on each
fhoulder ; fhe fhall be as crooked as the Crefcent ;

her one eye fhall roll like the Bull's in Cox's Mufæum
—fhe fhall have a fkin like a mummy, and the beard
of a Jew—fhe fhall be all this, firrah !—yet I'll make
you ogle her all day, and fit up all night to write
fonnets on her beauty.

Abf. This is reafon and moderation indeed !

Sir Anth. None of your fneering, puppy! no grin-
ning, jackanapes !

Abf. Indeed, Sir, I never was in a worfe humour
for mirth in my life.

Sir Anth. 'Tis falfe, Sir, I know you are laughing in your fleeve : I know you'll grin when I am
gone, firrah !

Abf. Sir, I hope I know my duty better.

Sir Anth. None of your paffion, Sir! none of
your violence, if you pleafe.——It won't do with
me, I promife you.

Abf. Indeed, Sir, I never was cooler in my life.

Sir Anth. 'Tis a confounded lie !—I know you
are in a paffion in your heart; I know you are, you
hypocritical young dog! but it won't do.

Abf. Nay, Sir, upon my word.

Sir Anth. So you will fly out! can't you be cool,
like me ? What the devil good can *Paffion* do !—*Paffion* is of no fervice, you impudent, infolent, over-
bearing Reprobate !—There you fneer again—don't
provoke me !—but you rely upon the mildnefs of my
temper—you do, you Dog! you play upon the
meeknefs of my difpofition ! Yet take care—the patience of a faint may be overcome at laft !—but mark!
I give you fix hours and a half to confider of this :
if you then agree, without any condition, to do

every thing on earth that I choose, why—confound
you! I may in time forgive you——If not, z—ds!
don't enter the same hemisphere with me! don't
dare to breathe the same air, or use the same light
with me; but get an atmosphere and a sun of your
own! I'll strip you of your commission; I'll lodge a
five-and-threepence in the hands of trustees, and you
shall live on the interest.—I'll disown you, I'll disin-
herit you, I'll unget you! and d—n me! if ever I
call you Jack again!   [*Exit* Sir Anthony.

ABSOLUTE, *solus*.

Abs. Mild, gentle, considerate father——I kiss
your hands.—What a tender method of giving his
opinion in these matters Sir Anthony has! I dare
not trust him with the truth.——I wonder what old,
wealthy Hag it is that he wants to bestow on me!—
yet he married himself for love! and was in his youth
a bold Intriguer, and a gay Companion!

Enter FAG.

Fag. Assuredly, Sir, our Father is wrath to a degree; he comes down stairs eight or ten steps at a
time—muttering, growling, and thumping the ban-
nisters all the way: I, and the Cook's dog, stand
bowing at the door—rap! he gives me a stroke on
the head with his cane; bids me carry that to my
master, then kicking the poor Turnspit into the
area, d—ns us all, for a puppy triumvirate!—Upon
my credit, Sir, were I in your place, and found my
father such very bad company, I should certainly
drop his acquaintance. —

Abf. Ceafe your impertinence, Sir, at prefent.—
Did you come in for nothing . more ?——Stand out
of the way !   [*Pufhes him afide, and Exit.*

FAG, *folus.*

Fag. Soh ! Sir Anthony trims my Mafter; He is
afraid to reply to his Father—then vents his fpleen
on poor Fag !——When one is vexed by one perfon,
to revenge one's felf on another, who happens to
come in the way—is the vileft injuftice : Ah ! it
fhews the worft temper—the bafeft———

Enter ERRAND BOY.

Boy. Mr. Fag ! Mr. Fag ! your mafter calls
you.

Fag. Well ! you little, dirty puppy, you need
not baul fo !—The meaneft difpofition ! the———
Boy. Quick, quick, Mr. Fag.   .

Fag. Quick ! quick ! you impudent Jackanapes !
am I to be commanded by you too? you little, impertinent, infolent, kitchen-breed———

[*Exit, kicking and beating him.*

SCENE II.

The North Parade.

Enter LUCY.

Lucy. So—I fhall have another rival to add to my
miftrefs's lift—Captain Abfolute.———However, I

shall not enter his name till my purse has n
notice in form. - ,Poor Acres is dismissed !—V
have done him a laft friendly office, in lettir
know that Beverley was here before him.–
Lucius is generally more punctual, when he (
to hear from his *dear Dalia*, as he calls her :—
der he's not here !—I have a little scruple of
ence from this deceit ; tho' I should not be
well, if my hero knew that *Delia* was near fifi
her own miftrefs.

Enter Sir Lucius O'Trigger.

Sir Luc. Hah ! my little embaffadrefs—uɲ
confcience I have been looking for you; l ha
on the South Parade this half-hour.

Lucy. (*Speaking fimply*) O gemini ! and
been waiting for your worship here on the No:

Sir Luc. Faith !—may be, that was the re;
did not meet ; and it is very comical too, h
could go out and L not fee you—for I w
taking a nap at the Parade-Coffee-houfe,
chofe the *window* on purpofe that I might ɪ
you.

Lucy. My ftars ! Now I'd wager a fix-;
went by while you were afleep.

Sir Luc. Sure enough it muft have been ʄ
I never dreamt it was fo late, till I waked.
but my little girl, have you got nothing for ɪ

Lucy. Yes, but I have——I've got a letter
in my pocket.

Sir Luc. O faith ! I guefsed you weren'

·empty-handed—well—let me fee what the dear creature fays.

Lucy. There, Sir Lucius.   [*Gives him a letter.*

Sir Luc. (Reads) " *Sir—there is often a fudden incentive impulfe in love, that has a greater induction than years of domeflic combination : fuch was the commotion I felt at the firft fuperfluous view of Sir Lucius O'Trigger.*" Very pretty, upon my word. *Female punctuation forbids me to fay more ; yet let me add, that it will give me joy infallible to find Sir Lucius worthy the laft criterion of my affections.*

" DELIA."

Upon my confcience! Lucy, your lady is a great miftrefs of language.—Faith, fhe's quite the queen of the dictionary!—for the devil a word dare refufe coming at her call—though one would think it was quite out of hearing.

Lucy. Aye, Sir, a lady of her experience.

Sir Luc. Experience! what, at feventeen?

Lucy. O true, Sir—but then fhe reads fo—my ftars! how fhe will read off hand!

Sir Luc. Faith, fhe muft be very deep read to write this way—though fhe is rather an arbitrary writer too—for here are a great many poor words preffed into the fervice of this note, that would get their *habeas corpus* from any court in Chriftendom.

Lucy. Ah! Sir Lucius, if you were to hear how fhe talks of you!

Sir Luc. O tell her, I'll make her the beft hufband in the world, and Lady O'Trigger into the bargain!—But we muft get the old gentlewoman's confent—and do every thing fairly.

Lucy. Nay, Sir Lucius, I thought you wa'n't rich enough to be fo nice !

Sir Luc. Upon my word, young woman, you have hit it :—I am fo poor that I can't afford to do a dirty action.——If I did not want money I'd fteal your miftrefs and her fortune with a great deal of plea· fure.——However, my pretty girl, *(gives her mo- ney)* here's a little fomething to buy you a ribband ; and meet me in the evening, and I'll give you an anfwer to this.   So, huffy, take a kifs before-hand, to put you in mind.   -   [*Kiffes her.*

Lucy. O Lud ! Sir Lucius—I never feed fuch a gemman ! My lady won't like you if you're fo im· pudent.

Sir Luc. Faith fhe will, Lucy——that fame—— pho ! what's the name of it ?—*Modefty !*—is a qua- lity in a lover more praifed by the women than liked ; fo, if your miftrefs afks you whether Sir Lucius ever gave you a kifs, tell her fifty——my dear.

Lucy. What, would you have me tell her a lie ?

Sir Luc. Ah then, you baggage ! I'll make it a truth prefently.

Lucy. For fhame now ; here is fome one coming.

Sir Luc. O faith, I'll quiet your confcience !

[*Sees* Fag.—*Exit, humming a tune.*

Enter FAG.

Fag. So, fo, Ma'am.   I humbly beg pardon.

Lucy. O Lud !—now, Mr. Fag—you flurry one fo.

Fag. Come, come, Lucy, here's no one bye—
so a little less simplicity, with a grain or two more
sincerity, if you please——You play false with us,
Madam.——I saw you give the Baronet a letter.—
My Master shall know this—and if he don't call him
out—I will.

Lucy. Ha! ha! ha! you gentlemen's gentlemen
are so hasty.——That letter was from Mrs. Malaprop, simpleton.——She is taken with Sir Lucius's
address.

Fag. How! what tastes some people have!——
Why, I suppose I have walked by her window an
hundred times.——But what says our young lady?
Any message to my master?

Lucy. Sad news! Mr. Fag.—A worse Rival than
Acres! Sir Anthony Absolute has proposed his
son.

Fag. What, Captain Absolute?

Lucy. Even so.—I overheard it all.

Fag. Ha! ha! ha!—very good faith—goodbye,
Lucy, I must away with this news.

Lucy. Well—you may laugh—but it is true, I
assure you.   [*Going.*
But—Mr. Fag—tell your master not to be cast down
by this.

Fag. O, he'll be so disconsolate!

Lucy. And charge him not to think of quarrel•
ling with young Absolute.

Fag. Never fear!—never fear!

Lucy. Be sure—bid him keep up his spirits.

Fag. We will—we will.   [*Exeunt severally.*

L

ACT III.   SCENE I.

The North Parade.

Enter ABSOLUTE.

ABSOLUTE.

'Tis juft as Fag told me, indeed.——Whimfical enough, faith! My Father wants to *force* me to marry the very girl I am plotting to run away with! —He muft not know of my connection with her yet a-while.——He has too fummary a method of proceeding in thefe matters.——However, I'll read my recantation inftantly.——My converfion is fomething fudden, indeed—but I can affure him it is very *fincere*.——So, fo—here he comes.—He looks plaguy gruff.   [*Steps afide.*

Enter SIR ANTHONY.

Sir Anth. No—I'll die fooner than forgive him. —*Die*, did I fay? I'll live thefe fifty years to plague him.——At our laft meeting, his impudence had almoft put me out of temper.——An obftinate, paffionate, felf-will'd boy!—Who can he take after? This is my return for getting him before all his brothers and fifters!—for putting him, at twelve years old, into a marching regiment, and allowing him fifty pounds a-year, befide his pay ever fince!—But *I have* done with him;—he's any body's fon for me.

——I never will fee him more—never—never—never —never.

Abf. Now for a penitential face.

Sir Anth. Fellow, get out of my way.

Abf. Sir, you fee a penitent before you.

Sir Anth. I fee an impudent fcoundrel befoie me.

Abf. A fincere penitent.——I am come, Sir, to acknowledge my ·error, and to fubmit entirely to your will.

Sir Anth. What's that?

Abf. I have been revolving, and reflecting, and confidering on your paft goodnefs, and kindnefs· and condefcenfion to me.

Sir Anth. Well, Sir?

Abf. I have been likewife weighing and balancing what you were pleafed to mention concerning duty, and obedience, and authority.

Sir Anth. Well, Puppy?

Abf. Why then, Sir, the refult of my reflections is—a refolution to facrifice every inclination of my own, to your fatisfaction.

Sir Anth. Why now, you talk fenfe—abfolute fenfe—I never heard any thing more fenfible in my life.——Confound you; you fhall be Jack again.

Abf. I am happy in the appellation.

Sir Anth. Why, then, Jack, my dear Jack, I will now inform you—who the lady really is.—— Nothing but your paffion and violence, you filly fellow, prevented my telling you at firft. Prepare,

Jack, for wonder and rapture—prepare.——What think you of Mifs Lydia Languifh?

Abf. Languifh? What, the Languifhes of Worcefterfhire?

Sir Anth. Worcefterfhire! No. Did you never meet Mrs. Malaprop and her Niece, Mifs Languifh, who came into our country juft' before you were laft ordered to your regiment.

Abf. Malaprop! Languifh! I don't remember ever to have heard the names before. Yet, ftay —I think I do recollect fomething.——*Languifh*? *Languifh!* She fquints, don't fhe?——A little red-haired girl?

Sir Anth. Squints?——A red-haired girl!—— Z——ds! no.

Abf. Then I muft have forgot; it can't be the fame perfon.

Sir Anth. Jack! Jack! what think you of blooming, love-breathing feventeen.

Abf. As to that, Sir, I am quite indifferent.—If I can pleafe you in the matter, 'tis all I defire.

Sir Anth. Nay, but Jack, fuch eyes! fuch eyes! fo innocently wild! fo bafhfully irrefolute! Not a glance but fpeaks and kindles fome thought of love! Then, Jack, her cheeks! her cheeks, Jack! fo deeply blufhing at the infinuations of her tell-tale eyes! Then, Jack, her lips!—O Jack, lips fmiling at their own difcretion; and if not fmiling, more fweetly pouting; more lovely in fullennefs!

Abf. That's fhe indeed.—Well done, old gentleman!

Sir Anth. Then, Jack, her neck.——O Jack ! Jack !

Abf. And which is to be mine, Sir, the Niece or the Aunt ?

Sir Anth. Why, you unfeeling, infenfible Puppy, I·defpife you.   When I was of your age, fuch a defcription would have made me fly like a rocket ! The *Aunt*, indeed !—Odds life ! when I ran away with your mother, I would not have touched any thing old or ugly to gain an empire.

Abf. Not to pleafe your father, Sir ?

Sir Anth. To pleafe my father !——Z—ds ! not to pleafe————O, my father————Oddfo !———— yes—yes ; if my father indeed had defired———— that's quite another matter.————Tho' he wa'n't the indulgent father that I am, Jack.

Abf. I dare fay not, Sir.

Sir Anth. But, Jack, you are not forry to find your miftrefs is fo beautiful.

Abf. Sir, I repeat it ; if I pleafe you in this affair, 'tis all I defire.   Not that I think a woman the worfe for being handfome ; but, Sir, if you pleafe to recollect, you before hinted fomething about a hump or two, one eye, and a few more graces of that kind —now, without being very nice, I own I fhould rather choofe a wife of mine to have the ufual number of limbs, and a limited quantity of back : and tho' *one eye* may be very agreeable, yet as the prejudice has always run in favour of *two*, I would not wifh to affect a fingularity in that article.

Sir Anth. What a phlegmatic fot it is ! Why, firrah, you're an Anchorite !——a vile in ftock.———You a foldier !—you're a walking-block, fit only to duft the company's regimentals on !——— Odds life ! I've a great mind to marry the girl my-felf.

Abf. I am entirely at your difpofal, Sir ; if you fhould think of addreffing Mifs Languifh your-felf, I fuppofe you would have me marry the *Aunt ;* or if you fhould change your mind, and take the old lady—'tis the fame to me—I'll marry the *Niece.*

Sir Anth. Upon my word, Jack, thou'rt either a very great hypocrite, or———but, come, I know your indifference on fuch a fubject muft be all a lie— I'm fure it muft—come, now—damn your demure face !—come, confefs, Jack—you have been lying— ha'n't you ? You have been playing the hypocrite, hey !—I'll never forgive you, if you ha'n't been lying and playing the hypocrite.

Abf. I'm forry, Sir, that the refpect and duty which I bear to you fhould be fo miftaken.

Sir Anth. Hang your refpect and duty ! But, come along with me, I'll write a note to Mrs. Malaprop, and you fhall vifit the lady directly. Her eyes fhall be the Promethian torch to you——— come along, I'll never forgive you, if you don't come back, ftark mad with rapture and impatience—if you don't, egad, I'll marry the girl myfelf ! [*Exeunt.*

SCENE II.

Julia's *Dreſſing-room.*

Faulkland, *ſolus.*

Faulk. They told me Julia would return directly; I wonder ſhe is not yet come !—How mean does this captious, unſatisfied temper of mine appear to my cooler judgment ! Yet I know not that I indulge it in any other point :—but on this one ſubject, and to this one ſubject, whom I think I love beyond my life, I am ever ungenerouſly fretful, and madly capricious !—I am conſcious of it—yet I cannot correct myſelf ! What tender, honeſt joy ſparkled in her eyes when we met !—How delicate was the warmth of her expreſſions !—I was aſhamed to appear leſs happy—though I had come reſolved to wear a face of coolneſs and upbraiding. Sir Anthony's preſence prevented my propoſed expoſtulations : yet I muſt be ſatisfied that ſhe has not been ſo *very* happy in my abſence.——She is coming !—Yes !——I know the nimbleneſs of her tread, when ſhe thinks her impatient Faulkland counts the moments of her ſtay.

Enter Julia.

Julia. I had not hop'd to ſee you again ſo ſoon.
Faulk. Could I, Julia, be contented with my firſt

welcome—reſtrained as we were by the preſence of a third perſon ?

Julia. O Faulkland, ˙when your kindneſs can make me thus happy, let me not think that I diſcovered ſomething of coldneſs in your firſt ſalutation.

Faulk. 'Twas but your fancy, Julia.—I *was* rejoiced to ſee you—to ſee you in ſuch health—Sure I had no cauſe for coldneſs?

Julia. Nay then, I ſee you have taken ſomething ill.—You muſt not conceal from me what it is.

Faulk. Well then—ſhall I own to you that my joy at hearing of your health and arrival here, by your neighbour Acres, was ſomewhat damped, by his dwelling much ˙on the high ſpirits you had enjoyed in Devonſhire—on your mirth—your ſinging—dancing, and I know not what!—For ſuch is my temper, Julia, that I ſhould regard every mirthful moment in your abſence as a treaſon to conſtancy :—The mutual tear that ſteals down the cheek of parting lovers is a compact, that no ſmile ſhall live there till they meet again.

Julia. Muſt I never ceaſe to tax my Faulkland with this teaſing minute caprice?—Can the idle reports of a ſilly boor weigh in your breaſt againſt my tried affection?

Faulk. They have no weight with me, Julia: no, no—I am happy if you have been ſo—yet only ſay, that you did not ſing with *mirth*—ſay that you *thought* of Faulkland in the dance.

Julia. I never can be happy in your abſence.——
If *I* wear a countenance of content, it is to ſhew that

my mind holds no doubt of my Faulkland's truth.—
If I feem'd fad—it were to make malice triumph ;
and fay, that I had fixed my heart on one, who left
me to lament his roving, and my own credulity.——
Believe me, Faulkland, I mean not to upbraid you,
when I fay, that I have often dreffed forrow in fmiles,
left my friends fhould guefs whofe unkindnefs had
caufed my tears.

Faulk. You were ever all goodnefs to me.—O, I
am a brute, when I but admit a doubt of your true
conftancy !

Julia. If ever, without fuch caufe from you, as I
will not fuppofe poffible, you find my affections veer-
ing but a point, may I become a proverbial fcoff for
levity, and bafe ingratitude.

Faulk. Ah ! Julia, that laft word is grating to
me. I would I had no title to your *gratitude !*
Search your heart, Julia ; perhaps what you have miftaken for Love, is but the warm effufion of a too
thankful heart !

Julia. For what quality muft I love you ?

Faulk. For no quality ! To regard me for any
quality of mind or underftanding, were only to *efteem* me. And for perfon—I have often wifh'd myfelf deformed, to be convinced that I owe no obligation *there* for any part of your affection.

Julia. Where Nature has beftowed a fhew of nice
attention in the features of a man, he fhould laugh
at it, as mifplaced. I have feen men, who in *this*
vain article perhaps might rank above you ; but
my heart has never afked my eyes if it were fo or
not.

Faulk. Now this is not well from *you*, Julia—I de-
spise perfon in a man——Yet if you lov'd me as I
wifh, though I were an Æthiop, you'd think none
fo fair.

Julia. I fee you are determined to be unkind—
The *contract* which my poor father bound us in
gives you more than a lover's privilege.

Faulk. Again, Julia, you raife ideas that feed and
juftify my doubts.——I would not have been more
free—no—I am proud of my reftraint.——Yet—yet
—perhaps your high refpect alone for this folemn
compact has fettered your inclinations, which elfe
had made a worthier choice.——How fhall I be fure,
had you remained unbound in thought and promife,
that I fhould ftill have been the object of your perfevering love ?

Julia. Then try me now.—Let us be free as
ftrangers as to what is paft :—*my* heart will not feel
more liberty !

Faulk. There now ! fo hafty, Julia ! fo anxious to
be free !—If your love for me were fixed and ardent,
you would not lofe your hold, even tho' I wifh'd
it !

Julia, O, you torture me to the heart !— I cannot
bear it.

Faulk. I do not mean to diftrefs you.—If I lov'd
you lefs, I fhould never give you an uneafy moment.
—But hear me.—All my fretful doubts arife from
this—Women are not ufed to weigh, and feparate
the motives of their affections : the cold dictates of
prudence, gratitude, or filial duty, may fometimes
be miftaken for the pleadings of the heart.——Ⱡ

would not boaft—yet let me fay, that I have neither age, perfon, or character, to found diflike on ;—my fortune, fuch as few ladies could be charged with *indifcretion* in the match.—O Julia, whẹn *Love* receives fuch countenance from *Prudence*, nice minds will be fufpicious of its Birth.

Julia. I know not whither your infinuations would tend :—But as they feem prefling to infult me—I will fpare you the regret of having done fo. —I have given you no caufe for this ! .

[*Exit in tears.*

Faulk. In Tears ! ftay Julia; ftay but for a mo‑ ment.——The door is faftened!—Julia ;—my foul —but for one moment : I hear her fobbing !—— 'Sdeath ! what a brute am I to ufe her thus ! Yet ftay.—Aye—fhe is coming now :—how little refolu‑ tion there is in woman !—how a few foft words can turn them !——No, faith !—fhe is *not* coming either. ——Why, Julia—my love—fay but that you forgive me—come but to tell me that—now, this is being *too* refentful : ftay ! fhe is coming too—I thought fhe would—no *fteadinefs* in any thing! her going away muft have been a mere trick then—fhe fha'n't fee that I was hurt by it.—I'll affect indifference— *(hums a tune : then liftens)*——No—Z—ds ! fhe's *not* coming !—nor don't intend it, I fuppofe.—This is not *fteadinefs*, but *obftinacy !* Yet I deferve it.— What, after fo long an abfence, to quarrel with her tendernefs!—'twas barbarous and unmanly !—I fhould be afhamed to fee her now.—I'll wait till her juft re‑ fentment is abated—and when I diftrefs her fo again,

may I lofe her for ever! and be linked inftead to
fome antique virago, whofe gnawing paffions, and
long-hoarded fpleen, fhall make me curfe my folly
half the day, and all the night!   [*Exit.*

SCENE III.

Mrs. Malaprop's *Lodgings.*

Mrs. MALAPROP, *with a letter in her hand, and*
Captain ABSOLUTE.

Mrs. Mal. Your being Sir Anthony's fon, Captain, would itfelf be a fufficient accommodation;
—but from the ingenuity of your appearance, I am
convinced you deferve the character here given of
you.

Abf. Permit me to fay, Madam, that as I never
yet have had the pleafure of feeing Mifs Languifh,
my principal inducement in this affair at prefent, is
the honour of being allied to Mrs. Malaprop; of whofe
intellectual accomplifhments, elegant manners, and
unaffected learning, no tongue is filent.

Mrs. Mal. Sir, you do me infinite honour!—I
beg, Captain, you'll be feated.—*(Sit)*—Ah! few
gentlemen, now-a-days, know how to value the inef-
fectual qualities in a woman! few think how a little
knowledge becomes a gentlewoman!—Men have no
fenfe now but for the worthlefs flower of beauty!

Abf. It is but too true indeed, Ma'am;—yet I

fear our ladies fhould fhare the blame—they think our admiration of *beauty* fo great, that *knowledge* in *them* would be fuperfluous. Thus, like garden-trees, they feldom fhew fruit, till time has robb'd them of the more fpecious bloffom.—Few like Mrs. Malaprop and the Orange-tree, are rich in both at once!

Mrs. Mal. Sir—you overpower me with good-breeding—He is the very Pine-apple of politenefs! You are not ignorant, Captain, that this giddy girl has fomehow contrived to fix her affections on a beggarly, ftrolling, eve's-dropping Enfign, whom none of us have feen, and nobody knows any thing of.

Abf. O; I have heard the filly affair before.—— I'm not at all prejudiced againft her on *that* account.

Mrs. Mal. You are very good, and very confiderate, Captain.—I am fure I have done every thing in my power fince I exploded the affair! long ago I laid my pofitive conjunctions on her, never to think on the fellow again;—I have fince laid Sir Anthony's prepofition before her;—but I am forry to fay fhe feems refolved to decline every particle that I enjoin her.

Abf. It muft be very diftreffing indeed, Ma'am.

Mrs. Mal. Oh! it gives me the hydroftatics to fuch a degree;—I thought fhe had perfifted from corresponding with him; but behold this very day, I have interceded another letter from the fellow; I believe I have it in my pocket.

Abf. O the devil! my laft note.   [Afide.

Mrs. Mal. Aye, here it is.

Abf. Aye, my note indeed! O the little traitrefs, Lucy.   [*Afide.*

Mrs. Mal. There, perhaps you may know the writing.   . [*Gives him the letter.*

Abf. I think I have feen the hand before—yes, I certainly muft have feen this hand before:——

Mrs. Mal. Nay, but read it, Captain.

Abf. (*Reads*) " *My foul's idol, my ador'd Ly-dia!*"—Very tender indeed !

Mrs. Mal. Tender! aye and prophane too, o'my confcience !

Abf. " *I am exceffively alarmed at the intelligence you* " *fend me, the more fo as my new rival*"——

Mrs. Mal. That's *you,* Sir.

Abf. " *Has univerfally the charaĉter of being an ac-* " *complifhed gentleman, and a man of honour.*"——— Well, that's handfome enough.

Mrs. Mal. O, the fellow has fome defign in writ-ing fo—

Abf. That he had, I'll anfwer for him, Ma'am.

Mrs. Mal. But go on, Sir—you'll fee prefent-ly.

Abf. " *As for the old weather-beaten fhe-dragon who* " *guards you*"—Who can he mean by that ?

Mrs. Mal. Me, Sir—*me*—he means *me* there—. what do you think now ?——but go on a little fur-ther.

Abf. Impudent fcoundrel!—" *it fhall go hard but* " *I will elude her vigilance, as I am told that the fame* " *ridiculous vanity, which makes her drefs up her coarfe*

" features, and deck her dull chat with hard words
" which she don't understand.——

Mrs. Mal. There, Sir! an attack upon my language! what do you think of that?—an afperfion upon my parts of fpeech! was ever fuch a brute! Sure if I reprehend any thing in this world, it is the ufe of my oracular tongue, and a nice derangement of epitaphs!

Abf. He deferves to be hang'd and quarter'd! let me fee—*" fame ridiculous vanity"*——

Mrs. Mal. You need not read it again, Sir.

Abf. I beg pardon, Ma'am, *" does alfo lay her open*
" to the groffeft deceptions from flattery and pretended
" admiration".—an impudent coxcomb! *" fo that I*
" have a fcheme to fee you fhortly with the old Har-
" ridan's confent, and even to make her a go-be-
" tween in our interviews."——Was ever fuch affurance!

Mrs. Mal. Did you ever hear any thing like it?—
he'll elude my vigilance, will he—yes, yes! ha! ha! he's very likely to enter thefe doors!—we'll try who can plot beft!

Abf. So we will, Ma'am—fo we will.—Ha! ha! ha! a conceited puppy, ha! ha! ha!—Well, but Mrs. Malaprop, as the girl feems fo infatuated by this fellow, fuppofe you were to wink at her corref-ponding with him for a little time—let her even plot an elopement with him—then do you connive at her efcape—while *I*, juft in the nick, will have the fel-low laid by the heels, and fairly contrive to carry her off in his ftead.

Mrs. Mal. I am delighted with the scheme, never was any thing better perpetrated !

Abs. But, pray, could not I see the lady for a few minutes now ?—I should like to try her temper a little.

Mrs. Mal. Why, I don't know—I doubt she is not prepared for a visit of this kind.——There is a decorum in these matters.

Abs. O Lord ! she won't mind *me*—only tell her Beverley——

Mrs. Mal. Sir !

Abs. Gently, good tongue.   [*Aside.*

Mrs. Mal. What did you say of Beverley ?

Abs. O, I was going to propose that you should tell her, by way of jest, that it was Beverley who was below—she'd come down fast enough then—ha ! ha ! ha !

Mrs. Mal. 'Twould be a trick she well deserves —besides, you know the fellow tells her he'll get my consent to see her—ha ! ha !—Let him if he can, I say again.—Lydia, come down here !   [*Calling.*
—He'll make me a *go-between in their interviews !* —ha ! ha ! ha ! Come down, I say, Lydia !—I don't wonder at your laughing, ha ! ha ! ha ! his impudence is truly ridiculous.

Abs. 'Tis very ridiculous, upon my soul, Ma'am, ha ! ha ! ha !

Mrs. Mal. The little huffy won't hear.—Well, I'll go and tell her at once who it is—she shall know that Captain Absolute is come to wait on her. —*And I'll* make her behave as becomes a young woman.

Abf. As you pleafe, Ma'am.

Mrs. Mal. For the prefent, Captain, your fervant —Ah! you've not done laughing yet, I fee—*elude my vigilance!* yes, yes, ha! ha! ha!   [*Exit.*

Abf. Ha! ha! ha! one would think now that I might throw off all difguife at once, and feize my prize with fecurity—but fuch is Lydia's, caprice, that to undeceive were probably to lofe her.—I'll fee whether fhe knows me.

[*Walks afide, and feems engaged in looking at the. piêlures.*

Enter LYDIA.

Lydia. What a fcene am I now to go thro'! furely nothing can be more dreadful than to be obliged to liften to the loathfome addreffes of a ftranger to one's heart.—I have heard of girls perfecuted as I am, who have appealed in behalf of their favoured lover to the generofity of his rival: fuppofe I were to try it— there ftands the hated rival—an officer too!—but O how unlike my Beverley!—I wonder he don't begin. —truly he feems a very negligent wooer!—quite at. his eafe, upon my word! I'll fpeak firft—Mr. Abfolute.

Abf. Ma'am.   [*Turns round.*

Lydia. O Heav'ns! Beverley!   ˜

Abf. Hufh!—hufh, my life! foftly! be not furprifed!

Lydia. I am fo aftonifhed! and fo terrified! and fo overjoyed!—for Heav'ns fake! how came you here?

Abf. Briefly—I have deceived your aunt—

informed that my new rival was to vifit here this evening, and contriving to have him kept away, have paffed myfelf on *her* for Capt. Abfolute.

Lydia. O, charming!—And fhe really takes you for young Abfolute?

Abf. O, fhe's convinced of it.

Lydia. Ha! ha! ha! l can't forbear laughing to think how her fagacity is over-reached!

Abf. But we trifle with our precious moments— fuch another opportunity may not occur—then let me now conjure my kind, my condefcending angel, to fix the time when l may refcue her from undeferv- ing perfecution, and with a licenfed warmth plead for my reward.

Lydia. Will you then, Beverley, confent to forfeit that portion of my paltry wealth?—that burden on the wings of love?

Abf. O come to me—rich only thus—in lovelinefs —Bring no portion to me but thy love—'twill be ge- nerous in you, Lydia—for well you know, it is the only dower your poor Beverley can repay.

Lydia. How perfuafive are his words!—how charming will poverty be with him!

Abf. Ah! my foul, what a life will we then live? Love fhall be our idol and fupport! we will worfhip him with a monaftic ftrictnefs; abjuring all worldly toys, to center every thought and action there.— Proud of calamity, we will enjoy the wreck of wealth; while the furrounding gloom of adverfity fhall make the flame of our pure love fhow doubly bright.—By Heav'ns! I would fling all goods of une from me with a prodigal hand, to enjoy the

scene where I might clasp my Lydia to my bosom,
and say, the world affords no smile to me—but
here————   ¯   [*Embracing her.*
If she holds out now, the devil is in it !   [*Aside.*
  Lydia. Now could. I fly with him to the Anti-
podes ! but my persecution is not yet come to a
crisis.

Enter Mrs. MALAPROP, *listening.*

  Mrs. Mal. I am impatient to know how the little
huffy deports herself.   [*Aside.*
  Abs. So pensive, Lydia !—is then your warmth
abated ?
  Mrs. Mal. Warmth abated !—so !—she has been
in a passion, I suppose.
  Lydia. No—nor ever can while I have life.
  Mrs. Mal. An ill-temper'd little devil !—She'll
be in a passion all her life—will she ?
  Lydia. Think not the idle threats of my ridiculous
aunt can ever have any weight with me.
  Mrs. Mal. Very dutiful, upon my word !
  Lydia. Let her choice be Capt. *Absolute*, but Be-
verley is mine.
  Mrs. Mal. I am astonished at her assurance !—to
his face—this is to his face !
  Abs. Thus then let me enforce my suit.
                              [*Kneeling.*
  Mrs. Mal. Aye—poor young man—down on
his knees entreating for pity !—I can contain no
longer.——Why, thou vixen !——I have overheard
you.
  Abs. O, confound her vigilance !

Mrs. Mal. Capt. *Abfolute*—I know not how to apologize for her fhocking rudenefs.

Abf. So—all's fafe, I find. [*Afide.*
I have hopes, Madam, that time will bring the young lady——

Mrs. Mal. O, there's nothing to be hoped for from her ! fhe's as headftrong as an allegory on the banks of Nile.

Lydia. Nay, Madam, what do you charge me with now ?

Mrs. Mal. Why, thou unblufhing rebel—didn't you tell this gentleman to his face that you loved another better ?—didn't you fay you never would be his ?

Lydia. No, Madam—I did not.

Mrs. Mal. Good Heav'ns ! what affurance !—Lydia, Lydia, you ought to know that lying don't become a young woman !—Didn't you boaft that *Beverley*—that ftroller *Beverley*, poffeffed your heart? —Tell me that, I fay.

Lydia. 'Tis true, Ma'am, and none but *Beverley*.——

Mrs. Mal. Hold ;—hold Affurance !—you fhall not be fo rude.

Abf. Nay, pray Mrs. Malaprop, don't ftop the young lady's fpeech :—fhe's very welcome to talk thus——it does not hurt *me* in the leaft, I affure you.

Mrs. Mal. You are *too* good, Captain—*too* amiably patient—but come with me, Mifs—let us fee you again foon, Captain—remember what we have fixed.

Abf. I fhall, Ma'am.

Mrs, Mal. Come, take a graceful leave of the gentleman.

Lydia. May every blefling wait on my *Beverley,* my lov'd *Bev*——

Mrs. Mal. Huffy! I'll choak the word in your throat!—come along—come along.

[*Exeunt feverally.*
[Beverley *kiffing his hand to* Lydia—*Mrs.* Malaprop *flopping her from fpeaking.*

SCENE IV.

Acres's *Lodgings.*

ACRES *and* DAVID.

ACRES *as juft drefs'd.*

Acres. Indeed, David—do you think I become it To?

David. You are quite another creature, believe me Mafter, by the Mafs! an' we've any luck we fhall fee the Devon monkeyrony in all the print-fhops in Bath!

Acres. Drefs *does* make a difference, David.

David. 'Tis all in all, I think—difference! why, an' you were to go now to Clod-Hall, I am certain the old lady wouldn't know you: Mafter Butler wouldn't believe his own eyes, and Mrs. Pickle would

would cry, " Lard prefarve me !" our dairy-maid would come giggling to the door, and I warrant Dolly Tefter, your Honour's favourite would blufh like my waiftcoat—Oons ! I'll hold a gallon, there an't a dog in the houfe but would bark, and I quef-tion whether *Phillis* would wag a hair of her tail !

Acres. Aye, David, there's nothing like polifh-ing.

David. So l fays of your Honour's boots ; but the boy never heeds me !

Acres. But, David, has Mr. *De-la-Grace* been here ? I muft rub up my balancing, and chafing, and boring.

David. I'll call again, Sir.

Acres. Do—and fee if there are any letters for me at the poft-office.

David. I will.—By the Mafs, I can't help looking at your head !—if I hadn't been by at the cooking, I wifh I may die if I fhould have known the difh again myfelf ! [*Exit.*

[Acres *comes forward, praftifing a dancing ftep.*

Acres. Sink, flide—coupee—Confound the firft inventors of cotillons ! fay I—they are as bad as al-gebra to us country gentlemen—I can walk a Minuet eafy enough when I am forced !—and I have been ac-counted a good ftick in a Country-dance.—Odds jiggs and tabors !—I never valued your crofs-over two couple—figure in—right and left—and I'd foot it with e'er a Captain in the county !—but thefe out-landifh heathen Allemandes and Cotillons are quite beyond me !—I fhall never profper at 'em, that's fure—mine are true-born Englifh legs—they don't

understand their curst French lingo!—their *Pas* this,
and *Pas* that, and *Pas* t'other!—damn me! my
feet don't like to be called Paws! no, 'tis certain I
have most Antigallican Toes!

Enter SERVANT.

Ser. Here is Sir Lucius O'Trigger to wait on you,
Sir.

Acres. Shew him in.

Enter Sir LUCIUS.

Sir Luc. Mr. Acres, I am delighted to embrace
you.

Acres. My dear Sir Lucius, I kiss your hands.

Sir Luc. Pray, my friend, what has brought you
so suddenly to Bath?

Acres. Faith! I have followed Cupid's Jack-a-
Lantern, and find myself in a quagmire at last.—In
short, I have been very ill-used, Sir Lucius.—I don't
choose to mention names, but look on me as on a
very ill-used gentleman.

Sir Luc. Pray what is the case?——I ask no
names.

Acres. Mark me, Sir Lucius, I fall as deep as
need be in love with a young lady——her friends take
my part—I follow her to Bath—send word of my arrival; and receive answer, that the lady is to be other-
wise disposed of.—This, Sir Lucius, I call being ill-
used.

Sir Luc. Very ill upon my conscience—Pray, can
you divine the cause of it?

Acres. Why, there's the matter: she has another

lover, one *Beverley*, who, I am told, is now in Bath.
—Odds flanders and lies! he must be at the bottom
of it.

Sir Luc. A rival in the case, is there?—and you
think he has supplanted you unfairly.

Acres. Unfairly! to be sure he has.—He never
could have done it fairly.

Sir Luc. Then sure you know what is to be
done!

Acres. Not I, upon my soul!

Sir Luc. We wear no swords here, but you understand me.

Acres. What! fight him!

Sir Luc. Aye, to be sure: what can I mean
else?

Acres. But he has given me no provocation.

Sir Luc. Now, I think he has given you the greatest provocation in the world.—Can a man commit a
more heinous offence against another than to fall in
love with the same woman? O, by my soul, it is the
most unpardonable breach of friendship!

Acres. Breach of friendship! Aye, aye; but I
have no acquaintance with this man. I never saw
him in my life.

Sir Luc. That's no argument at all—he has the
less right then to take such a liberty.

Acres. 'Gad, that's true—I grow full of anger,
Sir Lucius!—I fire apace! Odds, hilts and blades;
I find a man may have a deal of valour in him, and
not know it! But could not I contrive to have a little right of my side?

Sir Luc. What the Devil signifies right, when

your *honour* is concerned? Do you think *Achilles*, or
my little *Alexander the Great* ever inquired where the
right lay? No, by my foul, they drew their broad-
fwords, and left the lazy fons of peace to fettle the
juftice of it.

Acres. Your words are a grenadier's march to
my heart! I believe courage muft be catching!—
I certainly do feel a kind of valour rifing as it
were————a kind of courage, as I may fay——
Odds flints, pans, and triggers! I'll challenge him
directly.

Sir Luc. Ah, my little friend! if we had *Blunder-
bufs-Hall* here—I could fhew you a range of ancef-
try, in the O'Trigger line, that would furnifh the
new room; every one of whom had killed his man!
—For though the manfion-houfe and dirty acres
have flipt through my fingers, I thank Heav'n our
honour, and the family-pictures, are as frefh as
ever.

Acres. O Sir Lucius! I have had anceftors too!
every man of 'em colonel or captain in the militia?
——Odds balls and barrels! fay no more—I'm
brac'd for it.—The thunder of your words has foured
the milk of human kindnefs in my breaft!————
Z—ds! as the man in the play fays, " I could do
" fuch deeds————"

Sir Luc. Come, come, there muft be no paffion
at all in the cafe—thefe things fhould always be done
civilly.

Acres. I muft be in a paffion, Sir Lucius——I
muft be in a rage——Dear Sir Lucius let me be
M

a rage, if you love me.——Come, here's pen and
paper.   [*Sits down to write.*
I would the ink were red !——Indite, I say indite !
—How shall I begin ! Odds bullets and blades ! I'll
write a good bold hand, however.

Sir Luc. Pray compose yourself.

Acres. Come—now shall I begin with an oath ?
Do, Sir Lucius, let me begin with a damme.

Sir Luc. Pho ! pho ! do the thing decently and
like a Chriftian.   Begin now——" *Sir*——

Acres. That's too civil by half.

Sir Luc. " *To prevent the confufion that might
arife.*"

Acres. Well——

Sir Luc. " *From our both addreffing the fame lady.*"

Acres. Aye—there's the reason—" *fame lady*"—
Well—

Sir Luc. " *I fhall expect the honour of your company.*"——

Acres. Z—ds ! I'm not afking him to dinner.

Sir Luc. Pray be eafy.

Acres. Well then, " honour of your company"

Sir Luc. " *To fettle our pretenfions.*"

Acres. Well.

Sir Luc. Let me fee, aye, *King's Mead-fields* will
do.——" *in King's Mead-fields.*"

Acres. So that's done ——Well, I'll fold it up
prefently ; my own creft—a hand and dagger fhall be
the feal.

Sir Luc. You fee now this little explanation will
put a ftop at once to all confufion or mifunderftanding
that might arife between you.

Acres. Aye, we fight to prevent any misunder-
standing,

Sir Luc. Now, I'll leave you to fix your own
time.—Take my advice, and you'll decide it this
evening if you can; then let the worst come of it,
'twill be off your mind to-morrow.

Acres. Very true.

Sir Luc. So I shall see nothing more of you, unless it be by letter, till the evening.——I would do
myself the honour to carry your message; but, to tell
you a secret, I believe I shall have just such another
affair on my own hands. There is a gay captain
here, who put a jest on me lately, at the expence of
my country, and I only want to fall in with the gentleman, to call him out.

Acres. By my valour, I should like to see you
fight first! Odds life! I should like to see you kill
him, if it was only to get a little lesson.

Sir Luc. I shall be very proud of instructing you.
—Well, for the present—but remember now, when
you meet your antagonist, do every thing in a mild
and agreeable manner.—Let your courage be as
keen, but at the same time as polished as your sword.

[*Exeunt severally.*

Acres. Ah! David, if you had heard Sir Lucius! —Odds fparks and flames! he would have rous'd your valour.

David. Not he, indeed. I hates fuch bloodthirfty cormorants. Lookk'ee, Mafter, if. you'd wanted a bout at boxing, quarter-ftaff, or fhortftaff, I fhould never be the man to bid you cry off: But for your curft fharps and fnaps, I never knew any good come of 'em.

Acres. But my honour, David, my honour! I muft be very careful of my honour.

David. Aye, by the Mafs! and I would be very careful of it; and I think in return my *honour* couldn't do lefs than to be very careful of *me*.

Acres. Odds blades! David, no gentleman will ... of his honour!

David. ... it would be but civil in honour

never to rifk the lofs of a *gentleman*.——Look'ee, Mafter, this *honour* feems to me to be a marvellous falfe friend : aye, truly, a very courtier-like fervant. ——Put the cafe, I was a gentleman (which thank God, no one can fay of me); well—my honour makes me quarrel with another gentleman of my ac- quaintance.—So—we fight. (Pleafant enough that) Boh!—I kill him—(the more's my luck.) Now, pray who gets the profit of it ?—Why, my *honour*. ——But put the cafe that he kills me !——by the Mafs ! I go to the worms, and my honour whips over to my enemy.

Acres. No, David—in that cafe !—Odds crowns and laurels !. your honour follows you to the grave.

David. Now, that's juft the place where I could make a fhift to do without it.

Acres. Z—ds ! David, you are a coward !——It doesn't become my valour to liften to you.—What, fhall I difgrace my anceftors ?—Think of that, Da- vid—think what it would be to difgrace my ancef- tors !

David. Under favour; the fureft way of not dif- gracing them, is to keep as long as you can out of their company. Look'ee now, Mafter, to go to them in fuch hafte—with an ounce of lead in your brains—I fhould think might as well be let alone. Our anceftors are very good kind of folks ; but they are the laft people I fhould choofe to have a vifiting acquaintance with.

Acres. But, David, now, you don't think is fuch very, very, very great danger, hey?

Odds' life! people often fight without any mifchief done!

David. By the Mafs, I think 'tis ten to one againft you!——Oons! here to meet fome lion-headed fellow, I warrant, with his d—n'd double-barrell'd fwords, and cut-and-thruft piftols! Lord blefs us! it makes me tremble to think o't.—Thofe be fuch defperate bloody-minded weapons! .Well, I never could abide 'em!—from a child I never could fancy 'em!—I fuppofe there a'nt been fo mercilefs a beaft in the world as your loaded piftol!

Acres. Z—ds! I *won't* be afraid—Odds fire and fury! you fhan't make me afraid.——Here is the challenge, and I have fent for my dear friend Jack Abfolute to carry it for me.

David. Aye, i'the name of mifchief, let *him* be the meffenger.—For my part, I wouldn't lend a hand to it for the beft horfe in your ftable. By the Mafs! it don't look like another letter!—It is, as I may fay, a defigning and malicious-looking letter!—and I warrant fmells of gunpowder like a foldier's pouch!—Oons! I wouldn't fwear it mayn't go off!

Acres. Out, you poltroon!—you ha'n't the valour of a grafs-hopper.

David. Well, I fay no more—'twill be fad news, to be fure, at Clod-Hall!—but I ha' done.—How Phyllis will howl when fhe hears of it!—Aye, poor bitch, fhe little thinks what fhooting her Mafter's after!——And I warrant old Crop, who ed your honour, field and road, thefe ten years, will curfe the hour he was born. [*Whimpering.*

Acres. It won't do, David—I am determined to
fight—fo get along, you coward, while I'm in the
mind.

Enter SERVANT.

Ser. Captain Abfolute, Sir.   ·
Acres. O! fhew him up.   [*Exit* Servant.
David. Well, Heaven fend we be all alive this .
time to morrow.
Acres. What's that!—Don't provoke me, Da-
vid!
David. Good bye, Mafter.   [*Whimpering.*
Acres. Get along, you cowardly, daftardly, ci oak-
ing raven.   [*Exit* David.

Enter ABSOLUTE.

Abf. What's the matter, Bob?
Acres. A vile, fheep-hearted blockhead :—If I
hadn't the valour of St. George and the dragon to
boot—
Abf. But what did you want with me, Bob?
Acres. O!—There—   [*Gives him the challenge.*
Abf. " *To Enfign Beverley.*" So—what's going
on now.   [*Afide.*
Well, what's this?
Acres. A challenge!
Abf. Indeed!——Why, you won't fight him;
will you, Bob?
Acres. 'Egad but I will, Jack.——Sir Lucius

has wrought me to it.   He has left me full of rage
—and I'll fight this evening, that so much good passion mayn't be wasted.

Abs. But what have I to do with this?

Acres. Why, as I think you know something of
this fellow, I want you to find him out for me, and
give him this mortal defiance.

Abs. Well, give it to me, and trust me he gets
it.

Acres. Thank you, my dear friend, my dear
Jack; but it is giving you a great deal of trouble.

Abs. Not in the least—I beg you won't mention
it.—No trouble in the world, I assure you.

Acres. You are very kind.——What it is to have
a friend!——You couldn't be my second—could you,
Jack?

Abs. Why no, Bob—not in *this* affair—it would
not be quite so proper.

Acres. Well then, I must get my friend Sir
Lucius. I shall have your good wishes, however,
Jack.

Abs. Whenever he meets you, believe me.

Enter SERVANT.

Ser. Sir Anthony Absolute is below, inquiring
for the Captain.

Abs. I'll come instantly.——Well, my little
hero, success attend you.   [*Going.*

Acres. Stay—stay Jack.——If Beverley should
ask you what kind of a man your friend Acres is,

do, tell him I am a devil of a fellow—will you,
Jack?

Abf. To be fure I fhall.——I'll fay you are a determined dog—hey, Bob!

Acres. Aye, do, do—and if that frightens him,
'gad perhaps he mayn't come.   So tell him I generally kill a man a week; will you, Jack?

Abf. I will, I will; I'll fay you are called in the
country " *Fighting Bob.*"

Acres. Right, right—'tis all to prevent mifchief;
for I don't want to take his life if I clear my
honour.

Abf. No!—that's very kind of you.

Acres. Why, you don't wifh me to kill him—do
you, Jack?

Abf. No, upon my foul, I do not.—But a devil
of a fellow, hey?   [*Going.*

Acres. True, true—but ftay—ftay, Jack—you
may add that you never faw me in fuch a rage before
—a moft devouring rage!

Abf. I will, I will.

Acres. Remember, Jack——a determined dog!

Abf. Aye, aye, " *Fighting Bob.*"

[*Exeunt feverally.*

M 5

SCENE II.

Mrs. Malaprop's *Lodgings.*

Mrs. MALAPROP *and* LYDIA.

Mrs. Mal. Why, thou perverfe one!—tell me
what you can object to him?—Isn't he a handfome
man?—tell me that.—A genteel man? a pretty figure
of a man?

Lydia. She little thinks whom fhe is praifing!
(Afide.)—So is Beverley, Ma'am.

Mrs. Mal. No caparifons, Mifs, if you pleafe!—
Caparifons don't become a young woman.—No!
Captain Abfolute is indeed a fine gentleman!

Lydia. Aye, the Captain Abfolute *you* have feen.
[*Afide.*

Mrs. Mal. Then he's *fo* well bred;—*fo* full of ala-
crity, ind adulation!—and has *fo much* to fay for
himfelf.—in fuch good language too!—His phyfi-
ognomy fo grammatical!—Then his prefence is fo
noble!—I protect, when I faw him, I thought of
what Hamlet fays in the Play:——" Hefperian
" curls—the front of *Job* himfelf!—an eye, like
" *March,* to threaten at command!—a Station,
" like Harry Mercury, new—" Something about
kiffing—on a hill—however, the fimilitude ftruck
me directly.

Lydia. How enraged fhe'll be prefently when fhe
difcovers her miftake! [*Afide.*

Enter SERVANT.

Ser. Sir Anthony, and Captain Abfolute are below, Ma'am.

Mrs. Mal. Shew them up here.   [*Exit* Servant.
Now, Lydia, I infift on your behaving as becomes
a young woman.—Shew your good breeding at leaft,
though you have forgot your duty.

Lydia. Madam, I have told you my refolution!—
I fhall not only give him no encouragement, but I
won't even fpeak to, or look at him.

[*Flings herfelf into a chair, with her face from
the door.*

Enter Sir ANTHONY *and* ABSOLUTE.

Sir Anth. Here we are, Mrs. Malaprop; come
to mitigate the frowns of unrelenting beauty—
and difficulty enough I had to bring this fellow.
—I don't know what's the matter; but if I had
not held him by force, he'd have given me the
flip.

Mrs. Mal. You have infinite trouble, Sir Anthony, in the affair.—I am afhamed for the caufe!
Lydia, Lydia, rife I befeech you!—pay your refpects!   [*Afide to her.*

Sir Anth. I hope, Madam, that Mifs Languifh
has reflected on the worth of this gentleman, and
the regard due to her Aunt's choice, and *my* alliance.
—Now, Jack, fpeak to her!   [*Afide to him.*

Abf. What the d—l fhall I do!   [*Afide.*
—You fee, Sir, fhe won't even look at me whilft

you are here.——I knew fhe wouldn't!—I told
you fo—Let me intreat you, Sir, to leave us together !

[Abfolute *feems to expoftulate with his Father.*

Lydia. (*Afide.*) l wonder I ha'n't heard my Aunt
exclaim yet ! fure fhe can't have look'd at him——
perhaps their regimentals are alike, and fhe is fomething blind.

Sir Anth. I fay, Sir, I won't ftir a foot yet.

Mrs. Mal. I am forry to fay, Sir Anthony, that
my affluence over my Niece is very fmall.—Turn
round Lydia, I blufh for you !   [*Afide to her.*

Sir Anth. May I not flatter myfelf, that Mifs
Languifh will affign what caufe of diflike fhe can
have to my fon!—Why don't you begin, Jack ?—
Speak, you puppy—fpeak !   [*Afide to him.*

Mrs. Mal. It is impoffible, Sir Anthony, fhe
can have any.——She will not fay fhe has.——
Anfwer, huffy ! why don't you anfwer?

[*Afide to her.*

Sir Anth. Then, Madam, I truft that a childifh
and hafty predilection will be no bar to Jack's happinefs.——Z—ds! firrah! why don't you fpeak?

[*Afide to him.*

Lydia. (*Afide.*) I think my lover feems as little
inclined to converfation as myfelf.—How ftrangely
blind my Aunt muft be!

Abf. Hem! hem! Madam—hem! (Abfolute
attempts to fpeak, then returns to Sir Anthony)——
Faith! Sir, I am fo confounded!—and fo—fo—
confufed!—I told you I fhould be fo, Sir—I knew

it.—The-the tremor of my paffion, entirely takes away my prefence of mind.

Sir Anth. But it don't take away your voice, fool, does it?—Go up, and fpeak to her directly!

[*Abfolute makes figns to Mrs.* Malaprop *to leave them together.*

Mrs. Mal. Sir Anthony, fhall we leave them together?—Ah! you ftubborn, little vixen!

[*Afide to her.*

Sir Anth. Not yet, Ma'am, not yet!—what the d—l are you at? unlock your jaws, firrah, or—

[*Afide to him.*

[Absolute *draws near* Lydia.]

Abf. Now, Heav'n fend fhe may be too fullen to look round!—I muft difguife my voice.

[*Afide.*

[*Speaks in a low hoarfe tone.*

—Will not Mifs Languifh lend an ear to the mild accents of true love?—Will not———

Sir Anth. What the d—l ails the fellow?—Why don't you fpeak out?—not ftand croaking like a frog in a quinfey!

Abf. The-the-excefs of my awe, and my-my-my modefty, quite choak me!

Sir Anth. Ah! your *modefty* again!—I'll tell you what, Jack; if you don't fpeak out directly, and glibly too, I fhall be in fuch a rage!—Mrs. Malaprop, I wifh the lady would favour us with fomething more than a fide-front.

[*Mrs.* Malaprop *feems to chide* Lydia.

Abf. So!—all will out I fee!

[*Goes up to* Lydia, *fpeaks foftly.*

Be not furprifed, my Lydia, fupprefs all furprife at
prefent.

Lydia. (*Afide.*) Heav'ns! 'tis Beverley's voice!
—Sure he can't have impos'd on Sir Anthony too!
　　　　　[*Looks round by degrees, then ftarts up.*
Is this poffible!—my Beverley!—how can this
be?—my Beverley?'

Abf. Ah! 'tis all over.　　　　　　[*Afide.*

Sir Anth. Beverley!—the devil—Beverley!——
What can the girl mean?—This is my fon, Jack
Abfolute.

Mrs. Mal. For fhame, huffy! for fhame!—your
head runs fo on that fellow, that you have him always in your eyes!—beg Captain Abfolute's pardon
directly.

Lydia. I fee no Captain Abfolute, but my lov'd
Beverley!

Sir Anth. Z—ds! the girl's mad!—her brain's
turn'd by reading!

Mrs. Mal. O' my confcience, I believe fo!——
what do you mean by Beverley, huffy?—You faw
Captain Abfolute before to-day; there he is—your
hufband that fhall be.

Lydia. With all my foul, Ma'am—when I refufe
my Beverley——

Sir Anth. O! fhe's as mad as Bedlam:—or has
this fellow been playing us a rogue's trick!—Come
here, firrah, who the d—I are you?

Abf. Faith, Sir, I am not quite clear myfelf; but
I'll endeavour to recollect.

Sir Anth. Are you my fon, or not?—anfwer for
your mother, you dog, if you won't for me.

Mrs. Mal. Aye, Sir, who are you? O mercy! I begin to fufpe{ct}!—

Abf. Ye Powers of Impudence befriend me! *(Afide.)* Sir Anthony, moft affuredly I am your wife's fon; and that I fincerely believe myfelf to be *your's* alfo, I hope my duty has always fhewn.—Mrs. Malaprop, I am your moft refpectful admirer—and fhall be proud to add affectionate nephew.—I need not tell my Lydia, that fhe fees her faithful *Beverley*, who, knowing the fingular generofity of her temper, affum'd that name, and a ftation, which has proved a teft of the moft difinterefted love, which he now hopes to enjoy in a more elevated character.

Lydia. So!—there will be no elopement after all!

                                [*Sullenly.*

Sir Anth. Upon my foul, Jack, thou art a very impudent fellow! to do you juftice, I think I never faw a piece of more confummate affurance!

Abf. O, you flatter me, Sir—you compliment—'tis my *modefty* you know, Sir—my *modefty* that has ftood in my way.

Sir Anth. Well, I am glad you are not the dull, infenfible varlet you pretended to be, however!—I'm glad you have made a fool of your father, you dog—I am———So this was your *penitence*, your *duty*, and *obedience!*—I thought it was d—n'd fudden!—You *never heard their names before*, not you!—*What*, The Languishes *of* Worcefterfhire, hey? —*if you could pleafe me in the affair, 'twas all you defired!*——Ah! you diffembling villain!—What! *(pointing to* Lydia*) fhe fquints, don't fhe?*—a little *red-haired girl!*—hey?—Why, you hypocritical

young rafcal—I wonder you a'n't afhamed to hold up
your head !

Abf. 'Tis with difficulty, Sir—I *am* confus'd—
very much confus'd, as you muft perceive.

Mrs. Mal. O Lud! Sir Anthony!—a new light
breaks in upon me!—hey!—how! what! Captain,
did *you* write the letters then?—What!—am I to
thank *you* for the elegant compilation of ' *an old weather-beaten fhe-dragon*'—hey?—O mercy!—was it *you*
that reflected on my parts of fpeech?

Abf. Dear Sir! my modefty will be overpower'd
at laft, if you don't affift me.—I fhall certainly not be
able to ftand it!

Sir Anth. Come, come, Mrs. Malaprop, we muft
forget and forgive;—odds'life! matters have taken
fo clever a turn all of a fudden, that I could find in
my heart, to be fo good-humour'd! and fo gallant!
—hey! Mrs. Malaprop!

Mrs. Mal. Well, Sir Anthony, fince *you* defire
it, we will not anticipate the paft;—fo mind young
people—our retrofpection will now be all to the future.

Sir Anth. Come, we muft leave them together;
Mrs. Malaprop, they long to fly into each other's
arms, I warrant!—Jack—is'n't the cheek as I faid,
hey?—and the eye, you rogue!—and the lip—hey?
Come, Mrs. Malaprop, we'll not difturb their tendernefs—their's is the time of life for happinefs!——
" *Youth's the feafon made for joy*"—(fings)—hey!—
Odds'life! I'm in fuch fpirits—I don't know what I
could not do!—Permit me, Ma'am—*(gives his hand
to Mrs, Malaprop.)* *(fings)* Tol-de-rol—'gad I

fhould like to have a little fooling myfelf—Tol-de-
rol! de-rol! [*Exit finging, and handing Mrs.* Malaprop.
    [LYDIA *fits fullenly in her chair.*]
Abf. So much thought bodes me no good *(afide)*
—So grave, Lydia!

Lydia. Sir!

Abf. So!—egad! I thought as much!—that
d—n'd monofyllable has froze me! *(afide)*—What,
Lydia, now that we are as happy in our friends confent, as in our mutual vows——

Lydia. Friends confent, indeed·!   [*Peevifhly.*

Abf. Come, come, we muft lay afide fome of our
romance—a little *wealth* and *comfort* may be endured
after all. And for your fortune, the lawyers fhall
make fuch fettlements as——

Lydia. Lawyers! I hate lawyers!

Abf. Nay then, we will not wait for their linger-
ing forms, but inflantly procure the licence, and—

Lydia. The *licence!*—I hate licence!

Abf. O my Love! be not fo unkind!—thus let
me intreat——   [*Kneeling.*

Lydia. Pfhaw!—what fignifies kneeling, when
you know I *muft* have you?

Abf. (Rifing) Nay, Madam, there fhall be no
conftraint upon your inclinations, I promife you.
—If I have loft your heart—I refign the reft.—
'Gad, I muft try what a little *fpirit* will do.
        [*Afide.*

Lydia. (Rifing) Then, Sir, let me tell you, the
intereft you had there was acquired by a mean, un-
manly impofition, and deferves the punifhment of
fraud.—What, you have been treating me like

child !—humouring my romance ! and laughing, I
fuppofe at your fuccefs !

Abf. You wrong me, Lydia, you wrong me—
only hear————

Lydia. So, while *I* fondly imagined we were de-
ceiving my relations, and flatter'd myfelf that I
fhould outwit and incenfe them All—behold ! my
hopes are to be crufh'd at once, by my Aunt's confent and approbation—and *I* am myfelf the only dupe
at laft !   [*Walking about in a heat.*
But here, Sir, here is the picture—*Beverley's* picture ! *(taking a miniature from her bofom)* which I
have worn night and day, in fpite of threats and
entreaties?————There, Sir, *(flings it to him)* and
be affured I throw the original from my heart as
eafily.

Abf. Nay, nay, Ma'am, we will not differ as to
that—Here, *(taking out a picture)* here is Mifs
Lydia Languifh.—What a difference !—aye, *there* is
the heav'nly affenting fmile, that firft gave foul and
fpirit to my hopes—thofe are the lips which feal'd a
vow, as yet fcarce dry in Cupid's calendar !—and
there the half refentful blufh, that *would* have check'd
the ardour of my thanks—Well, all that's paft !—all
over indeed !—There, Madam—in beauty, that copy
is not equal to you, but in my mind it's merit over
the original; in being ftill the fame, is fuch—that—
I cannot find in my heart to part with it.

[*Puts it up again.*

Lydia. *(Softening)* 'Tis your own doing, Sir—I,
I, I fuppofe you are perfectly fatisfied.

Abf. O moft certainly—fure now this is muchbet

ter than being in love !—ha ! ha ! ha!—there's fome
fpirit in *this* !—What fignifies breaking fome fcores
of folemn promifes :—all that's of no confequence you
know.—To be fure, people will fay, that Mifs didn't
know her own mind—but never mind that :—or perhaps they may be ill-natur'd- enough to hint, that
the gentleman grew tired of the lady and forfook her
—but don't let that fret you.

Lydia. There's no bearing his infolence.

[*Burfts into tears.*

Enter Mrs. MALAPROP *and* Sir ANTHONY.

Mrs. Mal. (*Entering*) Come, we muft interrupt
your billing and cooing a while.

Lydia. This is worfe than your treachery and deceit, you bafe ingrate.   [*Sobbing.*

Sir Anth. What the devil's the matter now ?——
Z—ds ! Mrs. Malaprop, this is the *oddeft billing* and
cooing I ever heard !—but what the deuce is the meaning of it ?—I'm quite aftonifh'd !

Abf. Afk the lady, Sir.

Mrs. Mal. O mercy !—I'm quite analys'd for my
part !—why, Lydia, what is the reafon of this ?

Lydia. Afk the gentleman, Ma'am.

Sir Anth. Z—ds ! I fhall be in a phrenzy !—why,
Jack, you are not come out to be any one elfe, are
you ?

Mrs. Mal. Aye, Sir, there's no more trick, is
there ?—you are not like Cerberus, *three* Gentlemen
at once, are you ?

Abf. You'll not let me fpeak—I fay the lady can
account for this much better than I can.

Lydia. Ma'am, you once commanded me never to think of Beverley again—there is the man—I now obey you :—for, from this moment, I renounce him for ever.   [*Exit* Lydia.

Mrs. Mal. O mercy! and miracles! what a turn here is—why fure, Captain, you haven't behaved difrefpectfully to my Niece.

Sir Anth. Ha! ha! ha!—ha! ha! ha!—now I see it.—Ha! ha! ha!—now I fee it—you have been too lively, Jack.

Abf. Nay, Sir, upon my word——

Sir Anth. Come, no lying, Jack—I'm fure 'twas fo.

Mrs. Mal. O Lud! Sir Anthony!—O fie, Captain!

Abf. Upon my foul, Ma'am——

Sir Anth. Come, no excufes, Jack ;—why, your father, you rogue, was fo before you :—the blood of the Abfolutes was always impatient.—Ha! ha! ha! poor little Lydia!—why, you've frighten'd her, you dog, you have.

Abf. By all that's good, Sir——

Sir Anth. Z—ds! fay no more, I tell you—— Mrs. Malaprop fhall make your peace.—You muft make his peace, Mrs. Malaprop :—you muft tell her 'tis Jack's way—tell her 'tis all our ways—it runs in the blood of our family!—Come, away Jack—ha! ha! ha! Mrs. Malaprop—a young villain!

[*Pufhes him out.*

Mrs. Mal. O! Sir Anthony!—O fie, Captain!

[*Exeunt feverally.*

SCENE IV.

The North Parade.

Enter Sir LUCIUS O'TRIGGER.

Sir Luc. I wonder where this Capt. Absolute hides himself.—Upon my conscience!—these officers are always in one's way in love affairs :—I remember I might have married Lady Dorothy Carmine, if it had not been for a little rogue of a Major, who ran away with her before she could get a fight of me !— And I wonder too what it is the ladies can fee in them to be so fond of them—unless it be a touch of the old serpent in 'em, that makes the little creatures be caught, like vipers with a bit of red cloth.—Hah! —isn't this the Captain coming?—faith it is !— There is a probability of succeeding about that fellow, that is mighty provoking !—Who the devil is he talking to ?   *[Steps aside.*

Enter Captain ABSOLUTE.

Abf. To what fine purpose I have been plotting ! a noble reward for all my schemes, upon my soul !— a little gypsey !—I did not think her romance could have made her so d—n'd absurd either—S'death, I never was in a worse humour in my life !—I could cut my own throat, or any other person's, with the greatest pleasure in the world !

Sir Luc. O, faith! I'm in the luck of it—I never could have found him in a sweeter temper for my purpose—to be sure I'm just come in the nick! now to enter into conversation with him, and so quarrel genteely.   [Sir Lucius *goes up to* Absolute.

——With regard to that matter, Captain, I must beg leave to differ in opinion with you.

Abs. Upon my word then, you must be a very subtle disputant :—because, Sir, I happen'd just then to be giving no opinion at all.

Sir Luc. That's no reason.—For, give me leave to tell you, a man may *think* an untruth as well as speak one.

Abs. Very true, Sir, but if a man never utters his thoughts, I should think they might stand a chance of escaping controversy.

Sir Luc. Then, Sir, you differ in opinion with me, which amounts to the same thing.

Abs. Hark'ee, Sir Lucius—if I had not before known you to be a gentleman, upon my soul, I should not have discovered it at this interview :—for what you can drive at, unless you mean to quarrel with me, I cannot conceive!

Sir Luc. I humbly thank you, Sir, for the quickness of your apprehension,   [*Bowing.*
—you have nam'd the very thing I would be at.

Abs. Very well, Sir—I shall certainly not baulk your inclinations :————but I should be glad you would please to explain your motives.

Sir Luc. Pray, Sir, be easy—the quarrel is a very pretty quarrel as it stands—we should only spoil it, by trying to explain it.—However, your memory is very short—or you could not have forgot an affront you passed on me within this week.—So no more, but name your time and place.

Abs. Well, Sir, since you are so bent on it, the sooner the better:—let it be this evening—here by the Spring-Gardens.—We shall scarcely be interrupted.

Sir Luc. Faith! that same interruption in affairs of this nature, shews very great ill-breeding.———— I don't know what's the reason, but in England, if a thing of this kind gets wind, people make such a pother, that a gentleman can never fight in peace and quietness.—However, if it's the same to you, Captain, I should take it as a particular kindness, if you'd let us meet in King's-Mead Fields, as a little business will call me there about six o'clock, and I may dispatch both matters at once.

Abs. 'Tis the same to me exactly.———A little after six, then we will discuss this matter more seriously.

Sir Luc. If you please, Sir, there will be very pretty small-sword light, tho' it won't do for a long shot.—So that matter's settl'd! and my mind's at ease.   [*Exit* Sir Lucius.

Enter FAULKLAND, *meeting* ABSOLUTE.

Abs. Well met.—I was going to look for you— O, Faulkland! all the Dæmons of spite and disappointment have conspired against me! I'm so vex'd, that if I had not the prospect of a resource in being knock'd o' the head by and bye, I should scarce have spirits to tell you the cause.

Faulk. What can you mean ?———Has Lydia chang'd her mind ?—I fhould have thought her duty and inclination would now have pointed to the fame object.

Abf. Aye, juft as the eyes do of a perfon who fquints :—when her love-eye was fixed on me— t'other—her eye of duty, was finely obliqued :—but when duty bid her point that the fame way—off t'other turn'd on a fwivel, and fecured its retreat with a frown !

Faulk. But what's the refource you———

Abf. O,. to wind up the whole, a good natured Irifhman here has *(mimicking* Sir Lucius) beg'd leave to have the pleafure of cutting my throat—and I mean to indulge him—that's all.

Faulk. Prithee, be ferious.

Abf. 'Tis fact, upon my foul.—Sir Lucius O'Trigger—you know him by fight—for fome af- front, which I am fure I never intended, has obliged me to meet him this evening at fix o'clock :—'tis on that account I wifhed to fee you—you muft go with me.

Faulk. Nay, there muft be fome miftake, fure.— Sir Lucius fhall explain himfelf—and I dare fay mat- ters may be accommodated :—but this evening, did you fay ?—I wifh it had been any other time.

Abf. Why ?—there will be light enough :—— there will (as Sir Lucius fays) " be very pretty fmall- fword light, tho' it won't do for a long fhot."— —Confound his long fhots !

Faulk. But I am myfelf a good deal ruffled, by a difference I have had with Julia—my vile tormenting temper has made me treat her fo cruelly, that I fhall not be myfelf till we are reconciled.

Abf. By Heav'ns, Faulkland, yon don't deferve her.

Enter SERVANT, *gives* FAULKLAND *a letter.*

Faulk. O Jack! this is from Julia—I dread to öpen it—I fear it may be to take a laft leave—per-haps to bid me return her letters—and reftore————— O! how I fuffer for my folly!

Abf. Here—let me fee.

[*Takes the letter and opens it.*

Aye, a final fentence indeed!—'tis all over with you, faith!

Faulk. Nay, Jack—don't keep me in fufpence.

Abf. Hear then.—" *As I am convinced that my " dear Faulkland's own reflections have already up- " braided him for his laft unkindnefs to me, I will not " add a word on the fubject.—I wifh to fpeak with you " as foon as poffible.—Yours ever and truly,* Julia."

—There's ftubbornnefs and refentment for you!

[*Gives him the letter.*

Why man, you don't feem one whit the happier at this.

Faulk. O, yes, I am—but—but————

Abf. Confound your *buts.*—You never hear any thing that would make another man blefs himfelf, but you immediately d—n it with a *but.*

Faulk. Now, Jack, as you are my friend, own honeftly—don't you think there is fomething forward —fomething indelicate in this hafte to forgive?— *Women fhould never fue for reconciliation:—that*

N

ſhould always come from us.—They ſhould retain their coldneſs till *woo'd* to kindneſs—and their *pardon,* like their *love,* ſhould " not unſought be won."

Abſ. I have not patience to liſten to you :—thou'rt incorrigible !—ſo ſay no more on the ſubject.—I muſt go to ſettle a few matters—let me ſee you before ſix—remember—at my lodgings.—A poor induſtri-ous devil like me, who have toil'd and drudg'd, and plotted to gain my ends, and am at laſt diſappointed by other people's folly—may in pity be allowed to ſwear and grumble a little !—but a captious ſceptic in love—a ſlave to fretfulneſs and whim—who has no difficulties but of his own creating—is a ſubject more fit for ridicule than compaſſion !   [*Exit* Abſolute.

Faulk. I feel his reproaches :—yet I would not change this too exquiſite nicety, for the groſs con-tent with which *he* tramples on the thorns of love.—His engaging me in this duel, has ſtarted an idea in my head, which I will inſtantly purſue.—I'll uſe it as the touch-ſtone of Julia's ſincerity and·diſintereſted-neſs—if her love prove pure and ſterling ore—my name will reſt on it with honour !—and once I've ſtamp'd it there, I lay aſide my doubts for ever :—but if the droſs of ſelfiſhneſs, the allay of pride pre-dominate—'twill be beſt to leave her as a toy for ſome leſs cautious Fool to ſigh for.

[*Exit* Faulkland.

ACT V. SCENE I.

Julia's *Dreffing-Room.*

JULIA, *fola.*

—How this meffage has alarmed me! what dreadful accident can he mean? why fuch charge to be
alone?———O Faulkland!—how many unhappy
moments!—how many tears have you coft me!

Enter FAULKLAND.

Julia. What means this?—why this caution,
Faulkland?

Faulk. Alas! Julia, I am come to take a long
farewell.

Julia. Heav'ns! what do you mean?

Faulk. You fee before you a wretch, whofe life is
forfeited.—Nay, ftart not!—the infirmity of my
temper has drawn all this mifery on me.—I left you
fretful and paffionate—an untoward accident drew me
into a quarrel—the event is, that I muft fly this kingdom inftantly.—O Julia, had I been fo fortunate as
to have call'd you mine entirely, before this mif-
chance had fallen on me, I fhould not fo deeply dread
my banifhment!—

Julia. My foul is opprefs'd with forrow at the
nature of your misfortune: had thefe adverfe circumftances arifen from a lefs fatal caufe, I fhould

have felt ftrong comfort in the thought that I could now chafe from your bofom every doubt of the warm fincerity of my love.————My heart has long known no other guardian—I now intruft my perfon to your honour—we will fly together.—When fafe from purfuit, my Father's will may be fulfilled—and I receive a legal claim to be the partner of your forrows, and tenderest comforter. Then on the bofom of your wedded Julia, you may lull your keen regret to flumbering ; while virtuous love, with a Cherub's hand, fhall fmooth the brow of upbraiding thought, and pluck the thorn from compunction.

Faulk. O Julia ! I am bankrupt in gratitude ! but the time is fo preffing, it calls on you for fo hafty a refolution.—Would you not wifh fome hours to weigh the advantages you forego, and what little compenfation poor Faulkland can make you befide his folitary love ?

Julia. I afk not a moment.—No, Faulkland, I have lov'd you for yourfelf: and if I now, more than ever, prize the folemn engagement which fo long has pledged us to each other, it is becaufe it leaves no room for hard afperfions on my fame, and puts the feal of duty to an act of love.—But let us not linger.—Perhaps this delay————.

Fulk. 'Twill be better I fhould not venture out again till dark.—Yet am I griev'd to think what numberlefs diftreffes will prefs heavy on your gentle difpofition !

Julia. Perhaps your fortune may be forfeited by this unhappy act.—I know not whether 'tis fo—but fure that alone can never make us unhappy.—The

little I have will be fufficient to fupport us; and ex-
ile never fhould be fplendid.

Faulk. Aye, but in fuch an abjeƈt ftate of life,
my wounded pride perhaps may increafe the natural
fretfulnefs of my temper, till I become a rude, mo-
rofe companion, beyond your patience to endure.
Perhaps the recolleƈtion of a deed my confcience cannot juftify, may haunt me in fuch gloomy and unfo-
cial fits, that I fhall hate the tendernefs that would
relieve me, break from your arms, and quarrel with
your fondnefs !

Julia. If your thoughts fhould affume fo unhappy
a bent, you will the more want fome mild and affectionate fpirit to watch over and confole you :—One
who, by bearing *your* infirmities with gentlenefs and
refignation, may teach you *fo* to bear the evils of your
fortune.

Faulk. Julia, I have proved you to the quick !
and with this ufelefs device I throw away all my
doubts. How fhall I plead to be forgiven this laft
unworthy effeƈt of my reftlefs, unfatisfied difpofition ?

Julia. Has no fuch difafter happened as you related ?

Faulk. I am afhamed to own that it was all pretended; yet in pity, Julia, do not kill me with re-
fenting a fault which never can be repeated : But
fealing, this once, my pardon, let me to-morrow, in
the face of Heaven, receive my future guide and mo-
nitrefs, and expiate my paft folly, by years of tender
adoration.

Faulk. Hold, Faulkland !—that you are free from

a crime, which I befoie fear'd to name, Heaven knows how fincerely I rejoice!—Thefe are tears of thankfulnefs for that! But that your cruel doubts fhould have urged you to an impofition that has wrung my heart, gives me now a pang, more keen, than I can exprefs!

Faulk. By Heav'ns! Julia———

Julia. Yet hear me.———My Father lov'd you, Faulkland! and you preferv'd the life that tender parent gave me; in his prefence I pledged my hand —joyfully pledged it—where before I had given my heart. When, foon after, I loft that parent, it feem'd to me that Providence had, in Faulkland, fhewn me whither to transfer, without a paufe, my grateful duty, as well as my affeftion: Hence I have been content to bear from you, what pride and deli-cacy would have forbid me from another.—I will not upbraid you, by repeating how you have trifled with my fincerity.———

Faulk. I confefs it all! yet hear———

Julia. After fuch a year of trial—I might have flattered myfelf that I fhould not have been infult-ed with a new probation of my fincerity, as cruel as unneceffary! I now fee it is not in your nature to be content, or confident in love. With this conviftion—I never will be yours. While I had hopes that my perfevering attention, and unreproach-ing kindnefs might in time reform your temper, I fhould have been happy to have gain'd a dearer influ-ence over you; but I will not furnifh you with a licenfed power to keep alive an incorrigible fault, at the expence of one who never would contend with you.

Faulk. Nay, but Julia, by my foul and honour, if after this———— .

Julia. But one word more.—As my faith has once been given to you, 1 never will barter it with another, —I shall pray for your happiness with the truest sincerity ; and the dearest blessing I can ask of Heaven to send you, will be to charm you from that unhappy temper, which alone has prevented the performance of our solemn engagement.—All I request of *you* is, that you will yourself reflect upon this infirmity, and when you number up the many true delights it has deprived you of—let it not be your *least* regret, that it lost you the love of one—who would have follow'd you in beggary through the world ! [*Exit.*

Faulk. She's gone !—for ever!—There was an aweful resolution in her manner, that riveted me to my place————O Fool !—Dolt !—Barbarian !—Curst as I am, with more imperfections than my fellow-wretches, kind Fortune sent a Heaven-gifted cherub to my aid, and, like a ruffian, I have driven her from my side !—I must now haste to my appointment.—Well, my mind is tuned for such a scene.— I shall wish only to become a principal in it, and reverse the tale my cursed folly put me upon forging here.————O Love !—Tormentor !—Fiend !—whose influence, like the Moon's, acting on men of dull souls, makes idiots of them, but meeting subtler spirits, betrays their course, and urges sensibility to madness !   [*Exit.*

Enter MAID *and* LYDIA.

Maid. My Miſtreſs, Ma'am, I know, was here,
juſt now—perhaps ſhe is only in the next room.
                                    [*Exit* Maid.

Lydia. Heigh ho !—Though he has uſed me ſo,
this fellow runs ſtrangely in my head. ˉ I believe one
lecture from my grave Couſin will make me recall
him.

Enter JULIA.

Lydia. O Julia, I am come to you with ſuch an
appetite for conſolation.—Lud ! Child, what's the
matter with you ?—You have been crying !—I'll be
hanged, if that Faulkland has not been tormenting
you !

Julia. You miſtake the cauſe of my uneaſineſs !—
Something has flurried me a little.—Nothing that
you can gueſs at.—I would not accuſe Faulkland to a
Siſter !   [*Aſide.*

Lydia. Ah ! whatever vexations you may have, I
can aſſure you mine ſurpaſs them.—You know who
Beverley proves to be ?

Julia. I will now own to you, Lydia, that Mr.
Faulkland had before informed me of the whole affair. Had young Abſolute been the perſon you took
him for, I ſhould not have accepted your confidence
on the ſubject, without a ſerious endeavour to coun-
teract your caprice.

Lydia. So then I ſee I have been deceived by

every - one!—but I don't care—I'll never have him.

Julia. Nay, Lydia———

Lydia. Why, is it not provoking? when I thought we were coming to the prettieft diftrefs imaginable, to find myfelf made a mere Smithfield bargain of at laft———There had I projeĉted one of the moft fentimental elopements!—fo becoming a difguife!—fo amiable a ladder of Ropes!—Confcious Moon—four horfes—Scotch parfon—with·fuch furprife to Mrs. Malaprop—and fuch paragraphs in the Newfpapers!———O, I fhall die with difappointment. ·

Julia. I don't wonder at it! ·

Lydia. Now—fad reverfe!—what have I to expeĉt, but, after a deal of flimfy preparations with a bifhop's licence, and my Aunt's bleffing, to go fimpering up to the Altar; or perhaps be cried three times in a country-church, and have an unmannerly fat clerk afk the confent of every butcher in the parifh to join John Abfolute and Lydia Languifh; Spinfter! O, that I fhould live to hear myfelf called · Spinfter!

Julia. Melancholy, indeed!

Lydia. How mortifying, to remember the dear delicious fhifts I ufed to be put to, to gain half a mi.- · nute's converfation with this fellow!———How often have I ftole forth, in the coldeft night in January, and found him in the garden, ftuck like a dripping ftatue!—There would he kneel to me in the fnow, and fneeze and cough fo pathetically! he fhivering with cold, and I with apprehenfion! and while the freezing blaft numb'd our joints, how warmly would

Julia. But who is there beſide Captain Abſolute, friend?

David. My poor Maſter—under favour for mentioning him fiıſt.—You know me, my Lady—I am David—and my Maſter of courſe is, or *was* Squire Acres.—Then comes Squire Faulkland.

Julia. Do, Ma'am, let us inſtantly endeavour to prevent miſchief.

Mrs. Mal. O fie—it would be very enelegant in us:—we ſhould only participate things.

David. Ah! do Mrs. 'Aunt, ſave a few lives— they are deſperately given, believe me.—Above all, there is that blood-thirſty Philiſtine, Sir Lucius O'Trigger.

Mrs. Mal. Sir Lucius O'Trigger!—O mercy! have they drawn poor little dear Sir-Lucius into the ſcrape?—Why, how you ſtand, girl! you have no more feeling than one of the Derbyſhire Putrefactions!

Lydia. What are we to do, Madam?

Mrs. Mal. Why, fly with the utmoſt felicity to be ſure, to prevent miſchief:—here, friend—you can ſhew us the place?

Fag. If you pleaſe, Ma'am, I will conduct you.. —David, do you look for Sir Anthony.

[*Exit* David.

Mrs. Mal. Come girls!—this gentleman will exhort us.—Come, Sir, you're our envoy—lead the way, and we'll precede.

Fag. Not a ſtep before the ladies for the world!

Mrs. Mal. You're ſure you know the ſpot.

Fag. I think I can find it, Ma'am; and one goes

thing is, we fhall hear the report of the piftols as we draw near, fo we can't well mifs them ; never fear, Ma'am, never fear.   ·   [*Exit, he talking.*

SCENE II.

· *South Parade.*

Enter ABSOLUTE, *putting his fword under his great coat.*

Abf. A fword feen in the. ftreets of Bath would raife as great an alarm as a mad-dog.—How provoking this is in Faulkland !—never punctual ! I fhall be obliged to go without him at laft.—O; the devil! here's Sir Anthony——how fhall I efcape him ?

[*Muffles up his face, and takes a circle to go off.*

Enter Sir ANTHONY.

Sir Anth. How one may be deceived at a little diftance ! only that I fee he don't know me, I could have fworn that was Jack !—Hey !—Gad's life ; it is.—Why Jack—what are you afraid of ?—hey ! fure I'm right.—Why, Jack—Jack Abfolute !

[*Goes up to him.*

Abf. Really, Sir, you have the advantage. of me :—I don't remember ever to have had the honour——my name is Saunderfon, at your fervice.

Sir Anth. Sir, I beg your pardon—I took you—hey!—why, z—ds! it is————Stay——

[*Looks up to his face.*

So, fo—your humble fervant, Mr. Saunderfon!—Why, you fcoundrel, what tricks are you after now?

Abf. O! a joke, Sir, a joke!—I came here on purpofe to look for you, Sir.

Sir Anth. You did! well, I am glad you were fo lucky:—but what are you muffled up fo for?—what's this for?—hey?

Abf. 'Tis cool, Sir, isn't it?—rather chilly fome-how:—but I fhall be late—I have a particular en-gagement.

Sir Anth. Stay.——Why, I thought you were looking for me?—Pray, Jack, where is't you are going.

Abf. Going, Sir!

Sir Anth. Aye—where are you going?

Abf. Where am I going?

Sir Anth. You unmannerly puppy!

Abf. I was going, Sir, to—to—to—to Lydia—Sir, to Lydia—to make matters up if I could;—and I was looking for you, Sir, to—to——

Sir Anth. To go with you, I fuppofe—Well, come along.

Abf. O! z—ds! no, Sir, not for the world!—I wifh'd to meet with you, Sir, to—to—to——You find it cool, I'm fure, Sir—you'd better not ftay out.

Sir Anth. Cool!—not at all—Well, Jack—and what will you fay to Lydia?

Abf. O, Sir, beg her pardon, humour her—pro-mife and vow :—but I detain you, Sir—confider the cold air on your gout.

Sir Anth. O, not at all!—not at all!—I'm in no hurry.—Ah! Jack, you youngfters when once you are wounded here.

[*Putting his hand to* Abfolute's *breaft.*
Hey! what the deuce have you got here?

Abf. Nothing, Sir—nothing.

Sir Anth. What's this?—here's fomething d—n'd hard.

Abf. O, trinkets, Sir! trinkets—a bauble for Lydia!

Sir Anth. Nay, let me fee your tafte.

[*Pulls his coat open, the fword falls.*
Trinkets!—a bauble for Lydia!—z—ds! firrah, you are not going to cut her throat, are you?

Abf. Ha! ha! ha!—I thought it would divert you, Sir, though I didn't mean to tell you till after-wards.

Sir Anth. You didn't?—Yes, this is a very divert-ing trinket, truly.

Abf. Sir, I'll explain to you.—You know, Sir, Lydia is romantic—dev'lifh romantic, and very ab-furd of courfe :——Now, Sir, I intend, if fhe re-fufes to forgive me—to unfheath this fword—and fwear—I'll fall upon its point, and expire at her feet!

Sir Anth. Fall upon a fiddle-ftick's end!—why, I fuppofe it is the very thing that would pleafe her—Get along, you Fool.—

Abf. Well, Sir, you fhall hear of my fuccefs—

Acres. No, Sir Lucius—but I fhould think forty or eight-and-thirty yards———

Sir Luc. Pho! pho! nonfenfe! three or four feet between the mouths of your piftols is as good as a mile.

Acres. Odds bullets, no!—by my valour! there is no merit in killing him fo near :—do, my dear Sir Lucius, let me bring him down at a long fhot :—a long fhot, Sir Lucius, if you love me!

Sir Luc. Well—the gentleman's friend and I muft fettle that.—But tell me now, Mr. Acres, in cafe of an accident, is there any little will or commiffion I could execute for you!

Acres. I am much obliged to you, Sir Lucius—but I don't underftand———

Sir Luc. Why, you may think there's no being fhot at without a little rifk—and if an unlucky bullet fhould carry a Quietus with it—I fay it will be no time then to be bothering you about family matters.

Acres. A Quietus!

Sir Luc. For inftance now—if that fhould be the cafe—would you chufe to be pickled and fent home? —or would it be the fame to you to lie here in the Abbey;—I'm told there is very fnug lying in the Abbey.

Acres. Pickled!—Snug lying in the Abbey!— Odds tremors! Sir Lucius, don't talk fo!

Sir Luc. I fuppofe, Mr. Acres, you never were engaged in an affair of this kind before?

Acres. No, Sir Lucius, never before.

Sir Luc. Ah! that's a pity!—there's nothing like

being ufed to a thing.—Pray now, how would you
receive the gentleman's fhot?

Acres. Odds files!—I've praĉtifed that—there
Sir Lucius—there   [*Puts himfelf in an attitude.*
—a fide-front, hey?—Odd! I'll make myfelf fmall
enough :—I'll ftand edge-ways.

Sir Luc. Now—you're quite out—for if you ftand
fo when I take my aim—   [*Levelling at him.*

Acres. Z—ds! Sir Lucius—are you fure it is not
cock'd?

Sir Luc. Never fear.

Acres. But—but—you don't know—it may go off
of its own head!

Sir Luc. Pho! be eafy—Well, now if I hit you
in the body, my bullet has a double chance—for if
it-miffes a vital part on your right fide—'twill be very
hard if it don't fucceed on the left!

Acres. A vital part!

Sir Luc. But, there—fix yourfelf fo—
                        [*Placing him.*
let him fee the broad-fide of your full front—there—
now a ball or two may pafs clean thro' your body,
and never do any harm at all. ·

Acres. Clean thro' me!—a ball or two clean thro'
me!

Sir Luc. Aye—may they—and it is much the gen-
teeleft attitude into the bargain.

Acres. Look'ee! Sir Lucius—I'd juft as leive be
fhot in an aukward pofture as a genteel one—fo, by
my valour! I will ftand edge-ways.

Sir Luc. (*Looking at his watch.*) Sure they don't

mean to difappoint us—Hah !—no. faith—I think I fee them coming.

Acres. Hey !—what !—coming !

Sir Luc. Aye—Who are thofe yonder getting over the ftile ?

Acres. There are two of them, indeed !—well— let them come—hey, Sir Lucius !—we—we—we— we—won't run.—

Sir Luc. Run !.

Acres. No—I fay—we *won't* run, by my va- lour !

Sir Luc. What the devil's the matter with you?

Acres. Nothing—nothing—my dear friend—my dear Sir Lucius—but I-I-I don't feel quite fo bold, fomehow—as I did.

Sir Luc. O fie !—confider your honour.

Acres. Aye—true—my honour—Do, Sir Lucius, . edge in a word or two every now and then about my honour.

Sir Luc. Well, here they're coming.   [*Looking.* .

Acres. Sir Lucius—if I wa'n't with you, I fhould almoft think I was afraid—if my valour fhould leave me !—Valour will come and go.

Sir Luc. Then pray keep it faft, while you have it.

Acres. Sir Lucius—I doubt it is going—yes— my valour is certainly going !—it is fneaking off !— I feel it oozing out as it were at the palms of my hands !

Sir Luc. Your honour—your honour.—Here they are.

Acres. O mercy!—now—that I was fafe at *Clod-Hall!*—or could be fhot before I was aware!

Enter FAULKLAND *and* ABSOLUTE.

Sir Luc. Gentlemen, your moft obedient—hah!—what, Captain Abfolute!—So, I fuppofe, Sir, you are come here, juft like myfelf—to do a kind office, firft for your friend—then to proceed to bufinefs on your own account.

Acres. What, Jack!—my dear Jack!—my dear fiiend!

Abf. Hark'ee, Bob, *Beverley's* at hand.

Sir Luc. Well, Mr. Acres—I don't blame your faluting the gentleman civilly.—So, Mr. Beverley, *(to* Faulkland) if you'll choofe your weapons, the Captain and I will meafure the ground.

Faulk. My Weapons, Sir.

Acres. Odds life! Sir Lucius, I'm not going to fight Mr. Faulkland; thefe are my particular friends.

Sir Luc. What, Sir, did not you come here to fight Mr. Acres?

Faulk. Not I, upon my word, Sir.

Sir Luc. Well, now, that's mighty provoking! But I hope, Mr. Faulkland, as there are three of us come on purpofe for the game—you won't be fo cantanckerous as to fpoil the party by fitting out.

Abf. O pray, Faulkland, fight to oblige Sir Lucius.

Faulk, Nay, if Mr. Acres is fo bent on the matter.

Acres. No, no, Mr. Faulkland—I'll bear my dif-pointment like a Chriftian—Look'ee, Sir Lucius, there's no occafion at all for me to fight ; and if it is the fame to you, I'd as lieve let it alone.

Sir Luc. Obferve me, Mr. Acres—I muft not be trifled with. You have certainly challenged fome-body—and you came here to fight him—Now, if that gentleman is willing to reprefent him—I can't fee, for my foul, why it isn't juft the fame thing.

Acres. Why no—Sir Lucius—I tell you, 'tis one Beverley I've challenged—a fellow, you fee, that dare not fhew his face ! If *he* were here, I'd make him give up his pretenfions directly !—

Abf. Hold, Bob—let me fet you right—there is no fuch man as *Beverley* in the cafe.—The per-fon who affumed that name is before you ; and as his pretenfions are the fame in both characters, he is ready to fupport them in whatever way you pleafe.

Sir Luc. Well, this is lucky—Now you have an opportunity—

Acres. What, quarrel with my dear friend Jack Abfolute—not if he were fifty Beverleys ! Z—ds ! Sir Lucius, you would not have me be fo unnatu-ral.

Sir Luc. Upon my confcience, Mr. Acres, your valour has *oozed* away with a vengeance !

Acres. Not in the leaft ! Odds Backs and Abet-tors ! I'll be your fecond with all my heart—and if you fhould get a *Quietus,* you may command me entirely. I'll get you *fnug lying* in the *Abbey here;*

or *pickle* you, and fend you over to Blunderbufs-
hall, or any thing of the kind with the greateft pleafure.

Sir Luc. Pho! pho! you are little better than a
coward.

Acres. Mind, gentlemen, he calls me a *Coward;*
·Coward was the word, by my valour !

Sir Luc. Well, Sir?

Acres. Look'ee, Sir Lucius, 'tisn't that I mind
the word Coward—*Coward* may be faid in joke—
But if you had call'd me a *Poltroon*, Odds Daggers
_and Balls——

Sir Luc. Well, Sir?

Acres. ——I fhould have thought you a very ill-
bred man.

Sir Luc. Pho! you are beneath my Notice.

Abf. Nay, Sir Lucius, you can't have a better
fecond than my friend, Acres——He is a moft
determined dog—call'd in the country, *Fighting Bob.*
——He generally *kills a man a week ;* don't you,
Bob ?

Acres. Aye—at home !—

Sir Luc. Well then, Captain, 'tis we muft begin
·—fo come out, my little counfellor,

[*Draws his fword.*

and afk the gentleman, whether he will refign the
lady, without forcing you to proceed againft him ?

Abf. Come on then, Sir; *(draws)* fince you
won't let it be an amicable fuit, here's my reply.

Enter Sir Anthony, David, *and the* Women.

David. Knock 'em all down, fweet Sir Anthony, knock down my Mafter in particular—and bind his hands over to their good behaviour !

Sir Anth. Put up, Jack, put up, or I fhall be in a phrenzy—how came you in a duel, Sir ?

Abf. Faith, Sir, that gentleman can tell you better than I; 'twas he call'd on me, and you know, Sir, I ferve his Majefty.

Sir Anth. Here's a pretty fellow! I catch him going to cut a man's throat, and he tells me, he ferves his Majefty !——Zounds ! firrah, then how durft you draw the King's fword againft one of his fubjects ?

Abf. Sir, I tell you ! That gentleman call'd me out, without explaining his reafons.

Sir Anth. Gad ! Sir, how come you to call my fon out, without explaining your reafons ?

Sir Luc. You fon, Sir, infulted me in a manner which my honour could not brook.

Sir Anth. Zounds ! Jack, how durft you infult the gentleman in a manner which his honour could not brook ?

Mrs. Mal. Come, come, let's have no Honour before ladies—Captain Abfolute, come here—How could you intimidate us fo ?—Here's Lydia has been terrified to death for you.

Abf. For fear I fhould be kill'd, or efcape, Ma'am ?

Mrs. Mal. Nay, no delusions to the past—Lydia is convinc'd ; speak child.

Sir Luc. With your leave, Ma'am, I must put in a word here—I believe I could interpret the young Lady's silence—Now mark—

Lydia. What is it you mean, Sir ?

Sir Luc. Come, come, Delia, we must be serious now—this is no time for trifling.

Lydia. 'Tis true, Sir ; and your reproof bids me offer this gentleman my hand, and solicit the return of his affections.

Abf. O ! my little angel, say you so ?—Sir Lucius—I perceive there must be some mistake here —with regard to the affront which you affirm I have given you. I can only say, that it could not have been intentional.——And as you must be convinced, that I should not fear to support a real injury—you shall now see that I am not ashamed to atone for an inadvertency—I ask your pardon.— But for this lady, while honour'd with her approbation, I will support my claim against any man whatever.

Sir Anth. Well said, Jack, and I'll stand by you, my Boy.

Acres. Mind, I give up all my claim—I make no pretensions to any thing in the world—and if I can't get a wife, without fighting for her, by my Valour ! I'll live a batchelor.

Sir Luc. Captain, give me your hand—an ffront handsomely acknowledged becomes an ob-

O

ligation—and as for the Lady—if she chooses to
deny her own hand-writing here—

[*Takes out letters.*

Mrs. Mal. O, he will diſſolve my myſtery !—Sir
Lucius, perhaps there's ſome miſtake—perhaps, I
can illuminate—

Sir Luc. Pray, old gentlewoman, don't interfere,
where you have no buſineſs.—Miſs Languiſh, are
you my Delia, or not ?

Lydia. Indeed, Sir Lucius, I am not.

[Lydia *and* Abſolute *walk aſide.*

Mrs. Mal. Sir Lucius O'Trigger—ungrateful as
you are—I own the ſoft impeachment—pardon my
bluſhes, I am Delia.

Sir Luc. You Delia—pho ! pho ! be eaſy.

Mrs. Mal. Why, thou barbarous Vandyke—
thoſe letters are mine—When you are more ſenſible
of my benignity—perhaps I may be brought to encourage your addreſſes.

Sir Luc. Mrs. Malaprop, I am extremely ſenſible
of your condeſcenſion ; and whether you or Lucy
have put this trick upon me, 1 am equally beholden to you.—And to ſhew you I'm not ungrateful, Captain Abſolute ! ſince you have taken
that lady from me, I'll give you my Delia into the
bargain.

Abſ. 1 am much obliged to you, Sir Lucius ;
but here's my friend, fighting Bob, unprovided
for.

Sir Luc. Hah ! little Valour—here, will you
make your fortune ?

Acres. Odds Wrinkles ! No.—But give me your

hand, Sir Lucius, forget and forgive; but if ever I give you a chance of *pickling* me again, fay Bob Acres is a Dunce, that's all.

Sir Anth. Come, Mrs. Malaprop, don't be caft down—you are in your bloom yet.

Mrs. Mal. O Sir Anthony!—men are all barbarians—   [*All retire but* Julia *and* Faulkland.

Julia. He feems dejected and unhappy—not fullen—there was fome foundation, however, for the tale he told me——O woman! how true fhould be your judgment, when your refolution is fo weak!

Faulk. Julia!—how can I fue for what I fo little deferve? I dare not prefume—yet Hope is the Child of Penitence.

Julia. Oh! Faulkland, you have not been more faulty in your unkind treatment of me, than I am now in wanting inclination to refent it. As my heart honeftly bids me place my weaknefs to the account of love, I fhould be ungenerous not to admit the fame plea for your's.

Faulk. Now I fhall be bleft indeed!——

[Sir Anthony *comes forward.*

Sir Anth. What's going on here?—So you have been quarrelling too, I warrant.——Come, Julia, I never interfered before; but let me have a hand in the matter at laft.—All the faults I have ever feen in my friend Faulkland, feemed to proceed from what he calls the *delicacy* and *warmth* of his affection for you——There, marry him directly. Julia, you'll find he'll mend furprifingly!

[*The reft come forward.*

A

T R I P

TO

S C A R B O R O U G H.

A

COMEDY.

BY R. B. SHERIDAN, ESQ.

ADAPTED FOR

THEATRICAL REPRESENTATION,

AS PERFORMED AT THE

THEATRE-ROYAL,

DRURY-LANE.

ALTERED FROM

Vanbrugh's Relapfe ; or, Virtue in Danger.

REGULATED FROM THE PROMPT-BOOK.

By Permiffion of the Managers.

DUBLIN ;

PRINTED BY WILLIAM PORTER,

FOR WILLIAM JONES, NO. 86, DAME-STREET.

M DCC XCIII.

A
T R I P
TO
S C A R B O R O U G H.
A
COMEDY.

BY R. B. SHERIDAN, ESQ.

ADAPTED FOR

THEATRICAL REPRESENTATION,

AS PERFORMED AT THE

THEATRE-ROYAL,

DRURY-LANE.

ALTERED FROM

Vanbrugh's Relapse ; or, Virtue in Danger.

REGULATED FROM THE PROMPT-BOOK.

By Permiffion of the Managers.

" The Lines diftinguifhed by inverted Commas, are omitted in the Reprefentation.'

DUBLIN ;

PRINTED BY WILLIAM PORTER,

FOR WILLIAM JONES, NO. 86, DAME-STREET.

M DCC XCIII.

PROLOGUE.

WRITTEN BY DAVID GARRICK, ESQ.

SPOKEN BY MR. KING.

WHAT various transformations we remark,
From Eaſt Whitechapel to the Weſt Hyde-park !
Men, women, children, houſes, ſigns, and faſhions,
State, ſtage, trade, taſte, the humours and the paſſions ;
Th' Exchange, 'Change-alley, whereſoe'er your ranging,
Court, city, country, all are chang'd, or changing ;
The ſtreets ſometime ago, were pav'd with ſtones,
Which, aided by a hackney coach, half broke your bones,
The pureſt lovers then indulg'd no bliſs ;
They run great hazard if they ſtole a kiſs—
One chaſte falute—the Damſel cry'd, O fye !
As they approach'd, ſlap went the coach away,
—Poor Sylvia got a bump, and Damon a black eye.
But now weak nerves in hackney coaches roam,
And the cramm'd glutton ſnores unjolted home :
Of former times that poliſh'd thing a Beau,
Is metamorphos'd now, from top to toe ;
Then the full flaxen wig, ſpread o'er the ſhoulders,
Conceal'd the ſhallow head from the beholders !
But now the whole's revers'd—each fop appears,
Cropp'd, and trimm'd up—expoſing head and ears ;
The buckle then it's modeſt limits knew—
Now, like the ocean, dreadful to the view,
Hath broke it's bounds, and ſwallows up the ſhoe ;

O 5

DRAMATIS PERSONÆ.

Men.

Lord FOPPINGTON,	Mr. Dodd.
YOUNG FASHION,	Mr. Palmer.
LOVELESS,	Mr. Smith.
Colonel TOWNLEY,	Mr. Brereton.
Sir TUNBELLY CLUMSEY,	Mr. Moody.
PROBE,	Mr. Parfons.
LORY,	Mr. Baddeley.
LA VAROLE,	Mr. Burton.
SHOEMAKER,	Mr. Carpenter.
TAYLOR,	Mr. Baker.
HOSIER,	Mr. Norris.
JEWELLER,	Mr. La Mafh.
SERVANTS, &c.	

Women.

BERINTHIA,	Mifs Farren.
AMANDA,	Mrs. Robinfon.
Mrs. COUPLER,	Mrs. Booth.
NURSE,	Mrs. Bradfhaw.
Mifs HOYDEN,	Mrs. Abington.

A
TRIP TO SCARBOROUGH.

ACT I. SCENE I.

The Hall of an Inn.

Enter YOUNG FASHION *and* LORY—Poftillion *following with a Portmanteau.*

Y. FASHION.

LORY, pay the poft-boy, and take the portmanteau.

Lory. Faith, Sir, we had better let the poft-boy
take the portmanteau and pay himfelf.

Y. Faf. Why, fure there's fomething left in it.

Lory. Not a rag, upon my honour, Sir—we eat
the laft of your wardrobe at Newmalton—and if we
had had twenty miles farther to go, our next meal
muft have been off the cloak-bag.

Y. Faf. Why, 'fdeath it appears full.

Lory. Yes, Sir—I made bold to ftuff it with hay,
to fave appearances, and look like baggage.

Enter Colonel TOWNLY.

My dear Colonel, I am rejoiced to meet you here.

Townly. Dear Tom, this is an unexpected pleasure—what, are you come to Scarbro' to be present
at your brother's wedding?

Lory. Ah, Sir, if it had been his funeral, we
should have come with pleasure.

Townly. What, honest Lory, are you with your
master still?

Lory. Yes, Sir, I have been starving with him ever
since I saw your honour last.

T. Faf. Why, Lory is an attach'd rogue; there's
no getting rid of him.

Lory. True, Sir, as my master says, there's no
seducing me from his service, 'till he's able to pay
me my wages.   [*Afide.*

T. Faf. Go, go, Sir—and take care of the baggage.

Lory. Yes, Sir—the baggage!—O Lord!—I
suppose,. Sir, I must charge the landlord to be very
particular where he stows this.

T. Faf. Get along, you rascal.

[*Exit* Lory, *with the Portmanteau.*

But, Colonel, are you acquainted with my proposed
sister-in-law?

Townly. Only by character—her father, Sir Tunbelly Clumsey, lives within a quarter of a mile of this
place, in a lonely old house, which nobody comes
near. She never goes abroad, nor sees company at

home; to prevent all misfortunes, she has her breeding within doors; the parson of the parish teaches her to play upon the dulcimer; the clerk to sing, her nurse to dress, and her father to dance:—in short, nobody has free admission there but our old acquaintance, Mother Coupler, who has procured your brother this match, and is, I believe, a distant relation of Sir Tunbelly's.

Y. Fash. But is her fortune so considerable?

Townly. Three thousand a year, and a good sum of money independent of her father beside.

Y. Fash. 'Sdeath! that my old acquaintance, dame Couplet, could not have thought of me as well as my brother for such a prize.

Townly. Egad I wouldn't swear that you are too late—his Lordship, I know, hasn't yet seen the lady, and, I believe, has quarrelled with his patroness.

Y. Fash. My dear Colonel, what an idea have you started?

Townly. Pursue it if you can, and I promise you, you shall have my assistance; for besides my natural contempt for his Lordship, I have at present the enmity of a rival towards him.

Y. Fash. What, has he been addressing your old flame, the sprightly Widow Berinthia?

Townly. Faith, Tom, I am at present most whimsically circumstanced—I came here near a month ago to meet the lady you mention; but she failing in her promise, I, partly from pique, and partly from idleness, have been diverting my chagrin by offering up

chaſte incenſe to the beauties of Amanda, our friend
Lovelefs's wife.

T. Faſ. I have never ſeen her, but have heard her
ſpoken of as a youthful wonder of beauty and prudence.

Townly. She is ſo indeed ; and Lovelefs being too
carelefs and infenſible of the treaſure he poſſeſſes—my
lodging in the ſame houſe has given me a thouſand
opportunities of making my aſſiduities acceptable ;
ſo that in lefs than a fortnight, I began to bear
my diſappointment from the widow, with the moſt
Chriſtian reſignation.

T. Faſ. And Berinthia has never appear'd ?

Townly. O there's the perplexity ; for juſt as I
began not to care whether I ever ſaw her again or
not, laſt night ſhe arrived.

T. Faſ. And inſtantly reaſſumed her empire.

Townly. No faith—we met—but the lady not con-
deſcending to give me any ſerious reaſons for having
fool'd me for a month, I left her in a huff.

T. Faſ. Well, well, I'll anſwer for't, ſhe'll ſoon
reſume her power, eſpecially as friendſhip will prevent your purſuing the other too far—but my coxcomb of a brother, is an admirer of Amanda's too, is
he ?

Townly. Yes ; and I believe is moſt heartily de-
ſpiſed by her—but come with me, and you ſhall ſee
her and your old friend Lovelefs.

T. Faſ. I muſt pay my reſpects to his Lordſhip
—perhaps you can direct me to his lodgings.

Townly. Come with me, I ſhall paſs by it.

Y. Faf. I wifh you could pay the vifit for me; or could tell me what I fhould fay to him.

Townly. Say nothing to him—apply yourfelf to his bag, his fword, his feather, his fnuff-box; and when you are well with them, defire him to lend you a thoufand pounds, and I'll engage you prof-per.

Y. Faf. 'Sdeath and furies! why was that cox-comb thruft into the world before me? O Fortune! Fortune! thou art a jilt, by Gad.   [*Exit.*

SCENE II.

A Dreffing-Room.

Lord FOPPINGTON, *in his Night Gown, and* LA VAROLE.

L. Fop. Well, 'tis an unfpeakable pleafure to be a man of quality—ftrike me dumb!—even the boors of this Northern fpa have learn'd the refpeſt due to a title—La Varole!

La Var. Mi Lor——

L. Fop. You han't yet been at Muddy-Moat-Hall to announce my arrival, have you?

La Var. Not yet, mi Lor.

L. Fop. Then you need not go till Saturday.
    [*Exit* La Varole.

as l am in no particular hafte to view my intended Spofa—I fhall facrifice a day or two more to the purfuit of my friend Lovelefs's wife—Amanda is a charming creature—ftrike me ugly ; and if I have any difcernment in the world, fhe thinks no lefs of my Lord Foppington.

Enter LA VAROLE.

La Var. Mi Lor, de fhoemaker, de taylor, de hofier, de fempftrefs, de peru, be all ready, if your lordfhip pleafe to drefs.

L. Fop. 'Tis well, admit them.

L. Var. Hey, Meffieurs, entrez.

Enter TAYLOR, &c. &c.

L. Fop. So, gentlemen, I hope you have all taken pains to fhew yourfelves mafters in your profeffions.

Tayl. 1 think I may prefume to fay, Sir——

La Var. My Lor, you clown you !

Tayl. My Lord, I afk your Lordfhip's pardon, my Lord. I hope, my Lord, your Lordfhip will pleafe to own, 1 have brought your Lordfhip as accomplifhed a fuit of clothes as ever Peer of England wore, my Lord—will your Lordfhip pleafe to try 'em now ? .

L. Fop. Ay; but let my people difpofe the glaffes fo, that I may fee myfelf before and behind ; for I love to fee myfelf all round.

[*Whilſt he puts on his clothes,* enter YOUNG FASHION
and LORY.]

Y. Faſ. Hey-day! What the devil have we here?
—Sure my gentleman's grown a favourite at court,
he has got ſo many people at his levee.

Lory. Sir, theſe people come in order to make
him a favourite at court—they are to eſtabliſh him
with the ladies.

Y. Faſ. Good Heav'n! to what an ebb of taſte
are women fallen, that it ſhould be in the power
of a laced coat to recommend a gallant to them!

Lory. Sir, Taylors and Hair-dreſſers are now become the bawds of the nation—'tis they that debauch
all the women.

Y. Faſ. Thou ſay'ſt true; for there's that fop now
has not, by nature, wherewithal to move a cook
maid: and by the time theſe fellows have done with
him, egad he ſhall melt down a Counteſs—but now
for my reception.

·L. Fop. Death and eternal tortures! Sir—I ſay
the coat is too wide here by a foot.

Tayl. My Lord, if it had been tighter, 'twould
neither have hook'd nor button'd.

L. Fop. Rat the hooks and buttons, Sir, can any
thing be worſe than this?—As Gad ſhall jedge me!
it hangs on my ſhoulders like a chairman's ſur-
tout.

Tayl. 'Tis not for me to diſpute your Lordſhip's
fancy.

Lory. There, Sir, obſerve what reſpeâ does.

Y. Faf. Refpect!—D—n him for a coxcomb—but let's accoft him.—Brother, I'm your humble fervant.

L. Fop. O Lard, Tam, I did not expect you in England—Brother, I'm glad to fee you—but what has brought you to Scarbro', Tam?—Look you, Sir, *(To the* Taylor) I fhall never be reconciled to this naufeous wrapping gown; therefore, pray get me another fuit with all poffible expedition; for this is my eternal averfion—Well, but Tam, you don't tell me what has driven you to Scarbro'?—Mrs. Callicoe, are not you of my mind?

Sempf. Directly, my Lord.—I hope your Lordfhip is pleafed with your ruffles?

L. Fop. In love with them, ftab my vitals!—Bring my bill, you fhall be paid to-morrow.

Sempf. I humbly thank your Lordfhip.

[*Exit* Sempftrefs.

L. Fop. Heark thee, fhoemaker, thefe fhoes a'nt ugly, but they don't fit me.

Shoemaker. My Lord, I think they fit you very well.

L. Fop. They hurt me juft below the inftep.

Shoemaker. *(Feeling his foot.)* No, my Lord, they don't hurt you there.

L. Fop. I tell thee they pinch me execrably.

Shoemaker. Why then, my Lord, if thofe fhoes pinch you, I'll be d—n'd.

L. Fop. Why, wilt thou undertake to perfuade me I cannot feel?

Shoemaker. Your Lordfhip may pleafe to feel what

you think fit, but that fhoe does not hurt you—I think I underftand my trade.

L. Fop. Now, by all that's good and powerful, thou art an incomprehenfible coxcomb—but thou makeft good fhoes, and fo I'll bear with thee.

Shoemaker. My Lord, I have work'd for half the people of quality in this town thefe twenty years, and 'tis very hard I fhouldn't know when a fhoe hurts, and when it don't.

L. Fop. Well, prithee be gone about thy bufinefs.

[*Exit* Shoemaker.

Mr. Mendlegs, a word with you. The calves of thefe ftockings are thicken'd a little too much; they make my legs look like a porter's.

Mendlegs. My Lord, methinks they look mighty well.

L. Fop. Aye, but you are not fo good a judge of thofe things as I am—I have ftudy'd them all my life, —therefore pray let the next be the thicknefs of a crown-piece lefs.

Mendlegs. Indeed, my Lord, they are the fame kind I had the honour to furnifh your Lordfhip with in town.

L. Fop. Very poffibly, Mr. Mendlegs; but that was in the beginning of the winter; and you fhould always remember, Mr. Hofier, that if you make a Nobleman's fpring legs as robuft as his autumnal calves, you commit a monftrous impropriety, and make no allowance for the fatigues of the winter.

Jew. I hope, my Lord, thofe buckles have had the unfpeakable fatisfaction of being honoured with your Lordfhip's approbation?

L. Fop. Why, they are of a pretty fancy; but don't you think them rather of the fmalleft?

Jew. My Lord, they could not well be larger to keep on your Lordſhip's ſhoe.

L. Fop. My good Sir, you forget that theſe matters are not as they uſed to be: formerly, indeed, the buckle was a ſort of machine, intended to keep on the ſhoe; but the caſe is now quite reverſed, and the ſhoe is of no earthly uſe, but to keep on the buckle.—Now, give me my watches, and the buſineſs of the morning will be pretty well over.

Y. Faſh. Well, Lory, what doſt think on't?—a very friendly reception from a brother after three years abſence!

Lory. Why, Sir, 'tis your own fault—here you have ſtood ever ſince you came in, and have not commended any one thing that belongs to him.

Y. Faſh. Nor ever ſhall, while they belong to a coxcomb.—Now your people of buſineſs are gone, brother, I hope I may obtain a quarter of an hour's audience of you?

L. Fop. Faith, Tam, I muſt beg you'll excuſe me at this time, for I have an engagement which I would not break for the ſalvation of mankind. Hey! —there!—is my carriage at the door?—You'll excuſe me, brother.   [*Going.*

Y. Faſh. Shall you be back to dinner?

L. Fop. As Gad ſhall jedge me, I can't tell, for it is paſſible I may dine with ſome friends at Donner's.

Y. Faſh. Shall I meet you there? for I muſt needs talk with you.

L. Fop. That I'm afraid may'nt be quite fo pra-
per;—for thofe I commonly eat with are a people
of nice converfation; and you know, Tam, your
education has been a little at large—but there are
other ordinaries in town—very good beef ordinaries
—I fuppofe, Tam, you can eat beef?—However,
dear Tam, I'm glad to fee thee in England, ftap my
vitals ! •   [*Exit.*

Y. Faf. Hell and furies ! Is this to be borne ?

Lory. Faith, Sir, I could almoft have given him
a knock o' the pate myfelf.

Y. Faf. 'Tis enough ; I will now fhew you the ex-
cefs of my paffion, by being very calm.—Come, Lory, lay your loggerhead to mine, and, in cold blood,
let us contrive his deftruction.

Lory. Here comes a head, Sir, would contrive it •
better than us both, if fhe would but join in the con-
federacy.

Y. Faf. By this light, Madam Coupler; fhe
feems diffatisfied at fomething: let us obferve
her.

Enter COUPLER.

Coup. Soh ! I am likely to be well rewarded for
my fervices, truly ; my fufpicions, I find, were but
too juft —What ! refufe to advance me a paltry fum,
when I am upon the point of making him mafter of a
Galloon ! But let him look to the confequences, an
ungrateful, narrow-minded coxcomb.

Y. Faf. So he is, upon my foul, old lady: it
muft be my brother you fpeak of.

Coup. Hah !—ftripling, how came you here?
D

What, has fpent all, hey? And art thou come to
dun his Lordfhip for affiftance?

T. Faf. No;—I want fomebody's affiftance to
cut his Lordfhip's throat, without the rifque of being
hang'd for him.

Coup. Egad, firrah, I could help thee to do him
almoft as good a turn without the danger of being
burnt in the hand for't.

T. Faf. How—how, old Mifchief?

Coup. Why, you muft know I have done you the
kindnefs to make up a match for your brother.

T. Faf. I'm very much beholden to you, truly.

Coup. You may before the wedding-day yet: the
lady is a great heirefs, the match is concluded, the
writings are drawn, and his lordfhip is come hither
to put the finifhing hand to the bufinefs.

T. Faf. I underftand as much.

Coup. Now you muft know, ftripling, your brother's a knave.

T. Faf. Good.

Coup. He has given me a bond of a thoufand
pounds for helping him to his fortune, and has promifed me as much more in ready money upon the day
of the marriage; which, I underftand by a friend,
he never defigns to pay me; and his juft now refuf-
ing to pay me a part, is a proof of it. If, therefore, you will be a generous young rogue, and fecure me five thoufand pounds, I'll help you to the
lady.

T. Faf. And how the devil wilt thou do that?

Coup. Without the devil's aid, I warrant thee.
Thy brother's face not one of the family ever faw;

the whole bufinefs has been managed by me, and all·
the letters go thro' my hands.   Sir Tunbelly Clumfey, my relation, (for that's the old gentleman's
name) is apprized of his Lordfhip's being down here,
and expects him to-morrow to receive his daughter's
hand; but the Peer, I find, means to bait here a
few days longer, to recover the fatigue of his journey, I fuppofe.   Now you fhall go to Muddymoat-
hall in this place.   I'll give you a letter of introduc-
tion; and if you don't marry the girl before fun-fet,
you deferve to be hang'd before morning.

Y. Faf. Agreed, agreed; and for thy reward—

Coup. Well, well;—tho' I warrant thou haft not
a farthing of money in thy pocket now—no—one
may fee it in thy face.

Y. Faf. Not a foufe, by Jupiter.

Coup. Muft I advance then?—well, be at my
lodgings next door this evening, and I'll fee what
may be done—We'll fign and feal, and when I have
given thee fome farther inftructions, thou fhalt hoift
fail and be gone.   [*Exit* Coupler.

Y. Faf. So, Lory; Providence thou feeft at laft·
takes care of merit: we are in a fair way to be great
people.

Lory. Aye, Sir, if the devil don't ftep between
the cup and the lip, as he ufes to do.

Y. Faf. Why, faith, he has play'd me many a
damn'd trick to fpoil my fortune; and, egad, I'm·
almoft afraid he's at work about it again now! but if
I fhould tell thee how, thou'dft wonder at me.

Lory. Indeed, Sir, I fhould not.

Y. Faf. How doft know?

Lory. Becaufe, Sir, I have wondered at you fo often, I can wonder at you no more.

T. Faf. No! what wouldft thou fay if a qualm of confcience fhould fpoil my defign?

Lory. I would eat my words, and wonder more than ever!

T. Faf. Why faith, Lory, tho' I am a young Rake-hell, and have play'd many a rogueifh trick, this is fo full-grown a cheat, I find I muft take pains to come up to't——I have fcruples.

Lory. They are ftrong fymptoms of death. If you find they encreafe, Sir, pray make your will.

T. Faf. No, my confcience fhan't ftarve me neither, but thus far I'll liften to it. Before I execute this projeCt, I'll try my brother to the bottom. If he has yet fo much humanity about him as to affift me (tho' with a moderate aid) I'll drop my projeCt at his feet, and fhew him how I can do for him much more than what I'd afk he'd do for me. This one conclufive trial of him I refolve to make.—

Succeed or fail, ftill viCtory's my lot,
If I fubdue his heart, 'tis well—if not
I will fubdue my confcience to my plot.

Exeunt.

ACT II. SCENE I.

Enter Loveless *and* Amanda.

Loveless.

How do you like thefe lodgings, my dear? For my part, I am fo well pleas'd with them, I fhall hardly remove whilſt we ſtay here, if you are fatisfied.

Aman. I am fatisfied with every thing that pleafes you, elfe I had not come to Scarbro' at all.

Lovel. O! a little of the noife and folly of this place, will fweeten the pleafures of our retreat ; we fhall find the charms of our retirement doubled when we return to it.

Aman. That pleafing profpeƈt will be my chiefeſt entertainment, whilſt, much againſt my will, I engage in thofe empty pleafures which 'tis fo much the fafhion to be fond of.

Lovel. I own moſt of them are, indeed, but empty ; yet there are delights, of which a private life is deſtitute, which may divert an honeſt man, and be a harmlefs entertainment to a virtuous woman : good mufic is one ; and truly, (with fome fmall allowance) the plays, I think, may be efteemed another.

Aman. Plays, I muſt confefs, have fome fmall charms, and would have more, would they reſtrain that loofe encouragement to vice, which fhocks, if not the virtue of fome women, at leaſt the modeſty of all.

Lovel. But, 'till that reformation can be wholly made, 'twould furely be a pity to exclude the productions of fome of our beft writers, for want of a little wholefome pruning; which might be effected by any one who poffeffed modefty enough to believe that we fhould preferve all we can of our deceafed authors, at leaft 'till they are outdone by the living ones.

Aman. What do you think of that you faw laft night?

Lovel. To fay truth, I did not mind it much; my attention was for fome time taken off to admire the workmanfhip of Nature, in the face of a young lady who fat fome diftance from me, fhe was fo exquifitely handfome!

Aman. So exquifitely handfome!

Lovel. Why do you repeat my words, my dear?

Aman. Becaufe you feem'd to fpeak them with fuch pleafure, I thought I might oblige you with their echo.

Lovel. Then you are alarm'd, Amanda.

Aman. It is my duty to be fo when you are in danger.

Lovel. You are too quick in apprehending for me. I view'd her with a world of admiration, but not one glance of love.

Aman. Take heed of trufting to fuch nice diftinctions. But were your eyes the only things that were inquifitive? Had I been in your place, my tongue, I fancy, had been curious too. I fhould have afk'd her, where fhe liv'd (yet ftill without defign) who was fhe, pray?

Lovel. Indeed, I cannot tell.

Aman. You will not tell.

Lovel. By all that's facred then, I did not afk.

Aman. Nor do you know what company was with her?

Lovel. I do not; but why are you fo earneft?

Aman. I thought I had caufe.

Lovel. But you thought wrong, Amanda; for turn the cafe, and let it be your ftory: fhould you come home and tell me you had feen a handfome man, fhould I grow jealous becaufe you had eyes?

Aman. But fhould I tell you he was *exquifitely* fo, and that I had gazed on him with admiration, fhould you not think 'twere poffible I might go one ftep further, and enquire his name?

Lovel. (*Afide*) She has reafon on her fide, I have talk'd too much; but I muft turn off another way. (*To her.*) Will you then make no difference, Amanda, between the language of our fex and yours? There is a modefty reftrains your tongues, which makes you fpeak by halves when you commend, but roving flattery gives a loofe to ours, which makes us ftill fpeak double what we think. You fhould not, therefore, in fo ftrict a fenfe, take what I faid to her advantage.

Aman. Thofe flights of flattery, Sir, are to our faces only; when women are once out of hearing, you are as modeft in your commendations as we are; but I fhan't put you to the trouble of farther excufes;——if you pleafe, this bufinefs fhall reft here, only give me leave to wifh, both for your peace and

mine, that you may never meet this miracle of beauty more.

Lovel. I am content.

Enter SERVANT.

Serv. Madam, there is a lady at the door in a
chair, defires to know whether your Ladyfhip fees
company? her name is Berinthia.

Aman. O dear!—'tis a relation I have not feen
thefe five years, pray her to walk in. [*Exit* Servant.
Here's another beauty for you; fhe was, when I faw
her laft, reckoned extremely handfome.

Lovel. Don't be jealous now, for I fhall gaze upon
her too.

Enter BERINTHIA.

Lovel. (*Afide.*) Ha!—by Heav'ns, the very woman.

Ber. (*Saluting* Amanda.) Dear Amanda, I did
not expect to meet with you in Scarbro'.

Aman. Sweet coufin, I'm overjoyed to fee you.
(*To* Lovelefs) Mr. Lovelefs, here's a relation and a
friend of mine, I defire you'll be better acquainted
with.

Lovel. (*Saluting* Berinthia.) If my wife never defires a harder thing, Madam, her requeft will be
eafily granted.

Enter SERVANT.

Serv. Sir, my Lord Foppington prefents his
humble fervice to you, and defires to know how

you do.   He's at the next door, and if it be not inconvenient to you, he'll come and wait upon you.

Lovel. Give my compliments to his Lordſhip, and I ſhall be glad to ſee him.   [*Exit* Servant. If you are not acquainted with his Lordſhip, Madam, you will be entertained with his character.

Aman. Now it moves my pity more than my mirth, to ſee a man whom Nature has made no fool, be ſo very induſtrious to paſs for an aſs.

Lovel. No, there you are wrong, Amanda ; you ſhould never beſtow your pity upon thoſe who take pains for your contempt; pity thoſe whom Nature abuſes, never thoſe who abuſe Nature.

Enter Lord Foppington.

L. Fop. Dear Loveleſs, I am your moſt humble ſervant.

Lovel. My Lord, I'm your's.

L. Fop. Madam, your Ladyſhip's very humble ſlave.

Lovel. My Lord, this lady is a relation of my wife's.

L. Fop. (*Saluting her.*) The beautifulleſt race of people upon earth, rat me.   Dear Loveleſs, I am overjoyed that you think of continuing here.   I am, ſtap my vitals.   (*To* Amanda.)   For God's ſake, Madam, how has your Ladyſhip been able to ſubſiſt thus long, under the fatigue of a country life?

Aman. My life has been very far from that, my Lord, it has been a very quiet one.

P 5

L. Fop. Why that's the fatigue I fpeak of, Madam; for 'tis impoffible to be quiet, without thinking: now thinking is to me the greateft fatigue in the world.

Aman. Does not your Lordfhip love reading then?

L. Fop. Oh, paffionately, Madam, but I never think of what I read.

Ber. Why, can your Lordfhip read without thinking?

L. Fop. O Lard, can your Ladyfhip pray without devotion, Madam?

Aman. Well, I muft own, I think books the beft entertainment in the world.

L. Fop. I am fo much of your Ladyfhip's mind, Madam, that I have a private gallery in town, where I walk fometimes, which is furnifhed with nothing but books and looking-glaffes. Madam, I have gilded them, and ranged them fo prettily, before Gad, it is the moft entertaining thing in the world, to walk and look at them.

Aman. Nay, I love a neat library too, but 'tis, I think, the infide of a book fhould recommend it moft to us.

L. Fop. That, I muft confefs, I am not altogether fo fand of; far to my mind, the infide of a book is to entertain one's felf with the forced product of another man's brain. Now I think a man of quality and bieeding may be much more diverted with the natural fprauts of his own; but to fay the truth, Madam, let a man love reading never fo well, when ce he comes to know the tawn, he finds fo many

better ways of paffing away the four-and-twenty
hours, that it were ten thoufand pities he fhould confume his time in that.   Far example, Madam, now
my life, my life, Madam, is a perpetual ftream of
pleafure, that glides through with fuch a variety of
entertainments, I believe the wifeft of our anceftors
never had the leaft conception of any of 'em.   I rife,
Madam, when in town, about twelve o'clock.   I
don't rife fooner, becaufe it is the worft thing in the
world for the complexion; nat that I pretend to be a
beau, but a man muft endeavour to look decent, left
he makes fo odious a figure in the fide-bax, the ladies
fhould be compelled to turn their eyes upon the play;
fo at twelve o'clock I fay I rife.   Naw, if I find it
a good day, I refalve to take the exercife of riding,
fo drink my chocolate, and draw on my boots by
two.   On my return, I drefs; and after dinner,
lounge, perhaps to the Opera.

Ber. Your Lordfhip, I fuppofe, is fond of mufic?

L. Fop. O, paffionately, on Tuefdays and Satur-
days, provided there is good company, and one is
not expected to undergo the fatigue of liftening.

Aman. Does your Lordfhip think that the cafe at
the Opera?

L. Fop. Moft certainly, Madam; there is my
Lady Tattle, my Lady Prate, my Lady Titter, my
Lady Sneer, my Lady Giggle, and my Lady Grin
—thefe have boxes in the front, and while any favourite air is finging, are the prettieft company in
the waurld, ftap my vitals! May'nt we hope for
the honour to fee you added to our fociety, Madam?

Aman. Alas, my Lord, I am the worſt company in the world at a concert, I'm ſo apt to attend to the muſic.

L. Fop. Why, Madam, that is very pardonable in the country, or at church; but a monſtrous inattention in a polite aſſembly. But I am afraid I tire the company?

Lovel. Not at all; pray go on.

L. Fop. Why then, ladies, there only remains to add, that I generally conclude the evening at one or other of the Clubs, nat that I ever play deep; indeed I have been for ſome time tied up from loſing above five thouſand pawnds at a fitting.

Lovel. But is'nt your Lordſhip ſometimes obliged to attend the weighty affairs of the nation?

L. Fop. Sir, as to weighty affairs, I leave them to weighty heads; I never intend mine ſhall be a burthen to my body.

Ber. Nay, my Lord, but you are a pillar of the ſtate.

L. Fop. An ornamental pillar, Madam; for ſooner than undergo any part of the burthen, rat me, but the whole building ſhould fall to the ground.

Aman. But, my Lord, a fine gentleman ſpends a great deal of his time in his intrigues; you have given us no account of them yet.

L. Fop. (Aſide.) Soh! She would enquire into my amours, that's jealouſy; poor ſoul! I ſee ſhe's in love with me. *(To her.)* Why, Madam, I ſhould have mentioned my intrigues, but I am really afraid I begin to be troubleſome with the length of my viſit.

Aman. Your Lordſhip is too entertaining to grow troubleſome any where.

L. Fop. (*Aſide.*) That now was as much as if ſhe had ſaid, pray make love to me. I'll let her ſee I'm quick of apprehenſion. (*To her.*) O Lard, Madam, I had like to have forgot a ſecret I muſt needs tell your Ladyſhip. (*To* Lovelefs.) Ned, you muſt not be ſo jealous now as to liſten.

Lovel. Not I, my Lord, I am too faſhionable a huſband to pry into the ſecrets of my wife.

L. Fop. (*To* Amanda, *ſqueezing her hand.*) I am in love with you to defperation, ſtrike me ſpeechlefs !

Aman. (*Giving him a box o' the ear.*) Then thus I return your paſſion—an impudent fool !

L. Fop. Gad's curſe, Madam, I'm a Peer of the Realm.

Lovel. Hey, what the Devil do you affront my wife, Sir? Nay then——   [*Draws and fight.*

Aman. Ah ! What has my folly done ?—Help ! murder ! help ! Part them, for Heaven's ſake.

L. Fop. (*Falling back, and leaning on his ſword.*) Ah ! quite through the body, ſtap my vitals !

Enter SERVANTS.

Lovel. (*Running to him.*) I hope I han't killed the fool, however—bear him up—where's your wound ?

L. Fop. Juſt thro' the guts.

Lovel. Call a ſurgeon, there—unbutton him quickly.

L. Fop. Ay, pray make haſte.

Lovel. This miſchief you may thank yourſelf for.

dumb!—*(aside)* but thou haft an impertinent wife, ſtap my vitals!

Probe. So—carry him off—carry him off—we ſhall have him prate himſelf into a fever by and by—carry him off.

[*Exit with* Lord Foppington *and* Probe.

Aman. Now on my knees, my dear, let me aſk your pardon for my indiſcretion—my own I never ſhall obtain.

Lovel. Oh, there's no harm done—you ſerv'd him well.

Aman. He did indeed deſerve it ; but 1 tremble to think how dear my indiſcreet reſentment might have coſt you.

Lovel. O, no matter—never trouble yourſelf about that.

Enter Colonel Townly.

Town. So, ſo, I'm glad to find you all alive—I met a wounded Peer carrying off—for Heav'ns ſake what was the matter?

Lovel. O, a trifle—he would have made love to my wife before my face, ſo ſhe obliged him with a box o'the ear, and I run him through the body, that was all.

Town. Bagatelle on all ſides—but pray, Madam, how long has this noble Lord been an humble ſervant of your's?

Aman. This is the firſt I have heard on't—ſo I ſuppoſe 'tis his quality more than his love has brought him into this adventure. He thinks his title an authentic paffport to every woman's heart,. below the degree of a Peerefs.

Town. He's coxcomb enough to think any thing; but I would not have you brought into trouble for him—I hope there's no danger of his life?

Lovel. None at all—he's fallen into the hands of a roguifh furgeon, who, I perceive, defigns to frighten a little money out of him—but I faw his wound—'tis nothing—he may go to the ball to-night if he pleafes.

Town. I am glad you have corrected him without farther mifchief, or you might have deprived me of the pleafure of executing a plot againſt his Lordſhip, which I have been contriving with an old acquaintance of yours.

Lovel. Explain——

Town. His brother, Tom Faſhion, is come down here, and we have it in contemplation to fave him the trouble of his intended wedding; but we want your affiſtance. Tom would have called, but he is preparing for his enterprize, fo I promifed to bring you to him—fo, Sir, if thefe ladies can fpare you—

Lovel. I'll go with you with all my heart—*(afide)* —though I could wifh, methinks, to ſtay and gaze a little longer on that creature—Good Gods! how engaging ſhe is—but what have I to do with beauty? —I have already had my portion, and muſt not covet more.——*(To Townly)* Come, Sir, when you pleafe.

Town. Ladies, your fervant.

Aman. Mr. Lovelefs, pray one word with you before you go.

notwithftanding all thefe jars, did not his death at laft extremely trouble you?

Ber. O yes.—I was forced to wear an odious Widow's band a twelve-month for't.

Aman. Women, I find, have different inclinations:. —prithee, Berinthia, inftruct me a little farther— for I'm fo great a novice, I'm almoft afham'd on't. —Not, Heav'n knows, that what you call intrigues have any charms for me.—the practical part of all unlawful love is——

Ber. O 'tis abominable—but for the fpeculative,. that we muft all confefs is entertaining enough.

Aman. Pray, be fo juft then to me, to believe, 'tis with a world of innocence, I would enquire whether you think thofe, we call Women of Reputation, do really efcape all other men, as they do thofe fhadows of beaux?

Ber. O no, Amanda—there are a fort of men make dreadful work amongft 'em—men that may be called the Beaus Antipathy—for they agree in nothing but walking upon two legs. Thefe have brains —the beau has none.—Thefe are in love with their miftrefs—the beau with himfelf.—They take care of their reputation—he's induftrious to deftroy it.— They are decent—he's a fop.—They are men—he's an afs.

Aman. If this be their character, I fancy we had here e'en now a pattern of 'em both.

Ber. His Lordfhip and Colonel Townly?

Aman. The fame.

Ber. As for the Lord, he's eminently fo; and for the other, I can affure you there's not a man in town who has a better intereſt with the women, that are worth having an intereſt with.

Aman. He anſwers then the opinion I had ever of ·him—Heav'ns! what a difference there is between a -man like him, and that vain nauſeous fop, Lord Foppington—*(taking her hand)* I muſt acquaint you with a ſecret, couſin—'tis not that fool alone has ·talked to me of love.—Townly has been tampering .too.

Ber. *(Aſide.)* So, ſo!—here the myſtery comes ·out!—Colonel Townly!—impoſſible, my dear!

Aman. 'Tis true, indeed!—though he has done it ·in vain; nor do I think that all the merit of ·mankind ·combined, could ſhake the tender love I bear my huſ- .band; .yet I will own to you, Berinthia, I did not ·ſtart at his addreſſes, as when they came from one whom I contemned.

Ber. *(Aſide.)* O this is better and better—well ·ſaid innocence!—and you really think, my dear, ·that nothing could abate your conſtancy and attach- ·ment to your huſband.

.·*Aman.* Nothing, I am convinced.

Ber. What if you found he lov'd another woman .better?

Aman. Well!

Ber. Well!—why were I that thing they call a ſlighted wife; ſomebody ſhould run the riſk of being that thing they call—a huſband.

.·*Aman.* O fie, Berinthia, no revenge ſhould ever be ·taken againſt a huſband—but to wrong his bed is a vengeance, which of all vengeance——

Ber. Is the fweeteft!—Ha! ha! ha!—don't I talk madly?

Aman. Madly indeed!

Ber. Yet I'm very innocent.

Aman. That I dare fwear you are.—I know how to make allowances for your humour—but you refolve then never to marry again?

Ber. O no!—I refolve I will?

Aman. How fo?

Ber. That I never may.

Aman. You banter me.

Ber. Indeed I don't—but I confider I'm a woman, and form my refolutions accordingly.

Aman. Well, my opinion is, form what refolution you will, matrimony will be the end on't.

Ber. I doubt it—but A Heav'ns!—I have bufinefs at home, and am half an hour too late.

Aman. As you are to return with me, I'll juft give fome orders, and walk with you.

Ber. Well, make hafte, and we'll finifh this fubject as we go.   [*Exit* Amanda.
Ah! poor Amanda, you have led a country life! Well, this difcovery is lucky!—bafe Townly!—at once falfe to me, and treacherous to his friend! and my innocent, demure, coufin, too!—I have it in my power to be revenged on her, however. Her hufband, if I have any fkill in countenance, would be as happy in my fmiles, as Townly can hope to be in her's.—I'll make the experiment, come what will on't.—The woman who can forgive the being robb'd of a favour'd lover, muft be either an ideot or a wanton.

ACT III. SCENE I.

Enter LORD FOPPINGTON *and* LA VAROLE.

L. Fop.

HEY, fellow—let my vis-a-vis come to the door.

La Var. Will your Lordfhip venture fo foon to expofe yourfelf to the weather?

L. Fop. Sir, I will venture as foon as I can to expofe myfelf to the ladies.

La Var. I wifh your Lordfhip would pleafe to keep houfe a little longer; I'm affraid your honour does not well confider your wound.

L. Fop. My wound!—I would not be in eclipfe another day, though I had as many wounds in my body as I have had in my heart.   So mind, Varole, let thefe cards be left as directed.   For this evening I fhall wait on my father-in-law, Sir Tunbelly, and I mean to commence my devoirs to the lady, by giving an entertainment at her father's expence; and heark thee, tell Mr. Lovelefs I requeft he and his company will honour me with their prefence, or I fhall think we are not friends.

La Var. I will be fure.   [*Exit.*

Enter YOUNG FASHION.

Y. Faf. Brother, your fervant, how do you find yourfelf to-day?

L. Fop. So well, that I have ardered my coach

the door ;—fo there's no danger of death this baut, Tam.

Y. Faf. I'm very glad of it.

L. Fop. (Afide.) That I believe's a lye.—Prithee, Tam, tell me one thing—did not your heart cut a caper up to your mauth, when, you heard I was ran through the bady ?

Y. Faf. Why do you think it fhould ?

L. Fop. Becaufe I remember mine did fo when I heard my uncle was fhot through the head.

Y. Faf. It then did very ill.

L. Fop. Prithee, why fo ?

Y. Faf. Becaufe he ufed you very well.

L. Fop. Well !—Naw, ftrike me dumb, he ftarv'd me—he has let me want a thaufand women, for want of a thaufand pound.

Y. Faf. Then he hinder'd you from making a great many ill bargains—for I think no woman worth money that will take money.

L. Fop. If I was a younger brother, I fhould think fo too.

Y. Faf. Then you are feldom much in love ?

L. Fop. Never, ftap my vitals.

Y. Faf. Why then did you make all this buftle about Amanda ?

L. Fop. Becaufe fhe was a woman of an infolent virtue—and I thought myfelf piqu'd in honour to debauch her.

Y. Faf. (Afide.) Very well. Here's a rare fellow for you, to have the fpending of five thoufand pounds a year. But now for my bufinefs with him. ——Brother, though I know to talk of bufinefs (efpecially of money) is a theme not quite fo entertaining to you as that of the ladies, my neceffities are fuch, I hope you'll have patience to hear me.

L. Fop. The greatnefs of your neceffities, Tam, is the worft argument in the warld for your being patiently heard.   I do believe you are going to make a very good fpeech, but ftrike me dumb, it has the worft beginning of any fpeech 1 have heard this twelvemonth.

Y. Faf. I'm forry you think fo.

L. Fop. I do believe thou art—but come, let's know the affair quickly.

Y. Faf. Why then, my cafe in a word is this.— The neceffary expences of my travels have fo much exceeded the wretched income of my annuity, that I have been forced to mortgage it for five hundred pounds, which is fpent.   So unlefs you are fo kind as to affift me in redeeming it, I know no remedy but to take a purfe.

L. Fop. Why, faith, Tam, to give you my fenfe of the thing, I do think taking a purfe the beft remedy in the warld—for if you fucceed you are relieved that way, if you are taken—you are relieved t'other.

Y. Faf. I'm glad to fee you are in fo pleafant a humour ; I hope I fhall find the effects on't.

L. Fop. Why, do you then really think it a reafonable thing that I fhould give you five hundred pawnds?

Y. Faf. I do not afk it as a due, brother, I am willing to receive it as a favour.

L. Fop. Then thou art willing to receive it any bow, ftrike me fpeechlefs.—But thefe are d——

Q

times to give money in ; taxes are fo great, repairs
fo exorbitant, tenants fuch rogues, and bouquets fo
dear, that the Devil take me, I am reduced to that
extremity in my cafh, I have been forced to retrench
in that one article of fweet pawder, till I have brought
it dawn to five guineas a maunth—now judge, Tam,
whether I can fpare you five hundred pawnds?

T. Faf. If you can't I muſt ſtarve, that's all.
(Afide.) Damn him.

L. Fop. All I can fay is, you fhould have been a
better hufband.

T. Faf. Ouns!—If you can't live upon ten thoufand a-year, how do you think I fhould do't upon
two hundred ?

L. Fop. Don't be in a paffion, Tam, for paffion
is the moft unbecoming thing in the warld—to the
face.   Look you, I don't love to fay any thing to
you to make you melancholy, but upon this occafion
I muſt take leave to put you in mind, that a running-
horfe does require more attendance than a coach-horfe.
—Nature has made fome difference 'twixt you and
me.

T. Faf. Yes.—She has made you older.   *(Afide.)*
Plague take her.

L. Fop. That is not all, Tam.

T. Faf. Why, what is there elfe ?

*L. Fop. (Looking firſt upon himſelf, and then upon
his brother.)* Afk the ladies.

T. Faf. Why, thou Effence-bottle, thou Mufk
Cat—doſt thou then think thou haſt any advantage
over me but what fortune has given thee ?

Fop. I do, ſtap my vitals.

Y. Faf. Now, by all that's great and powerful, thou art the Prince of Coxcombs.

L. Fop. Sir, I am proud at being at the head of fo prevailing a party.

Y. Faf. Will nothing then provoke thee ?—Draw, Coward.

L. Fop. Look you, Tam,, you know I have always taken you for a mighty dull fellow, and here is one of the foolifheft plats broke out, that I have feen a lang time. Your poverty makes life fo burthenfome to you, you would provoke me to a quarrel, in hopes either to flip through my lungs into my eftate, or to get yourfelf run through the guts, to put an end to your pain, but I will difappoint you in both your de-figns ; far with the temper of a Philafapher, and the difcretion of a Statefman—I fhall leave the room with my fword in the fcabbard.   [*Exit.*

Y. Faf. So! farewell brother ; and now confci-ence I defy thee.——Lory.

Enter LORY.

Lory. Sir ?

Y. Faf. Here's rare news, Lory, his Lordfhip has given me a pill has purged off all my fcru-ples.

Lory. Then my heart's at eafe again. For I have been in a lamentable fright, Sir, ever fince your confcience had the impudence to intrude into your company.

Y. Faf. Be at peace ; it will come there no more, my brother has given it a wring by the nofe, and I

have kick'd it down ftairs. ' So run away to the
inn, get the chaife ready quickly, and bring it to
dame Coupler's without a moment's delay.

Lory. Then, Sir, you are going ftraight about the
fortune ?

Y. Faf. I am.—Away—fly, Lory.

Lory. The happieft day I ever faw. I'm upon
the wing already.   [*Exeunt feverally.*

SCENE II.

A Garden.

Enter LOVELESS *and* SERVANT.

Lovel. Is my wife within ?

Ser. No, Sir, fhe has been gone out this half
hour.

Lovel. Well, leave me.   [*Exit* Servant.
How ftrangely does my mind run on this widow—
never was my heart fo fuddenly feiz'd on before—that
my wife fhould pick out her, of all woman-kind, to
be her playfellow.—But what fate does, let fate anfwer for—I fought it not—foh !—by heav'ns ! here
fhe comes.

Enter BERINTHIA.

Ber. What makes you look fo thoughtful, Sir ? I
hope you are not ill.

4

Lovel. I was debating, Madam, whether I was so or not, and that was it which made me look so thoughtful.

Ber. Is it then so hard a matter to decide?——I thought all people were acquainted with their own bodies, though few people know their own minds.

Lovel. What if the diftemper I fufpect be in the mind?

Ber. Why then I'll undertake to prefcribe you a cure.

Lovel. Alas! you undertake you know not what.

Ber. So far at leaft then you allow me to be a Phyfician.

Lovel. Nay, I'll allow you to be fo yet farther, for I have reafon to believe, fhould I put myfelf into your hands, you would increafe my diftemper.

Ber. How?

Lovel. Oh, you might betray my complaints to my wife.

Ber. And fo lofe all my practice.

Lovel. Will you then keep my fecret?

Ber. I will.

Lovel. I'm fatisfied. Now hear my fymptoms, and give me your advice. The firft were thefe when I faw you at the play; a random glance you threw, at firft alarm'd me. I could not turn my eyes from whence the danger came—I gaz'd upon you till my heart began to pant—nay, even now on your approaching me, my illnefs is fo increas'd, that if you do not help me I fhall, whilft you look on, confume to afhes.   [Taking her ba▮▮

Ber. *(Breaking from him.)* O Lord, let me go, 'tis the plague, and we shall be infected.

Lovel. Then we'll die together, my charming angel.

Ber. O Gad! the devil's in you. Lord, let me go—here's somebody coming.

Enter SERVANT.

Ser. Sir, my lady's come home, and desires to speak with you.

Lovel. Tell her I'm coming.   [*Exit* Servant, *(To* Berinthia) But before I go, one glass of nectar to drink her health.

Ber. Stand off, or I shall hate you, by heavens.

Lovel. *(Kissing her.)* In, matters of love, a woman's oath is no more to be minded than a man's.

[*Exit* Lovelefs.

Ber. Um!

Enter TOWNLY.

Townly. Soh! what's here—Berinthia and Lovelefs—and in such *clofe* converfation!—I cannot now wonder at her indifference in excufing herfelf to me!—O rare woman—well then, let Lovelefs look to his wife, 'twill be but the retort courteous on both fides. —*(To* Berinthia.) Your fervant, Madam, I need not afk how you do, you have got fo good a colour.

Ber. No better than I ufed to have, I fuppofe.

Townly. A little more blood in your cheeks.

Ber. I have been walking!

Townly. Is that all ? Pray, was it Mr. Loveless went from here juſt now?

Ber. O yes—he has been walking with me.

Townly. He has!'

Ber. Upon my word I think he is a very agreeable man !—and there is certainly ſomething particularly inſinuating in his addreſs !

Townly. So ! ſo ! ſhe has n't even the modeſty to diſſemble ! Pray, Madam, may I, without imperti⸲ nence, trouble you with a few ſerious queſtions ?

Ber. As many as you pleaſe ; but pray let them be as little ſerious as poſſible.

Townly. Is it not two years ſince I have preſumed to addreſs you ?'

Ber. I don't know exactly—but it has been a tedious long time.

Townly. Have I not, during that period, had every reaſon to believe that my aſſiduities were far from being unacceptable ?

Ber. Why, to do you juſtice, you have been extremely troubleſome—and I confeſs I have been more civil to you than you deſerved.

Townly. Did I not come to this place at your expreſs deſire ? and for no purpoſe but the honour of meeting you ?—and after waſting a month in diſappointment, have you condeſcended to explain, or in the ſlighteſt way apologize, for your conduct ?

Ber. O heav'ns! apologize for my conduct !—apologiſe to you !—O you barbarian !—But pray now, my good ſerious Colonel, have you any thing more to add ?

Townly. Nothing, Madam, but that after ſuch⸳

behaviour I am lefs furpris'd at what I faw juft now ; it is not very wonderful that the woman who can tri-fle with the delicate addreffes of an honourable lover, fhould be found coquetting with the hufband of her friend.

Ber. Very true—no more wonderful than it was for this *honourable* lover to divert himfelf in the ab-fence of this coquet, with endeavouring to feduce his friend's wife ! O Colonel, Colonel, don't talk of ho-nour or your friend, for heav'ns fake.

Townly. S'death ! how came fhe to fufpect this ? —Really, Madam, I don't underftand you.

Ber. Nay—nay—you faw I did not pretend to mifunderftand you.—But here comes the Lady— perhaps you would be glad to be left with her for an explanation.

Townly. O, Madam, this recrimination is a poor refource, and to convince you how much you are mif-taken, I beg leave to decline the happinefs you pro-pofe me.—Madam, your fervant.

Enter AMANDA. (TOWNLY *whiffers* AMANDA, *and exit.)*

Ber. He carries it off well, however—upon my word—very well !—how tenderly they part !——So, coufin—I hope you have not been chiding your ad-mirer for being with me—I affure you we have been talking of you.

Aman. Fie, Berinthia !—my admirer—will you never learn to talk in earneft of any thing ?

Ber. Why this fhall be in earneft, if you pleafe ; for my part I only tell you matter of fact.

Aman. I'm fure there's fo much jeft and earneft in what you fay to me on this fubject, I fcarce know how to take it.—I have juft parted with Mr. Lovelefs —perhaps it is my fancy, but I think there is an alteration in his manner, which alarms me.

Ber. And fo you are jealous? is that all?

Aman. That all!—is jealoufy then nothing?

Ber. It fhould be nothing, if I were in your cafe.

Aman. Why, what would you do?

Ber. I'd cure myfelf.

Aman. How?

Ber. Care as little for my hufband as he did for me. Look you, Amanda, you may build caftles in the air, and fume, and fret, and grow thin, and lean, and pale, and ugly, if you pleafe, but I tell you, no man worth having is true to his wife, or ever was, or ever will be fo.

Aman. Do you then really think he's falfe to me? for I did not fufpect him.

Ber. Think fo!—I am fure of it.

Aman. You are fure on't?

Ber. Pofitively—he fell in love at the play.

Aman. Right—the very fame—but who could have told you this?

Ber. Um——O—Townly!——I fuppofe your hufband has made him his confidant.

Aman. O bafe Lovelefs!—and what did Townly fay on't?

Ber. So, fo—why fhould fhe afk that?—— *(afide)*——fay!—why he abufed Lovelefs extremely, and faid all the tender things of you in the world.

Aman. Did he?—Oh! my heart!—I'm very ill
—I muſt go the chamber—dear Berinthia, don't
leave me a moment. *[Exit.*

Ber. No—don't fear.——So—there is certainly
ſome affection on her ſide at leaſt, towards Townly.
If it prove ſo, and her agreeable huſband perſeveres
—Heav'n ſend me reſolution!—Well—how this buſineſs will end I know not—but I ſeem to be in as fair
a way to loſe my gallant Colonel, as a boy *is* to be a
rogue, when he's put clerk to an attorney. *[Exit.*

SCENE III.

A Country Houſe.

Enter Young Fashion *and* Lory.

T. Faſ. So—here's our inheritance, Lory, if we
can but get into poſſeſſion—but methinks the ſeat of
our family looks like Noah's ark, as if the chief part
on't were deſigned for the fowls of the air, and the
beaſts of the field.

Lory. Pray, Sir, don't let your head run upon
the orders of building here—get but the heireſs, let
the devil take the houſe.

T. Faſ. Get but the houſe! let the devil take the
heireſs, I ſay—but come, we have no time to ſquan-
deʳ, knock at the door—

[Lory knocks two or three times.

What the devil, have they got no ears in this houfe?
—knock harder.

Lory. I'gad, Sir, this will prove fome inchanted
caftle—we fhall have the giant come out by and bye
with his club, and beat our brains out.

[*Knocks again.*

T. Faf. Hufh—they come—*(from within)* who is
there?

Lory. Open the door and fee—is that your country breeding?—

Ser. (Within.) Ay, but two words to that bargain—Tummas, is the blunderbufs prim'd?,

T. Faf. Ouns! give 'em good words, Lory—or
we fhall be fhot here a fortune-catching.

Lory. Egad, Sir, I think you're in the right on't
—ho!—Mr. what d'ye callum—will you pleafe to let
us in? or are we to be left to grow like willows by
your moat fide?

[Servant *appears at the window with a blunderbufs.*]

Ser. Weel naw, what's ya're bufinefs?

T. Faf. Nothing, Sir, but to wait upon Sir Tunbelly, with your leave.

Ser. To weat upon Sir Tunbelly?—why, you'll
find that's juft as Sir Tunbelly pleafes.

T. Faf. But will you do me the favour, Sir, to
know whether Sir Tunbelly pleafes or not?

Serv. Why look you d'ye fee, with good words
much may be done.—Ralph, go thy waes, and afk
Sir Tunbelly, if he pleafes to be waited upon—and
doft heer? call to nurfe, that fhe may lock up Mifs
Hoyden before the geats open.

T. Faf. D'ye hear that Lory?

Enter Sir Tunbelly, *with Servants, armed with guns, clubs, pitchforks,* &c.

Lory. O, *(Running behind his master.)* O Lord, O Lord, Lord, we are both dead men.

Y. Faf. Take heed fool, thy fear will ruin us.

Lory. My fear, Sir, 'sdeath, Sir, I fear nothing —*(Aside)*—would I were well up to the chin in a horse-pond.

Sir Tun. Who is it here has any business with me?

Y. Faf. Sir, 'tis I, if your name be Sir Tunbelly Clumsey?

Sir Tun. Sir, my name is Sir Tunbelly Clumsey, whether you have any business with me or not—so you see I am not ashamed of my name, nor my face either.

Y. Faf. Sir, you have no cause that I know of.

Sir Tun. Sir, if you have no cause either, I desire to know who you are; for 'till I know your name, I shan't ask you to come into my house: and when I do know your name, 'tis six to four I don't ask you then.

Y. Faf. (Giving him a letter.) Sir, I hope you'll find this letter an authentic passport.

Sir Tun. Cod's my life, from Mrs. Coupler.—I ask your Lordship's pardon ten thousand times—*(To his Servant.)*—Here, run in a doors quickly; get a Scotch coal fire in the great parlour—set all the Turkey work chairs in their places; get the brass candlesticks out, and be sure stick the socket full of laurel, run—*(Turning to* Young Fafhion) My Lord, I afk yourLordfhip's pardon—*(To* Serv.) and do you hear, run away to nurfe, bid her let Mifs Hoyden loofe again.   [*Exit* Servant..

(To Young Fafhion) I hope your honour will excufe the diforder of my family—we are not ufed to receive men of your Lordfhip's great quality every day—pray where are your coaches and fervants, my Lord?

T. Faf. Sir, that I might give you and your daughter a proof how impatient I am to be nearer a-kin to you, I left my equipage to follow me, and came away poft with only one fervant.

Sir Tun. Your Lordfhip does me too much honour—It was expofing your perfon to too much fatigue and danger, I proteft it was—but my daughter fhall endeavour to make you what amends fhe can—and though I fay it, that fhould not fay it, Hoyden has charms. ·

T. Faf. Sir, I am not a ftranger to them, though I am to her : common fame has done her juftice.

Sir Tun. My Lord, I am common Fame's very grateful humble fervant.—My Lord, my girl's young—Hoyden is young, my Lord; but this I muft fay for her, what fhe wants in art, fhe has by nature—what fhe wants in experience, fhe has in breeding—and what's wanting in her age, is made good in her conftitution—fo pray, my Lord, walk in ; pray, my Lord, walk in.

T. Faf. Sir, I wait upon you.

[*Exit through the gate.*

Miſs Hoyden, ſola.

Miſs. Sure, nobody was ever uſed as I am. I know well enough what other girls do, for all they think to make a fool of me. It's well I have a huſband a-coming, or I'cod I'd marry the baker, I would ſo.—Nobody can knock at the gate, but preſently I muſt be lock'd up—and here's the young greyhound can run looſe about the houſe all the day long, ſo ſhe can.—'Tis very well——

(Nurse, *without opening the door.*)

Nurſe. Miſs Hoyden, Miſs, Miſs, Miſs, Miſs Hoyden!

Enter Nurse.

Miſs. Well, what do you make ſuch a noiſe for, ha?—what do you din a body's ears for?—can't one be at quiet for you?

Nurſe. What do I din your ears for?—here's one come will din your ears for you.

Miſs. What care I who's come?—I care not a fig who comes, nor who goes, as long as I muſt be lock'd up like the ale cellar.

Nurſe. That, Miſs, is for fear you ſhould be drank before you are ripe.

Miſs. O, don't you trouble your head about that, I'm as ripe as you, though not ſo mellow.

Nurſe. Very well—now I have a good mind to lock you up again, and not let you ſee my Lord to-ight.

Miſs. My Lord! why is my huſband come?

Nurſe. Yes, marry is he, and a goodly perſon too.

Miſs. *(Hugging Nurſe.)* O my dear nurſe, for-give me this once, and I'll never miſuſe you again; no, if I do, you ſhall give me three thumps on the back, and a great pinch by the cheek.

Nurſe. Ah! the poor thing, ſee how it melts, its as full of good nature as an egg's full of meat.

Miſs. But my dear Nurſe, don't lie now, is he come by your troth?

Nurſe. Yes, by my truly is he.

Miſs. O Lord! I'll go and put on my laced tucker, though I'm lock'd up a month for't.

[*Exit running.*

ACT IV. SCENE I.

Enter Miſs Hoyden *and* Nurse.

Nurse.

Well, Miſs, how do you like your huſband that is to be?

Miſs. O Lord, Nurſe, I'm ſo overjoy'd, I can ſcarce contain myſelf.

. *Nurſe.* O but you muſt have a care of being too fond, for men now-a-days, hate a woman that loves 'em.

Miſs. Love him! Why do you think I love him, Nurſe? I'cod, I would not care if he was hang'd, ſo I were but once married to him.——No, that which pleaſes me, is to think what work I'll make when I get to London; for when I am a wife and a Lady both, I'cod I'll ſtaunt it with the beſt of 'em. Aye, and I ſhall have money enough to do ſo too, Nurſe.

Nurſe. Ah! there's no knowing that, Miſs, for though theſe Lords have a power of wealth, indeed, yet, as I have heard ſay, they give it all to their ſluts and their trulls, who joggle it about in their coaches, with a murrain to 'em, whilſt poor Madam ſits ſighing and wiſhing, and has not a ſpare half crown to buy her a Practice of Piety.

Miſs. O, but for that, don't deceive yourſelf, Nurſe, for this I muſt ſay of my Lord, he's as free as an open houſe at Chriſtmas. For this very morning he told me, I ſhould have ſix hundred a-year to buy pins. Now, Nurſe, if he gives me ſix hundred a-year to buy pins, what do you think he'll give me to buy fine petticoats?

Nurſe. Ah, my deareſt, he deceives thee fouly, and he's no better than a rogue for his pains. Theſe Londoners have got a gibberage with 'em, would confound a gipſey. That which they call pin-money, is to buy their wives every thing in the verſal world, down to their very ſhoe-knots.——Nay, I have heard folks ſay, that ſome ladies, if they will have gallants, as they call 'em, are forced to find them out of their pin-money too. But, look, look, if his *Honour* be not coming to you.——Now, if I were ſure

you would behave yourfelf handfomely, and not difgrace me that have brought you up, I'd leave you
alone together.

Mifs. That's my beft Nurfe, do as you'd be done
by—truft us together this once, and if I don't fhew
my breeding, may I never be married but die an old
maid.

Nurfe. Well, this once I'll venture you.—But if
you difparage me——

Mifs. Never fear.   [*Exit* Nurfe.

Enter YOUNG FASHION.

T. Faf. Your fervant, Madam, I'm glad to find
you alone, for I have fomething of importance to
fpeak to you about.

Mifs. Sir, (my Lord, I meant) you may fpeak
to me about what you pleafe, I fhall give you a civil
anfwer.

T. Faf. You give me fo obliging a one, it encou-
rages me to tell you in a few words, what I think
both for your intereft and mine.   Your father, I fuppofe you know, has refolved to make me happy in
being your hufband, and I hope I may depend on
your confent to perform what he defires.

Mifs. Sir, I never difobey my father in any thing
but eating green goofeberries.

T. Faf. So good a daughter muft needs be an admirable wife.—I am therefore impatient till you are
mine, and hope you will fo far confider the violence
of my love, that you won't have the cruelty to defer
my happinefs fo long as your father defigns it.

Mifs. Pray, my Lord, how long is that?

Y. Faf. Madam—a thoufand years—a whole week.

Mifs. A week !—Why I fhall be an old woman by that time.

Y. Faf. And I an old man.

Mifs. Why, I thought it was to be to-morrow morning, as foon as I was up. I'm fure nurfe told me fo.

Y. Faf. And it fhall be to-morrow morning, if you'll confent ?

Mifs. If I'll confent! Why I thought I was to obey you as my hufband ?

Y. Faf. That's when we are married. Till then I'm to obey you.

Mifs. Why then, if we are to take it by turns, it's the fame thing. I'll obey you now, and when we are married you fhall obey me.

Y. Faf. With all my heart. But I doubt we muft get Nurfe on our fide, or we fhall hardly prevail with the Chaplain.

Mifs. No more we fhan't indeed, for he loves her better than he loves his pulpit, and would always be a-preaching to her by his good will.

Y. Faf. Why then, my dear, if you'll call her hither, we'll try to perfuade her prefently.

Mifs. O Lord, I can tell you a way how to per-fuade her to any thing.

Y. Faf. How's that ?

Mifs. Why tell her fhe's a handfome, comely wo-man, and give her half-a-crown.

Y. Faf. Nay, if that will do, fhe fhall have half a score of them.

Mifs. O Gemini, for half that fhe'd marry you herfelf.—I'll run and call her.   [*Exit.*

Y. Faf. Soh, matters go fwimmingly. This is a rare girl I'faith. I fhall have a fine time on't with her at London. But no matter—fhe brings me an eftate will afford me a feparate maintenance.

Enter LORY.

Y. Faf. 'So, Lory, what's the matter?

Lory. Here, Sir; an intercepted packet from the enemy—your brother's poftillion brought it—I knew the livery, pretended to be a fervant of Sir Tunbelly's, and fo got poffeffion of the letter.

Y. Faf. (*Looking at it.*) Ouns!—He tells Sir Tunbelly here, that he will be with him this evening, with a large party to fupper—'egad I muft marry the girl directly.

Lory. O Zounds, Sir, directly to be fure! Here fhe comes.   [*Exit* Lory.

Y. Faf. And the old Jefabel with her. She has a thorough procuring countenance, however.

Enter Mifs HOYDEN *and* NURSE.

Y. Faf. How do you do, Mrs. Nurfe?—I defired your young lady would give me leave to fee you, that I might thank you for your extraordinary care and conduct in her education; pray accept of this fmall acknowledgment for it at prefent, and depend upon my farther kindnefs when I fhall be that happy thing her hufband.

Nurfe. (*Afide.*) Gold, by Maakins!—Your Ho

nour's goodnefs is too great. Alas! all I can boaft of is, I gave her pure good milk, and fo your Ho. nour would have faid, an you had feen how the poor thing thrived—and how it would look up in my face —and crow and laugh it would!

Mifs. (*To* Nurfe, *taikng her angrily afide.*) Pray one word with you. Prithee, Nurfe, don't ftand ripping up old ftories, to make one afhamed before one's love; do you think fuch a fine, proper gentleman as he is, cares for a fiddle-come tale of a child? If you have a mind to make him have a good opinion of a woman, don't tell him what one did then, tell him what one can do now. (*To him.*) I hope your Honour will excufe my mif-manners, to whifper before you, it was only to give fome orders about the family.

Y. Faf. O, every thing, Madam, is to give way to bufinefs; befides, good houfewifery is a very commendable quality in a young lady.

Mifs. Pray, Sir, are young ladies good houfewives at London town?—Do they darn their own linen.

Y. Faf. O no;—they ftudy how to fpend money, not to fave.

Mifs. I'cod, I don't know but that may be better fport, ha, Nurfe!·

Y. Faf. Well, you fhall have your choice when you come there.

Mifs. Shall I?—then by my troth I'll get there as faft as I can. (*To* Nurfe.) His Honour defires you'll be fo kind, as to let us be married to-morrow.

Nurfe. To-morrow, my dear Madam?

Y. Faf. Aye faith, Nurfe, you may well be fur-prifed at Mifs's wanting to put it off fo long—to-morrow! no, no—'tis now, this very hour, I would have the ceremony perform'd.

Mifs. I'cod, with all my heart.

Nurfe. O mercy, worfe and worfe.

Y. Faf. Yes, fweet Nurfe, now, and privately. For all things being figned and fealed, why fhould Sir Tunbelly make us ftay a week for a wedding din-ner?

Nurfe. But if you fhould be married now, what will you do when Sir Tunbelly calls for you to be wedded?

Mifs. Why then we will be married again.

Nurfe. What, twice, my child!

Mifs. I'cod, I don't care how often I'm married, not I.

Nurfe. Well—I'm fuch a tender-hearted fool, I find I can refufe you nothing. So you fhall e'en fol-low your own inventions.

Mifs. Shall I?—*(Afide.)* O Lord, I could leap over the Moon.

Y. Faf. Dear Nurfe, this goodnefs of your's fhan't go unrewarded. But now you muft employ your power with the Chaplain, that he may do his friendly office too, and then we fhall be all happy. Do you think you can prevail with him?

Nurfe. Prevail with him!—Or he fhall never pre-vail with me, I can tell him that.

Y. Faf. I'm glad to hear it; however, to ftrength-en *your intereft* with him, you may let him know,

I have feveral fat livings in my gift, and that the firft
that falls fhall be in your difpofal.

Nurfe. Nay then, I'll make him marry more folks
than one, I'll promife him.

Mifs. Faith do, Nurfe, make him marry you too,
I'm fure he'll do it for a fat living.

Y. Faf. Well, Nurfe, while you go and fettle
matters with him, your lady and I will go and take
a walk in the garden.   [*Exit* Nurfe.

Y. Faf. (Giving her his hand.) Come, Madam,
dare you venture yourfelf alone with me ?

Mifs. O dear, yes, Sir, I don't think you'll do
any thing to me I need be afraid on.   [*Exeunt.*

SCENE II.

Enter AMANDA, *her* WOMAN *following.*

Maid. If you pleafe, Madam, only to fay whether you'll have me buy them or not ?

Aman. Yes—no—go—Teazer !—I care not what
you do—prithee leave me.   [*Exit* Maid.

Enter BERINTHIA.

Ber. What, in the name of Jove's the matter with
you ?

Aman. The matter, Berinthia ? I'm almoft mad ;
I'm plagued to death.

Ber. Who is it that plagues you?

Aman. Who do you think should plague a wife, but her hufband?

Ber. O ho! is it come to that?—we shall have you wish yourself a widow, by and bye.

Aman. Would I were any thing but what I am! a bafe, ungrateful man, to ufe me thus!

Ber. What, has he given you frefh reafon to fuf- pect his wandering?

Aman. Every hour gives me reafon.

Ber. And yet, Amanda, you perhaps at this mo- ment caufe in another's breaft the fame tormenting doubts and jealoufies which you feel fo fenfibly your- felf.

Aman. Heaven knows I would not!

Ber. Why, you can't tell but there may be fome one as tenderly attached to Townly, whom you boaft of as your conqueft, as you can be to your huf- band.

Aman. I'm fure I never encouraged his preten- fions.

Ber. Pfhaw! Pfhaw!—No fenfible man ever per- feveres to love, without encouragement. Why have you not treated him as you have Lord Foppington?

Aman. Becaufe he has not prefumed fo far. But let us drop the fubject. Men, not women, are rid- dles. Mr. Lovelefs now follows fome flirt for variety, whom I'm fure he does not like fo well as he does me.

Ber. That's more than you know, Madam.

Aman. Why, do you know the ugly thing?

Ber. I think I can guefs at the perfon—but fhe's
no fuch ugly thing neither.

Aman. Is fhe very handfome?

Ber. Truly I think fo.

Aman. Whate'er fhe be, I'm fure he does not like
her well enough to beftow any thing more than a little outward gallantry upon her.

Ber. *(Afide.)* Outward gallantry.—I can't bear
this.—Come, come, don't you be too fecure, Amanda; while you fuffer Townly to imagine that you do
not deteft him for his defigns on you, you have no
right to complain, that your hufband is engaged elfe-
where.   But here comes the perfon we were fpeaking
of.

Enter TOWNLY.

Town. Ladies, as I come uninvited, I beg, if I
intrude, you will ufe the fame freedom in turning me
out again.

Aman. I believe, Sir, it is near the time Mr. Lovelefs faid he would be at home.   He talked of ac-
cepting of Lord Foppington's invitation to fup at Sir
Tunbelly Clumfey's.

Town. His Lordfhip has done me the honour to
invite me alfo.   If you'll let me efcort you, I'll let
you into a myftery as we go, in which you muft play
a part when we arrive.

Aman. But we have two hours yet to fpare—the
carriages are not ordered 'till eight—and it is not a
five minutes drive.   So, Coufin, let us keep the
Colonel to play piquet with us, till Mr. Lovelefs
comes home.

Ber. As you pleafe, Madam, but you know I have a letter to write.

Town. Madam, you know you may command me, though I'm a very wretched gamefter.

Aman. O, you play well enough to lofe your money, and that's all the ladies require—and fo without any more ceremony, let us go into the next room and call for cards and candles.   [*Exeunt.*

SCENE III.

Berinthia's *Dreffing-Room.*

Enter LOVELESS.

Lovel. So—thus far all's well—I have got into her dreffing-room, and it being dufk, I think nobody has perceived me fteal into the houfe. I heard Berinthia tell my wife fhe had fome particular letters to write this evening, before we went to Sir Tunbelly's, and here are the implements for correfpondence—how fhall I mufter up affurance to fhew myfelf when fhe comes?—I think fhe has given me encouragement—and to do my impudence juftice, 1 have made the moft of it.—1 hear a door open and fome one coming; if it fhould be my wife, what the Devil fhould I fay?—I believe fhe miftrufts me, and by my life I don't deferve her tendernefs; however I am determin ed to reform, though not yet.   Hah!—Berinthia-

R

ſo I'll ſtep in here till I ſee what ſort of humour ſhe
is in.   [*Goes into the Cloſet.*

Enter BERINTHIA.

Ber. Was ever ſo provoking a ſituation!—To
think I ſhould ſit and hear him compliment Amanda
to my face!—I have loſt all patience with them both.
I would not for ſomething have Lovelefs know what
temper of mind they have piqued me into, yet I can't
bear to leave them together. No—I'll put my papers away, and return, to diſappoint them. *(Goes
to the cloſet.)* O Lord! a ghoſt! a ghoſt! a ghoſt!

Enter LOVELESS.

Lovel. Peace, my Angel—it's no ghoſt—but one
worth a hundred ſpirits.

Ber. How, Sir, have you had the inſolence to
preſume to——run in again—here's ſomebody coming.

Enter MAID.

Maid. O Lord, Ma'am, what's the matter?

Ber. O Heav'ns! I'm almoſt frightened out of
my wits!—I thought verily I had ſeen a ghoſt, and
'twas nothing but a black hood pin'd againſt the wall.
—You may go again, I am the fearfuleſt fool!
                                    [*Exit* Maid.

Re-enter LOVELESS.

Lovel. Is the coaſt clear?

Ber. The coast clear !—Upon my word I wonder at your affurance !

Lovel. Why then you wonder before I have given you a proof of it.   But where's my wife ?

Ber. At cards.

Lovel. With whom ?

Ber. With Townly.

Lovel. Then we are fafe enough.

Ber. You are fo !—Some hufbands would be of another mind were he at cards with their wives.

Lovel. And they'd be in the right on't too—but I dare truft mine.

Ber. Indeed !—And fhe, I doubt not, has the fame confidence in you.   Yet do you think fhe'd be content to come and find you here ?

Lovel. 'Egad, as you fay, that's true—then for fear fhe fhould come, hadn't we better go into the next room out of her way ?

Ber. What—in the dark ?

Lovel. Aye—or with a light, which you pleafe.

Ber. You are certainly very impudent.

Lovel. Nay then—let me conduct you, my Angel.

Ber. Hold, hold, you are miftaken in your Angel, I affure you.

Lovel. I hope not, for by this hand I fwear.

Ber. Come, come, let go my hand, or I fhall hate you, I'll cry out as I live.

Lovel. Impoffible !—you cannot be fo cruel.

Ber. Ha !—here's fome one coming—begone inftantly.

Lovel. Will you promife to return if I remain here?

Ber. Never truft myfelf in a room with you again while I live.

Lovel. But I have fomething particular to communicate to you.

Ber. Well, well, before we go to Sir Tunbelly's I'll walk upon the lawn. If you are fond of a Moonlight evening, you will find me there.

Lovel. E'faith, they're coming here now.——I take you at your word.

[*Exit* Lovelefs *into the Clofet.*

Ber. 'Tis Amanda, as I live.—I hope fhe has not heaid his voice. Though I mean fhe fhould have her fhare of jealoufy.

Enter AMANDA.

Aman. Berinthia, why did you leave me?

Ber. I thought I only fpoil'd your party.

Aman. Since you have been gone, Townly has attempted to renew his importunities.—I muft break with him—for I cannot venture to acquaint Mr. Lovelefs with his conduct.

Ber. O no—Mr. Lovelefs muftn't know of it by any means.

Aman. O, not for the world.——I wifh, Berinthia, you would undertake to fpeak to Townly on the fubject.

Ber. Upon my word it would be a very pleafant fubject for me to talk to him on.—But come—let us go back—and you may depend on't, I'll not leave you together again, if I can help it. [*Exeunt.*

Enter Loveless.

Lovel. Soh—fo !—a pretty piece of bufinefs I have over-heard—Townly makes love to my wife—and I'm not to know it for the world—I muft enquire into this—and, by Heav'n, if I find that Amanda has in the fmalleft degree——Yet, what have I been at here ?——O, s'death ! that's no rule.

That wife alone, unfullied credit wins,
Whofe virtues can atone her hufband's fins ;
Thus while the man has other nymphs in view,
It fuits the woman to be doubly true.

[*Exit.*

ACT V.   SCENE I.

A Garden—Moon Light.

Enter Loveless.

LOVELESS.

Now, does fhe mean to make a fool of me, or not ? —I fhan't wait much longer, for my wife will foon be enquiring for me to fet out on our fupping party.— Sufpence is at all times the devil—but of all modes of fufpence, the watching for a loitering miftrefs is the worft—but let me accufe her no longer—fhe approaches with one ſmile to o'erpay the anxiety of a year.

(Enter Berinthia.)

O Berinthia, what a world of kindneſs are you in my debt!—had you ſtaid five minutes longer—

Ber. You would have been gone, I ſuppoſe.

Lovel. (Aſide.) Egad ſhe's right enough.

Ber. And I aſſure you, 'twas ten to one that I came at all. In ſhort, I begin to think you are too dangerous a Being to trifle with ; and as I ſhall pro-bably only make a fool of you at laſt, I believe we had better let matters reſt as they are. ‑

Lovel. You cannot mean it ſure ?

Ber. No!—why do you think you are really ſo irreſiſtable, and maſter of ſo much addreſs, as to deprive a woman of her ſenſes in a few days acquaint-ance ?

Lovel. O, no, Madam; 'tis only by your pre-ſerving your ſenſes that I can hope to be admitted into your favour—your taſte, judgment, and diſ-cernment, are what I build my hopes on.

Ber. Very modeſt, upon my word—and it cer-tainly follows, that the greateſt proof I can give of my poſſeſſing thoſe qualities, would be my admiring Mr. Lovelefs !

Lovel. O, that were ſo cold a proof—

Ber. What ſhall I do more ?—eſteem you ?

Lovel. O, no—worſe and worſe.—Can you be-hold a man, whoſe every faculty your attractions have engroſſed—whoſe whole ſoul, as by enchant-ment, you have ſeiz'd on—can you ſee him tremble at your feet, and talk of fo poor a return as your efteem!

Ber. What more would you have me give to a married man?

Lovel. How doubly cruel to remind me of misfortunes!

Ber. A misfortune to be married to fo charming a woman as Amanda!

Lovel. I grant all her merit, but—'fdeath, now fee what you have done by talking of her—fhe's here by all that's unlucky.

Ber. O Ged, we had both better get out of the way, for I fhould feel as aukward to meet her as you.

Lovel. Aye—but if I miftake not, I fee Townly coming this way alfo—I muft fee a little into this matter. *(Steps afide.)*

Ber. O, if that's your intention—I am no woman if I fuffer myfelf to be outdone in curiofity.

[*Goes on the other fide.*

Enter AMANDA.

Aman. Mr. Lovelefs come home and walking on the lawn!—I will not fuffer him to walk fo late, though perhaps it is to fhew his neglect of me——Mr. Lovelefs—ha!—Townly again!—how I am perfecuted!

Enter TOWNLY.

Town. Madam, you feem difturbed!

Aman. Sir, I have reafon.

Town. Whatever be the caufe, I would to Heaven it were in my power to bear the pain, or to remove the malady.

Aman. Your interference can only add to my diftrefs.

Town. Ah! Madam, if it be the fting of unre-
quited love you fuffer from, feek for your remedy in
revenge—weigh well the ftrength and beauty of your
charms, and roufe up that fpirit a woman ought to
bear—difdain the falfe embraces of a hufband—fee
at your feet a real lover—his zeal may give him
title to your pity, although his merit cannot claim
your love!

Lovel. (*Afide.*) So, fo, very fine, e'faith!

Aman. Why do you prefume to talk to me thus?
—is this your friendfhip to Mr. Lovelefs?—I perceive you will compel me at laft to acquaint him with
your treachery.

Town. He could not upbraid me if you were—he
deferves it from me—for he has not been more falfe
to you, than faithlefs to me.

Aman. To you!

Town. Yes, Madam; the lady for whom he now
deferts thofe charms which he was never worthy of,
was mine by right; and I imagined too, by inclination.—Yes, Madam, Berinthia, who now——

Aman. Berinthia!—impoffible!—

Town. 'Tis true, or may I never merit your attention.—She is the deceitful forcerefs who now holds
your hufband's heart in bondage.

Aman. I will not believe it.

Town. By the faith of a true lover, I fpeak from

conviction.—This very day I faw them together, and overheard——

Aman. Peace, Sir, I will not even liften to fuch flander—this is a poor device to work on my refentment, to liften to your infidious addreffes.   No, Sir:— though Mr. Lovelefs may be capable of error, I am convinced I cannot be deceived fo grofsly in him, as to believe what you now report ; and for Berinthia, you fhould have fixed on fome more probable perfon for my rival, than fhe who is my relation, and my friend: for while I am myfelf free from guilt, I will never believe that love can beget injury, or confidence create ingratitude. ·

Town. If I do not prove this to you——·

Aman. You never fhall have an opportunity—from the artful manner in which you firft fhew'd yourfelf to me, I might have been led, as far as virtue permitted, to have thought you lefs criminal than unhappy—but this laft unmanly artifice merits at once my refentment and contempt.   [*Exit.*

Town. Sure there's divinity about her ; and fhe has difpenfed fome portion of honour's light to me : yet can I bear to lofe Berinthia without revenge or compenfation ?—Perhaps fhe is not fo culpable as I thought her.   I was miftaken when I began to think lightly of Amanda's virtue, and may be in my cenfure of my Berinthia.—Surely I love her ftill ; for I feel I fhould be happy to find myfelf in the wrong.

[*Exit.*

Enter LOVELESS *and* BERINTHIA.

Ber. Your fervant, Mr. Lovelefs. . .

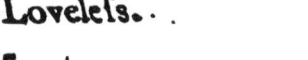

Lovel. Your servant, Madam.

Ber. Pray, what do you think of this?

Lovel. Truly, I don't know what to say.

Ber. Don't you think we steal forth two contemptible creatures?

Lovel. Why tolerable—so I must confess.

Ber. And do you conceive it possible for you ever to give Amanda the least uneasiness again?

Lovel. No, I think we never should, indeed.

Ber. We!—why, monster, you don't pretend that I ever entertain'd a thought.

Lovel. Why then, sincerely, and honestly, Berinthia, there is something in my wife's conduct which strikes me so forcibly, that if it were not for shame, and the fear of hurting you in her opinion, I swear I would follow her, confess my error, and trust to her generosity for forgiveness.

Ber. Nay, prithee don't let your respect for me prevent you; for as my object in trifling with you was nothing more than to pique Townly; and as I perceive he has been actuated by a similar motive, you may depend on't I shall make no mystery of the matter to him.

Lovel. By no means inform him—for though I may choose to pass by his conduct without resentment, how will he presume to look me in the face again?

Ber. How will you presume to look him in the face again?

Lovel. He—who has dared to attempt the honour of my wife!

Ber. You—who have dared to attempt the honour of his mistress!—Come, come, be ruled by me who affect more levity than I have, and don't think of anger in this caufe. A readinefs to refent injuries, is a virtue only in thofe who are flow to injure.

Lovel. Then I will be ruled by you—and when you fhall think proper to undeceive Townly, may your good qualities make as fincere a convert of him, as Amanda's have of me. When truth's extended from us, then we own the robe of virtue is a fecret habit.

Could women but our fecret counfels fcan—
Could they but reach the deep referve of man—
To keep our love—they'd rate their virtue high—
They live together, and together die !

[*Exit.*

SCENE II.

Sir Tunbelly's *Houfe.*

Enter MISS HOYDEN, NURSE, *and* Y. FASHION.

Y. Faf. This quick difpatch of the chaplain's I take fo kindly; it fhall give him claim to my favour as long as I live, I affure you.

Mifs. And to mine too, I promife you.

Nurfe. I moft humbly thank your honours ; and may your children fwarm about you, like bees about a honey-comb.

Mifs. I'cod with all my heart—the more the merrier, I fay—ha Nurfe ?

Enter LORY, *taking* Y. FASHION *haftily afide.*

Lory. One word with you, for Heav'ns fake.

Y. Faf. What the Devil's the matter?

Lory. Sir, your fortune's ruined, if you are not married—yonder's your brother, arrived with two coaches and fix horfes, twenty footmen, and a coat worth fourfcore pounds—fo judge what will become of your Lady's heart.

Y. Faf. Is he in the houfe yet?

Lory. No—they are capitulating with him at the gate—Sir Tunbelly luckily takes him for an impoftor, and I have told him that we had heard of this plot before.

Y. Faf. That's right: *(To* Mifs*)* My dear, here's a troublefome bufinefs my man tells me of, but don't be frighten'd, we fhall be too hard for the rogue.—Here's an impudent fellow at the gate (not knowing I was come hither incognito) has taken my name upon him, in hopes to run away with you.

Mifs. O the brazen-faced varlet, it's well we are married, or may-be we might never have been fo.

Y. Faf. (Afide.) Egad, like enough.—Prithee, Nurfe, run to Sir Tunbelly, and ftop him from going to the gate before I fpeak with him.

Nurfe. An't pleafe your honour, my Lady and I had beft lock ourfelves up till the danger be over.

Y. Faf. Do fo, if you pleafe.

Mifs. Not fo faft—I won't be lock'd up any more, now I'm married.

Y. Faf. Yes, pray, my dear do, till we have feiz'd this rafcal.

Mifs. Nay, if you'll pray me, I'll do any thing.

[*Exit Mifs and Nurfe.*

Y. Faf. (To Lory.) Hark you, firrah, things are better than you imagine. The wedding's over.

Lory. (*Aside.*) The Devil it is, Sir!

Y. Faf. Not a word—all's fafe—but Sir Tunbelly don't know it, nor muft not yet. So I am refolved to brazen the bufinefs out, and have the pleafure of turning the impoftor upon his Lordfhip, which I believe may eafily be done.

Enter Sir Tunbelly, *and* Servants, *armed with clubs, pitchforks,* &c.

Y. Faf. Did you ever hear, Sir, of fo impudent an undertaking?

Sir Tun. Never, by the Mafs—but we'll tickle him, I'll warrant you.

Y. Faf. They tell me, Sir, he has a great many people with him, difguifed like fervants.

Sir Tun. Ay, ay, rogues enow—but we have mafter'd them.—We only fired a few fhot over their heads, and the regiment fcower'd in an inftant.——— Here, Tommas, bring in your prifoner.

Y. Faf. If you pleafe, Sir Tunbelly, it will be beft for me not to confront the fellow yet, till you have heard how far his impudence will carry him.

Sir Tun. 'Egad, your Lordfhip is an ingenious perfon. Your Lordfhip then will pleafe to ftep afide.

Lory. (*Aside.*) 'Fore Heaven I applaud my mafter's modefty.   [*Exeunt* Y. Fafhion *and* Lory.

Enter Servants, *with* Lord Foppington, *difarmed.*

Sir Tun. Come—bring him along, bring him along.

L. Fop. What the pax do you mean, gentle

L. Fop. *(Aside.)* This muft be my wife, by her. natural inclination to her hufband.

Mifs. Pray, father, what do you intend to do with him—hang him?

Sir Tun. That, at leaft, child.

Nurfe. Aye, and it's e'en too good for him too.

L. Fop. *(Aside.)* Madame la Governante, I prefume; hitherto this appears to me to be one of the moft extraordinary families that ever man of quality match'd into.

Sir Tun. What's become of my Lord, daughter?

Mifs. He's juft coming, Sir.

L. Fop. *(Aside.)* My Lord!—What does he mean by that now?

Enter Y. Fashion *and* Lory.

L. Fop. Stap my vitals, Tam, now the dream's out.

Y. Faf. Is this the fellow, Sir, that defign'd to trick me of your daughter?

Sir Tun. This is he, my Lord; how do you like him? Is not he a pretty fellow to get a fortune?

Y. Faf. I find by his drefs, he thought your daughter might be taken with a beau.

Mifs. O gemini! Is this a beau? Let me fee him again. Ha! I find a beau is no fuch ugly thing neither.

Y. Faf. 'Egad, fhe'll be in love with him prefently.—I'll e'en have him fent away to gaol. *(To Lord Foppington.)* Sir, though your undertaking fhews you a perfon of no extraordinary modefty, I fuppofe you ha'n't confidence enough to expect much favour from me.

this is but a dream. Prithee, old father, wilt thou give me leave to aſk thee one queſtion?

Sir Tun. I can't tell whether I will or not, till I know what it is.

L. Fop. Why then it is, whether thou didſt not write to my Lord Foppington to come down and marry thy daughter?

Sir Tun. Yes, marry did I, and my Lord Foppington is come down, and ſhall marry my daughter before ſhe's a day older.

L. Fop. Now give me thy hand, old dad, I thought we ſhould underſtand one another at laſt.

Sir Tun. This fellow's mad—here, bind him hand and foot.   [*They bind him.*

L. Fop. Nay, prithee Knight, leave fooling, thy jeſt begins to grow dull.

Sir Tun. Bind him, I ſay—he's mad—bread and water, a dark room, and a whip, may bring him to his ſenſes again.

L. Fop. Prithee, Sir Tunbelly, why ſhould you take ſuch an averſion to the freedom of my addreſs, as to ſuffer the raſcals thus to ſkewer down my arms like a rabbit? 'Egad, if I don't waken quickly, by all that I can ſee, this is like to prove one of the moſt impertinent dreams that ever I dreamt in my life.   [*Aſide.*

Enter Miss Hoyden *and* Nurse.

Miſs. (*Going up to him.*) Is this he that would have run away with me? Fough! how he ſtinks of ſweets!—Pray, father, let him be dragged thro' the horſe-pond.

Lory. (*Aside.*) So, Sir, What will you do now?

Y. Faf. Be quiet—they are in the plot. (*To* Sir Tunbelly.) Only a few friends, Sir Tunbelly, whom I wifh'd to introduce to you.

L. Fop. Thou art the moſt impudent fellow, Tam, that ever Nature yet brought into the world. Sir Tunbelly, ſtrike me ſpeechleſs, but theſe are my friends and my gueſts, and they will ſoon inform thee, whether I am the true Lord Foppington or not.

Enter LOVELESS, TOWNLY, AMANDA, *and* BERINTHIA.

Y. Faf. So, gentlemen, this is friendly, I rejoice to ſee you.

Town. My Lord, we are fortunate in being the witneſſes of your Lordſhip's happineſs.

Lovel. But your Lordſhip will do us the honour to introduce us to Sir Tunbelly Clumſey?

Aman. And us to your Lady.

L. Fop. Ged take me, but they are all in a ſtory.

Sir Tun. Gentlemen, you do me great honour; my Lord Foppington's friends will ever be welcome to me and mine.

Y. Faf. My love, let me introduce you to theſe ladies.

Mifs. By goles, they look ſo fine and ſo ſtiff, I am almoſt aſham'd to come nigh 'em.

Aman. A moſt engaging lady, indeed!

Mifs. Thank ye, Ma'am!

Ber. And I doubt not, will ſoon diſtinguiſh herſelf in the Beau Monde.

Mifs. Where is that?

Y. Faf. You'll foon learn, my dear.

Lovel. But, Lord Foppington——

L. Fop. Sir!

Lovel. Sir! I was not addreffing myfelf to you, Sir; pray who is this gentleman? He feems rather in a fingular predicament.

Sir Tun. Ha, ha, ha!—So thefe are your friends and your guefts, ha, my adventurer?

L. Fop. I am ftruck dumb with their impudence, and cannot pofitively fay whether I fhall ever fpeak again or not.

Sir Tun. Why, Sir, this modeft gentleman wanted to pafs himfelf upon me for Lord Foppington, and carry off my daughter.

Lovel. A likely plot to fucceed, truly, ha, ha!

L. Fop. As Gad fhall judge me, Lovelefs, I did not expect this from thee; come, prithee confefs the joke; tell Sir Tunbelly that I am the real Lord Foppington, who yefterday made love to thy wife; was honour'd by her with a flap on the face, and afterward pink'd through the body by thee.

Sir Tun. A likely ftory, truly, that a Peer wou'd behave thus!

Lovel. A curious fellow indeed! that wou'd fcandalize the character he wants to affume; but what will you do with him, Sir Tunbelly?

Sir Tun. Commit him certainly, unlefs the bride and bridegroom choofe to pardon him.

L. Fop. Bride and bridegroom!—For Gad's fake, Sir Tunbelly, 'tis tarture to me to hear you call 'em fo.

Mifs. Why, you ugly thing, what would you have him call us? dog and cat!

L. Fop. By no means, Mifs; for that founds ten times more like man and wife, than t'other.

Sir Tun. A precious rogue this, to come a wooing!

Enter SERVANT.

Ser. There are fome more gentle folks below, to wait upon Lord Foppington.

Town. S'death, Tom, what will you do now?

L. Fop. Now, Sir Tunbelly, here are witneffes, who I believe are not corrupted.

Sir Tun. Peace, fellow!—Would your Lordfhip choofe to have your guefts fhewn here, or fhall they wait till we come to 'em?

Y. Faf. I believe, Sir Tunbelly, we had better not have thefe vifitors here yet; 'gad, all muft out!
                                                    [*Afide.*

Lovel. Confefs, confefs, we'll ftand by you.

L. Fop. Nay, Sir Tunbelly, I infift on your calling evidence on both fides, and if I do not prove that fellow an impoftor——

Y. Faf. Brother, I will fave you the trouble, by now confeffing, that I am not what I have paffed myfelf for;—Sir Tunbelly, I am a gentleman, and I flatter myfelf a man of character; but 'tis with great pride I affure, I am not Lord Foppington.

Sir Tun. Ouu's!—what's this!—an impoftor!— a cheat!—fire and faggots, Sir!—if you are not Lord Foppington, who the Devil are you?

Y. Faf. Sir, the beft of my condition is, I am your fon-in-law, and the worft of it is, I am brother to that noble Peer.

L. Fop. Impudent to the laft!

Sir Tun. My fon-in-law! Not yet, I hope?

Y. Faf. Pardon me, Sir, thanks to the goodnefs of your Chaplain, and the kind offices of this old gentlewoman.

Lory. 'Tis true, indeed, Sir; I gave your daughter away, and Mrs. Nurfe, here, was clerk.

Sir Tun. Knock that rafcal down!—But fpeak, Jezabel, how's this?

Nurfe. Alas, your honour, forgive me!—I have been over-reach'd in this bufinefs as well as you; your Worfhip knows, if the wedding dinner had been ready, you would have given her away with your own hands.

Sir Tun. But how durft you do this without acquainting me!

Nurfe. Alas, if your Worfhip had feen how the poor thing begg'd and pray'd, and clung and twin'd about me like ivy round an old wall, you would fay I who had nurs'd it and rear'd it, muft have had a heart of ftone to refufe it.

Sir Tun. Ouns! I fhall go mad! Unloofe my Lord there, you fcoundrels!

L. Fop. Why, when thefe gentlemen are at leifure, I fhou'd be glad to congratulate you on your fon-in-law, with a little more freedom of addrefs.

Mifs. 'Egad, though—I don't fee which is to be my hufband, after all.

Lovel. Come, come, Sir Tunbelly, a man of your underftanding muft perceive, that an affair of this kind is not to be mended by anger and reproaches.

Town. Take my word for it, Sir Tunbelly, you are only tricked into a fon-in-law you may be proud of; my friend, Tom Fafhion, is as honeft a fellow as ever breath'd.

Lovel. That he is, depend on't, and will hunt or drink with you moft affectionately ; be generous, old boy, and forgive them.

Sir Tun. Never—the huffey !—when I had fet my heart on getting her a title !

L. Fop. Now, Sir Tunbelly, that I am untrufs'd, give me leave to thank thee for the very extraordinary reception I have met with in thy damn'd, execrable manfion, and at the fame time to affure you, that of all the bumpkins and blockheads 1 have had the misfortune to meet with, thou art the moft obftinate and egregious, ftrike me ugly !

Sir Tun. What's this !—Ouns ! I believe you are both rogues alike !

L. Fop. No, Sir Tunbelly, thou wilt find to thy unfpeakable mortification, that I am the real Lord Foppington, who was to have difgraced myfelf by an alliance with a clod ; and that thou haft match'd thy girl to a beggarly younger brother of mine, whofe title deeds might be contained in thy tobacco-box.

Sir Tun. Puppy, puppy !—1 might prevent their being beggars if I choofe it ;—for I could give 'em as good a rent-roll as your Lordfhip.

Town. Well faid, Sir Tunbelly.

L. Fop. Aye, old fellow, but you will not do it ; for that would be acting like a Chriftian, and thou art a thorough barbarian, ftap my vitals.

Sir Tun. Udzookers ! Now fix fuch words more, and I'll forgive them directly.

Lovel. 'Slife, Sir Tunbelly, you fhou'd do it, and blefs yourfelf ; ladies what fay you ?

Aman. Good Sir Tunbelly, you muft confent.

Ber. Come, you have been young yourfelf, Sir Tunbelly.

Sir Tun. Well then, if I muft, 1 muft ;—but turn that fneering Lord out, however; and let me be re-venged on fomebody : but firft, look whether I am a barbarian, or not; there, children, I join your hands, and when I'm in a better humour, I'll give you my bleffing.

Lovel. Nobly done, Sir Tunbelly ; and we fhall fee you dance at a grandfon's wedding, yet.

Mifs. By goles though, 1 don't underftand this ; what, an't 1 to be a lady after all ? only plain Mrs. —What's my hufband's name, Nurfe ?

Nurfe. 'Squire Fafhion.

Mifs. 'Squire, is he ?—Well, that's better than nothing.

L. Fop. Now will I put on a Philofophic air, and fhew thefe people, that it is not poffible to put a man of my quality out of countenance. Dear, Tam, fince things are thus fallen out, prythee give me leave to wifh thee joy ; I do it *de bon coeur*, ftrike me dumb ! You have married into a family of great po-litenefs and uncommon elegance of manners ; and your bride appears to be a lady beautiful in perfon, modeft in her deportment, refined in her fentiments, and of nice morality, fplit my windpipe.

Mifs. By goles, hufband, break his bones, if he calls me names.

Y. Faf. Your Lordfhip may keep up your fpirits with your grimace, if you pleafe, I fhall fupport mine by Sir Tunbelly's favour, with this lady, and three thoufand pounds a year.

L. Fop. Well, adieu, Tam ; ladies, I kifs your

hands; Sir Tunbelly, I fhall now quit thy den, but while I retain my arms, I fhall remember thou art a favage, ftap my vitals! [*Exit.*

Sir Tun. By the mafs, 'tis well he's gone, for I fhould ha' been provok'd by and by, to ha' dun'un a mifchief:—Well, if this is a Lord, I think Hoyden has luck o' her fide, in troth!

Town. She has, indeed, Sir Tunbelly, but I hear the fiddles; his Lordfhip, I know, had provided 'em.

Lovel. O, a dance, and a bottle, Sir Tunbelly, by all means.

Sir Tun. I had forgot the company below; well, what—we muft be merry then, ha?—and dance and drink, ha?—Well, 'fore George, you fhan't fay I do things by halves; fon-in-law there looks like a hearty rogue, fo we'll have a night of it; and which of thefe gay ladies will be the old man's partner, ha?—Ecod, I don't know how I came to be in fo good a humour.

Ber. Well, Sir Tunbelly, my friend and I both will endeavour to keep you fo; you have done a generous action, and are entitled to our attention; and if you fhou'd be at a lofs to divert your new guefts, we will affift you to relate to them the plot of your daughter's marriage, and his Lordfhip's deferved mortification, a fubject which, perhaps, may afford no bad evening's entertainment.

Sir Tun. 'Ecod, with all my heart; though I am a main bungler at a long ftory.

Ber. Never fear, we will affift you, if the tale is judged worth being repeated; but of this you may be affured, that while the intention is evidently to pleafe, Britifh auditors will ever be indulgent to the errors of the performance.

Lightning Source UK Ltd.
Milton Keynes UK
UKHW021519090219
336936UK00007B/887/P

9 780483 587540